fP

THE
LONGEST
WAY HOME

*One Man's Quest
for the Courage
to Settle Down*

ANDREW McCARTHY

FREE PRESS

NEW YORK   LONDON   TORONTO   SYDNEY   NEW DELHI

FREE PRESS
A Division of Simon & Schuster, Inc.
1230 Avenue of the Americas
New York, NY 10020

NOTE TO READERS:
Names and identifying details of some of the people portrayed in this book have been changed.

Copyright © 2012 by Andrew McCarthy

All rights reserved, including the right to reproduce this book or portions thereof
in any form whatsoever. For information address Free Press Subsidiary Rights Department,
1230 Avenue of the Americas, New York, NY 10020.

This Free Press export edition September 2012

FREE PRESS and colophon are trademarks of Simon & Schuster, Inc.

For information about special discounts for bulk purchases,
please contact Simon & Schuster Special Sales at 1-866-506-1949
or business@simonandschuster.com.

The Simon & Schuster Speakers Bureau can bring authors to your live event.
For more information or to book an event contact the Simon & Schuster Speakers Bureau
at 1-866-248-3049 or visit our website at www.simonspeakers.com.

Designed by Mspace/Maura Fadden Rosenthal

Manufactured in the United States of America

3   5   7   9   10   8   6   4   2

Library of Congress Cataloging-in-Publication Data

McCarthy, Andrew.
The longest way home : one man's quest for the courage to settle down/
Andrew McCarthy. — 1st Free Press hardcover ed.
p. cm.
1. McCarthy, Andrew, 1962- 2. McCarthy, Andrew, 1962—Travel. 3. McCarthy, Andrew,
1962—Marriage. 4. Travel writers—United States—Biography. 5. Voyages and travels.
6. Travel—Psychological aspects. 7. Self-actualization (Psychology) 8. Actors—United States—
Biography. 9. Motion picture producers and directors—United States—Biography. I. Title.
CT275.M333A3 2012
920.073—dc23
2012010509

ISBN 978–1–4767–0955–0
ISBN 978–1–4516–6751–6 (ebook)

CONTENTS

CONTENTS

THE
LONGEST WAY
HOME

PROLOGUE

"Are you awake?" Something in the tone of the voice cut through to my sleeping brain.

"Coming," I called back.

"What time is it?" D murmured.

"Four fifteen. We're late." The night was still black. The canvas tent flapped in a dry breeze. I grabbed our bags, pulled at the zipper, and we were out. We slashed along a path through the dry bush lit by a waning moon, loaded into the jeep, and were gone in minutes. Occasionally, at the edges of the beam of light cast by the single working headlamp, a pair of shining red eyes was briefly lit in the darkness. We bounced on over the dirt track and after half an hour we came to a locked gate. From somewhere in the night a man appeared and opened it, and we drove into the Chitengo compound. A few limp fluorescent lights lit the area. A small young man grabbed our bags and threw them into the back of a decrepit minivan—the kind that are the lifeblood of Africa. He jumped behind the wheel; we climbed into the backseat.

"My name is Jonasse," the driver said—it was all the English he had.

We waited at another gate for a sleeping guard to be roused, and by the time we exited Gorongosa National Park we were forty-five minutes late. We still had a four-hour drive to catch our flight north.

If the road inside the park was potholed and scarred, the one outside the gates was worse. I set my jaw so as not to bite my tongue. Suddenly the wind blew strong and dust filled the van.

"Stop!" D shouted. "The boot is open." The back door of the van hadn't been properly closed, and all our bags had fallen onto the road. "My computer," D whispered.

The zipper of my bag had burst and my clothes were scattered along the dusty road into the dark. We scooped everything up as best we could and stuffed it back into the van.

"Do you want to check your computer?" I asked D.

"No, let's just go," she said.

When the sky began to soften we were driving through coarse bush. Dense and low trees crowded the road, which, impossibly, grew worse. We drove on. As we crested a small hill, D spoke again.

"Something's burning."

We stopped in the middle of the road and piled out. The right rear tire was flat. D and I looked at each other. The prospect of making our flight was slipping away. Then the untended van began to roll forward down the hill. Jonasse leapt behind the wheel and stopped the vehicle from going all the way. The minivan had no parking brake. D and I scavenged for pieces of wood to put in front of the tires to secure them. Jonasse retrieved the jack but didn't know how to work it. It didn't matter: the spare tire was flat.

We stood behind the van, looking up and down the road. No cars had passed us on our journey so far; none were coming now. We had no food and began to grow hungry. The sun broke the horizon and suddenly D burst into laughter. It was a laugh that took her entire body; it was raw and filled her completely. It was a laugh that made me realize I had done something right—to end up with a woman who could laugh like that.

"What is it?" I asked.

And then I heard it, too. Distant but distinct, the rhythmic pounding of drums filled the Mozambique dawn.

"I hope those aren't war drums," I said.

We had been married for less than a week, and just as I knew I had done something right, I also saw one of my biggest fears coming true—that I wouldn't be able to take care of this woman.

When the drumming faded we settled by the side of the road to wait. The sun climbed higher into the African sky; the day grew hot. Time passed. Our hunger became worse, and most unsettling of all, D fell silent. When I finally heard her voice again, it came from a deep, distant, and murky well of feeling. She looked straight ahead at the dusty road and spoke softly and slowly: "You owe me a honeymoon, buddy."

CHAPTER ONE

NEW YORK

"Wanted: Eighteen, Vulnerable and Sensitive"

We had traveled just nineteen miles west—my childhood was left behind. Gone were the backyard Wiffle ball games with my brothers that had defined my summer afternoons, as was the small maple tree in the front yard that I nearly succeeded in chopping down with a rubber ax when I was eight; over were the nights lying in bed talking to my older brother Peter across the room in the dark before sleep came. We had lived atop a small hill, safely in the center of a sub-urban block, in a three-bedroom colonial with green shutters; now we would live in a long and low house in a swale on a large corner lot a half hour and a world away.

"It looks like a motel," I said when I first saw our new home. Unwit-tingly, I had spoken to the temporary quality that our lives were about to take on. My eldest brother had just gone off to college, ending the daily battles with my father—no longer would my dad chase Stephen out the window and across the yard in a rage. Peter's star, which had burned so bright, grew suddenly and temporarily tarnished—driving and girlfriends usurped the passion for sports that had occupied his early years, yet he continued to look after me with a fierce protectiveness. My younger brother, Justin, eight years my junior, was slotted into a new school and tumbled in the wake left by the rest of us.

Instead of feeling more confident after our move into the larger home, my parents grew tense. More and more often, when the phone rang, I could hear my father's voice echoing from somewhere in the cavernous house, "I'm not here! I'm not here!" Whoever was looking for him, he did not want to be found. At the same time, my mother grew more remote due to an illness that we children knew of only vaguely—it was never discussed with us. In all this space, my family seemed to be coming apart. I was fourteen.

A quiet child, I'd had a rotation of friends and a cycle of movement in my old neighborhood, the loss of which left me untethered. There were woods across the road from our new home and I began to spend more and more time, alone, picking through the trees and building dams in the stream. Always in the shadow of my brother Peter's athletic ability, my passion for sports waned. I was never a diligent student, and as the work piled up, my interest faded. Noticing my rudderless unease, my mother suggested I try out for the school musical, *Oliver*. Reluctantly, I went along. When it came to the final audition for the role of the Artful Dodger, I surprised myself with how much I wanted the part. Pitted against another student who, it was made very clear, had a better singing voice and was more desired for the production, I threw myself into my performance in a way that left them no option but to reward me with the role.

In describing first love, the playwright Tennessee Williams once wrote, "It was like you suddenly turned a blinding light on something that had always been in half shadow." I experienced a similarly wondrous sense of discovery with that first role. I felt the power and belonging I had been searching for, without knowing that I had been searching at all. I knew my experience onstage was a profound one because I told no one of its effect on me.

A few years later, when the time came to apply to college, with few options because of my poor grades, I quietly took the train to Hoboken, then the PATH under the Hudson River, and went to a building off Washington Square in Greenwich Village. On the second floor of a windowless room I spoke a few paragraphs of a play I had read only a portion of, in front of a petite man with an effete manner who wore a bow tie and a waxed mustache.

"Sit down," he said when I was finished. He wanted to know why my grades were so bad and why I wanted to come to acting school. He asked if I had another monologue I could perform for him. I could do some of the lines from the Artful Dodger, I said. When I was finished he looked at me for a long while. "Okay," he said at last, "here's what we're going to do. I'm going to get you into this school, if I can. I'm sure they'll place you on academic probation to start. You're going to get good grades and be grateful to me for the rest of your life."

"Sounds good," I said, slipping on an attitude of casual indifference to mask the thrill I felt.

"No son of mine is going to be a fucking thespian," my father snapped when he learned of the audition—but when no other college accepted me, he had no choice.

This was the same man who then drove me into the city and knocked on door after door until we found an apartment for me to live in just off Washington Square Park when the university refused me housing. And it was during the buoyant ride back to New Jersey that we played "Thank God I'm a Country Boy" on his John Denver tape, over and over again. I bowed the air fiddle and he lowered the windows and the wind ripped through the car as we sang at the top of our lungs with our hearts wide open to each other.

As I packed my bags to leave home, my mother offered me a painting that I had always admired—a large canvas with the profile of a hawk, its golden eye staring boldly out at the viewer. When my father saw it leaning against the wall by the door, instead of on the living room wall, he grew enraged.

"That painting is not leaving this house," he barked. "That is my favorite piece of art."

My mother, who rarely engaged with my father when he lost his temper, pushed back. "I'm giving it to him," she declared. "He is leaving for school and I want him to have it."

A vicious fight ensued. I knew, even in the midst of the shouting, that this had nothing to do with a painting and everything to do with a mother losing her son in whom she had been overinvested, and a father who had resented their closeness.

A few months after I had settled in my apartment, my father made one of his many unscheduled visits, carrying the painting. He presented it as if it were a new idea to offer it to me. I tried to refuse but it was no use. When he left, I put the painting in the back of a closet, and when I moved from that apartment, I gave it away.

⚐

The man who had gone out on a limb and gotten me into NYU was Fred Gorlick. He rarely acknowledged me when I saw him at school, and he left shortly after I arrived. I never saw him again. I have been grateful to him for my entire life, but I could only keep half my word. Somehow I couldn't bring myself to attend my nonacting classes, and after two years, the powers that be at school asked me to leave.

A few months later another transient angel swept across my path.

"Wanted: Eighteen, vulnerable and sensitive" read the ad in the newspaper. I hadn't seen it, but a friend called and told me about the audition. I got on the number 1 train and went to the Upper West Side. I sat on the floor of a hallway in the Ansonia Hotel on Seventy-third Street and waited for three hours with several hundred other eighteen-year-old, vulnerable and sensitive hopefuls. I had never been to an "open call" before; I had never been to a movie audition.

When I was finally called into the room, I handed my headshot to a man with soft features who immediately flipped it over to look at my résumé. I had acted in exactly one professional play, for one weekend. The play was listed there, alone on the white page.

"You spelled the author's name wrong," the man with the soft features said.

"Oh," I responded meekly, "sorry."

Then he looked over his shoulder to a woman with a head full of untamed blond hair, who was busy with work of her own. She looked up, glanced at me briefly, and nodded. The man with the soft features turned back and said, "Come to our office tomorrow." He wrote the address and time on a piece of paper.

I went to the office the next day and was handed a scene from what I assumed was a movie script. I read it with the same man, whose name I learned was David, and went away. The following week I was summoned to meet the director of the film, Lewis Carlino, in his suite at a midtown hotel. He was a gentle, soft-spoken man with a trim gray beard. We chatted for a while, and then I left. As I waited by the elevator, David came out and asked me back to the office again the following day. We read the same scene I had before. This time,

Lewis was also present and they were recording me on videotape. I was nervous and knew I was performing poorly, unable to follow the director's suggestions. Worse, my eyes unwittingly opened wide, apparently giving me a look of frozen terror.

"Just relax your eyes," Lewis said kindly.

I didn't know what he was talking about.

I left, disheartened, knowing that I had lost any chance for the part.

Six weeks later I pushed the button on my roommate's new answering machine on the floor just inside his bedroom. And there was David's voice, asking if I could come in to the office yet again.

Marty Ransohoff, the film's producer, had seen the tape and saw something he liked. "He looks crazy, like Tony Perkins in *Psycho,*" Marty had said.

I was brought to Chicago to meet and screen-test with other actors, and finally I was flown out to Los Angeles to meet with Jacqueline Bisset—the role I was to play was that of her young lover and she needed to approve the choice.

At the Château Marmont hotel, beside the room where John Belushi had recently overdosed, I waited for the call. Marty picked me up in his Jaguar. He was an outsized man in every way, and as we drove up Benedict Canyon, he told me, "Just be yourself, kid."

A tall blond Adonis answered the door. He spoke with a thick Russian accent. "It is a pleasure to meet you," he said, and extended his well-tanned hand. It was Jacqueline Bisset's lover, the recently defected Russian ballet star Alexander Godunov.

I entered the Spanish-style bungalow and slouched on the couch in the sunken living room. Marty parked himself in a plush chair nearby. We sat in silence. He never took his eyes off me.

"Just relax, kid," Marty said after a while.

Then I heard a distant toilet flush, and I started to laugh. Jackie entered the room and sat on the ottoman across from me. She was gracious, interested, and extremely beautiful. I don't remember anything I said, but after a few minutes she turned to Marty and said, "He's cheeky," in her lush English accent. "I like him."

We were done—Marty drove me back down the hill and dropped me at a taxi stand to get a cab back to my hotel.

The film, called *Class,* was shot in Chicago. I lived in a hotel off Michigan Avenue for the duration of the shoot. I was nineteen. The acting work was the realization of my youthful dreams, but it was in that room, a yellow-walled junior suite with a king-size bed and a partial view of the lake, that I felt at home in a way that I hadn't before. Alone, far from everyone I knew, with work to do, I felt insulated and safe.

When the film ended, I returned to New York. I found no work for another year, except playing the role of Pepsi Boy in a Burger King commercial—it didn't matter. My life finally had direction, and I followed it unequivocally.

At twenty-one I landed a part in a movie called *Catholic Boys* (someone later changed it to *Heaven Help Us*), and the success that happened next happened fast. That I was unprepared, or ill-equipped, to best capitalize on my good fortune is something best decided in hindsight. My life was rushing forward; I was not interested in stopping it. Nor would I have been interested in anyone's advice on how I might do things differently, had anyone offered any. I was comfortable in my own company and convinced I knew my own mind.

Work led to more work and more travel. To Los Angeles, of course, and to Philadelphia and Kentucky, Kansas and Canada. I traveled to Paris and then London, to Italy and Brazil. Because of my natural inclination toward solitude I drifted away from the others after the workday ended and wandered the cities alone. I began to find comfort in the transience and invisibility of being a stranger in a strange place. Unnoticed and anonymous, I was relieved and excited as I discovered a world very different from the suburban New Jersey neighborhood of my childhood.

Success was something I craved—and yet it intimidated me. These mixed feelings were not new; ambivalence had already begun to assert itself in my life and had become hugely important in the most successful role of my early film work. I was an unlikely choice for the lead male role in *Pretty in Pink*—a now-iconic coming-of-age love story. At the time of filming, it seemed to me like a silly movie about a girl wanting to go to a dance. I was an oversensitive youth cast as a "hunk," a twenty-two-year-old, middle-class kid playing a seventeen-year-old boy of privilege. What gave my portrayal impact and contributed to the movie's popularity at the time, and its enduring relevance, was the ambivalence I brought to the role: the character's uncertainty regarding his place in the world echoed my own and spoke to a generation of young women and men.

In *St. Elmo's Fire,* that same ambivalence was amplified to an even greater degree and became the defining characteristic of a role that fit me better than any other. In that instance, because I was so actively living out my personal vacillations on-screen, I felt free—for the only time in my young life—to move fully toward a success I had decided I wanted. Only when the outlet of acting in that role was finished did my doubts and reservations return—and by then success was on its way.

Those films carried such weight with their intended audience because they gave credence to and took seriously the struggles of being young. Struggles I too was wrestling with at the time, and that I chose to ease through drinking. What began as a curiosity became a companion, then an emboldening habit, and finally an invisible albatross. Had I been interested in camaraderie, or allowing anyone to come close to me, someone might have pointed out that my drinking was in danger of derailing my plans—but it's doubtful I would have listened. Alcohol became my master with impunity.

While still in my mid-twenties, I wrapped up work on a film in Berlin and returned to my hotel room alone with a bottle of Jameson Irish Whiskey. I toasted myself in the mirror for a job well done and then awoke in a different room. I had no recollection of changing rooms. Confused and still groggy, I rolled over in bed and called the front desk. A man answered the phone in a language that wasn't German.

"Good morning," I croaked.

"Good afternoon," the accented voice corrected me.

"Oh, is it that late?" I asked, putting as much innocence into my voice as I could. "I must have overslept. What time is it?"

"It's half past four, sir."

"Oh, great," I said, hoping to make this appear in accordance with my plans. Sounding as reasonable as I could, I continued. "What day of the week is it? I've forgotten."

"Friday, sir," the voice on the phone said.

"Of course." I hadn't misplaced an entire day. But I still didn't know where I was. "Um, I'm just writing a postcard," I lied. "Could you remind me again of the name of the hotel?"

"Hotel L'Europe, sir," the voice on the phone said without hesitation.

This didn't help to determine my location either. "Yes," I said. "I didn't know if you used 'The' in the title or 'L.' Thanks."

"My pleasure, sir," the very reasonable man assured me.

I paused.

"Is there anything else, sir?"

"What city are we in?" I blurted out.

After only the slightest hesitation, the ever-friendly voice answered back cheerfully, "Amsterdam, of course, sir."

I hung up. "Fantastic," I thought. I had always wanted to visit Amsterdam. That I never paused to consider how I had traveled from Berlin to Amsterdam without recollection goes a long way to explaining the depth of the grip alcohol had on me at the time. I showered and ran off to the red-light district to look at the prostitutes in the windows. I met a man in the shadows who offered me cocaine. When I gave him fifty Dutch guilders for two small bags, he handed me only one and ran off. I chased after him, over canal bridges and down dark lanes, shouting. Eventually he stopped and turned and threw the second bag at me.

"You're fucking crazy," he yelled as the bag landed at my feet.

In a dark corner, I sniffed the powder, which burned my nose and did nothing to alter my mood, and then found a bar filled with dripping candles stuffed into wine bottles, where I settled in for the night.

I came home boasting of the benefits of "blackout travel." A few years later, I was not so cavalier, and the consequences of my drinking were not so easy to shrug off. At twenty-nine, I was played out. I traveled to Minnesota to get much-needed help with a drinking problem that had grown out of control.

A few years, and a lifetime, later, I was in a bookstore, gazing at a girl across the display table. She had sandy hair pulled back in a loose ponytail and wore a tight blue-and-white striped shirt—the kind the girls wore in French New Wave films. She had my full attention.

Eventually feeling eyes upon her, the young woman looked up and caught me staring. I panicked and grabbed the first book on the table in front of me.

"Here it is!" I shouted, and ran for the checkout counter like an idiot. Still flustered, I bought the book without thinking. Once out on the street, I recovered enough to take a look and see what I had just purchased. *Off the Road,* the title said. And then below it, *A Modern-Day Walk Down the Pilgrim's Route into Spain.* Nothing could have interested me less. I took the book home, put it on a shelf, and forgot about it.

A few months later I was taking a trip to Los Angeles, and halfway out the door, I grabbed the book for something to read on the plane. It was about a man who had decided to walk the Camino de Santiago in northern Spain. He walked from the south of France, over the Pyrenees, for five hundred miles to Santiago de Compostela, where, according to Catholic lore, the bones of Saint James had been discovered. In the eighth century, when this was news, thousands flocked across Spain to receive a plenary indulgence and get half their time in purgatory knocked off. The trail had fallen out of fashion in the last half dozen centuries, yet something about the author's tale of his modern-day pilgrimage spoke to me. Once again I was looking for something, I just didn't know what it was.

Two weeks later, on a bright and hot early summer morning, armed with a backpack and new hiking boots, I was crossing the border from France into Spain, high in the Pyrenees. By midafternoon I arrived, starving, with a blister forming on my right heel, at the monastery of Roncesvalles. Others who were walking the trail were already there, and we lodged together in a dormitory. Tentative allegiances were made and the next morning informal walking groups formed. I ended up with a Spaniard who was dressed in the costume of a pilgrim from centuries ago. He wore a draped brown robe and carried a long staff with a gourd affixed to the top. He looked like a seasoned Halloween trick-or-treater who knew where he was going and I followed close on his heels. He spoke no English and my schoolboy Spanish was hamstrung by self-consciousness. After three days of silent walking, my blisters became so bad that I had to stop in Pamplona for a week of rest, and my costumed guide left me behind without a word of good-bye.

I was miserable, lonely, and anxious. My long-established habit of solitude had left me completely isolated and without the resources to reach out. My worst fears about myself—among them that I just wasn't man enough to handle this—were proving to be true. I had come to Spain, I now saw, to determine whether I could take care of myself. As I sat in the Café Iruña on the Plaza del Castillo, the answer that was coming back to me was not good. I sipped coffee where Hemingway had sat and decided I would go home, my inadequacies of character and strength laid bare. Then the longer I sat, looking out on the plane trees that lined the square, the more I came to see how failure in this endeavor would later come to haunt me. This was a turning point and I knew it.

When my blisters stopped bleeding, I bought a pair of red Nike walking shoes, left my boots beside the sleeping figure of a homeless man who lived in an alcove of the ancient wall that still surrounded parts of the city, and walked on, alone. At night I often shunned the refuges where the other walkers gathered, choosing instead small inns or hotels where I could be by myself. When I did stay in the pilgrim hostels, I felt a great distance between myself and the others, as if a giant and opaque wall had been erected with me on one side and the rest of the world faintly visible but untouchable on the other. It was just such a barrier that I had once dissolved through drinking, but now, having been away from alcohol for a few years, my natural tendency toward isolation had me in its grip and I was trapped inside myself. I trudged on, hating every step.

A few weeks later, I was in the high plains of north central Spain, outside of the charmless village of Hornillos del Camino. The July heat had taken hold. The sun bore down as I marched mile after mile through low and sickly fields of wheat. The earth was parched and cracked. Sweat poured from my face and down my back under my heavy pack. A black raven circled overhead and then flew over the rise; I cursed the ease with which he covered a distance it would take me a day to accomplish. And then I was on my knees, weeping, sobbing, and then screaming—at God. I literally shook my fists at the heavens and demanded that this suffering stop. I insisted that someone come and pick me up, get me out of this—why couldn't it just be okay, like it seemed to be for all the other walkers? I cursed my isolation. Why did I feel this burden of separation? I sobbed some more; snot ran down my sweaty face.

I sank back onto my heels. My walking stick was twenty feet away, hurled aside during my tantrum. My pack had been likewise jettisoned. I picked at the hard-caked ground, embarrassed in front of no one but myself; looked up into the cloudless sky; and saw the raven had returned. He circled high above me twice and flew back over the horizon. I rose to my feet, retrieved my pack and stick, and shuffled after him.

In the sad-sack village of Castrojeriz I found a room and fell into twelve hours of dreamless sleep. When I awoke, I ate with appetite and set out again. The withering wheat I had marched through for days was behind me, and signs of life were beginning to return to the *camino*. After an hour I stopped, without reason, by the side of a barn and sat on an elevated plank. It was too early for my midmorning break, and yet I sat. Since breakfast I had had the feeling that I was forgetting something, that my pack felt lighter. I looked off toward the horizon, the distant spire of a church indicating the next village was nowhere in sight. I swilled some water and then began to feel a tingling between my shoulder blades. And suddenly I was smiling. It was the first time I remembered smiling since I left New York. And then I knew what was missing, what I hadn't carried with me that morning. Fear. The fear that had calcified between my shoulders was suddenly not there—fear that had been my center of gravity, fear that had been so ever present in my life that I was unaware of its existence until that moment of its first absence.

The tingling between my shoulders continued and grew. Soon my entire body felt as if it were vibrating. I felt physically larger, as if I had grown—or was growing. I breathed deep and spread my arms. I tilted my head back and began to sing. The Who's song "Getting in Tune" spilled from my lips. I had no recollection of ever singing it before and yet I knew all the words and sang without restraint.

Beside a barn in the middle of Spain, I had the same elation of being at home in myself as I had with the Artful Dodger and in that hotel room in Chicago, only this time I needed no work to hide behind. I was in my own skin and on my own terms.

The next two weeks went by in a blaze. Every step took me deeper into the landscape of my own being. I was in sync with the universe. I arrived at my chosen destination just before a downpour. I slept in and missed the pack of wild dogs that terrorized the early walkers. I met people I found fascinating. Where had they been hiding? I grew physically stronger each day, and by the time I strode into Santiago in late July I felt the way I always wanted to feel yet somehow never quite did. I needed no validation, no outside approval—I was myself, fully alive and satisfied in simply being.

I returned home changed by my experience. The acute euphoria of my trip faded, but my sense of self lingered and went deep. And so I began to travel, not for work, but for travel's sake. I returned to Europe, to the cities I had been to before, rewriting my drunken travel history and giving myself clear-eyed recollections. I began to take longer trips, to Southeast Asia and then Africa. Always alone. Often I arrived with no plan, no place to stay, knowing no one. I wanted to see how I would manage, if I could take care of myself, and inevitably found myself walking through fear and coming home the better for it. Success in acting had given me a persona and a shell of confidence; my travels helped me find myself beneath that persona and fill out that shell with belief. Through travel, I began to grow up.

🚶

Whenever I would tell people that I was going off on some trip or another, I was met with remarks like, "Oh, tough life," or, "That's rough." Even good friends reacted with outright hostile envy—"Must be nice," they often said. I used to try to explain and justify my travels. It was pointless.

Travel—especially by people who rarely do it—is often dismissed as a luxury and an indulgence, not a practical or useful way to spend one's time. People complain, "I wish I could afford to go away." Even when I did the math and showed that I often spent less money while on the road than staying home, they looked at me with skepticism. Reasons for not traveling are as varied and complex as the justification for any behavior.

Perhaps people feel this way about travel because of how it's so often perceived and presented. They anticipate and expect escape, from jobs and worries, from routines and families, but mostly, I think, from themselves—the sunny beach with life's burdens left behind.

For me, travel has rarely been about escape; it's often not even about a particular destination. The motivation is to go—to meet life, and myself, head-on along the road. There's something in the act of setting out that renews me, that fills me with a feeling of possibility. On the road, I'm forced to rely on instinct and intuition, on the kindness of strangers, in ways that illuminate who I am, ways that shed light on my motivations, my fears. Because I spend so much time alone when I travel, those fears, my first companions in life, are confronted, resulting in a liberation that I'm convinced never would have happened had I not ventured out. Often, the farther afield I go, the more at home I feel. That's not because the avenues of Harare are more familiar to me than the streets of New York, but because my internal wiring relaxes and finds an ease of rhythm that it rarely does when at home.

At some point in my travels I began to jot down notes. I had tried to keep a journal, but I found my reminiscences indulgent and silly. I found no joy in writing them and was embarrassed rereading them.

One day I wrote a scene of an encounter that I had with a young man who offered me a ride on his moped in Saigon. The scene captured the essence of my trip. Then a woman I saw behaving rudely in Laos shed light on my experience of that silent city. On New Year's Day in Malawi, the image of a small girl carrying a large umbrella in the sun stayed with me. I wrote it all down.

When I came home I put my notepads in the back of a drawer and didn't look at them. But the idea grew.

I knew someone who knew someone, and I met a man named Keith Bellows, the editor of *National Geographic Traveler* magazine. Keith is a barrel-chested lion of a man with a mane of silver hair— exactly the kind of man who had intimidated me in my youth. He agreed to meet me over drinks in an East Village bar, where I told him of my desire to write about travel for his magazine.

He looked at me funny. "You're an actor."

"I know that," I said. "I also know how to travel, and I know what it's done for me." I was forthright in a way that I never had been able to be when talking about my acting.

"Can you write?" He still wasn't giving the conversation much weight; he was looking at a young woman down the bar.

"I can tell a story." This got his attention. "That's what I've been doing for twenty years as an actor." I shrugged.

It took another year of cajoling, via e-mail, on the phone, and over dinners, during which we became friends. Finally, after a meal at a restaurant in SoHo, Keith looked at me and said, "I still don't understand why you would want to do this. You're not going to make any money. There's no glamour."

I shrugged and offered up a vague, "It'll be fun." As with my first acting role in high school, something was calling me, and I kept that knowledge to myself. I had no way of knowing where it might lead; all I knew was that it made sense to me.

"Where do you know well? What place speaks to you?"

"Ireland," I said quickly. "The west. There's a place in County Clare—"

"Then that's where I'm sending you."

And so a second career began, traveling and writing about those travels.

It was on that trip to Ireland, for my first writing assignment, that I met D for only the second time, and we decided to spend our life together.

The first time I saw D, she was in the lobby of the Great Southern Hotel in Galway, in the west of Ireland. Tall and striking, with a confident stride, she approached me as I waited for a taxi to take me to the airport.

"I really liked your film yesterday," she said, and stuck out her hand. (I had written and directed a short film adaptation of a Frank O'Connor story that was playing in a local festival.) I was acutely aware of her fingers wrapping around my own—the strength and presence of her grip galvanized my energy. I felt as if I'd been met— with her handshake, D reached in and pulled me from my isolation.

She too had shown a film at the festival—I hadn't seen it.

"Your taxi is here, sir," the doorman said.

I turned back to D, we exchanged first names, and I left.

She was beautiful and had a clear, direct manner that got my attention, but she wasn't the kind of woman I had ever dated. Yet her handshake stayed with me.

A few weeks later, I e-mailed the festival director and mentioned my meeting with a "fellow filmmaker." I'd lost her e-mail address, I lied. Would she be able to pass it on? Even in the moment, I was aware how out of character this was for me.

E-mail obtained, I wrote out a tentative query of reconnection while sitting in the business center in a hotel basement in Barcelona, Spain, where I was acting in a film. I remember clearly leaning back in the chair and saying aloud to the empty room, "What are you doing?"

And then I clicked "send."

Several weeks passed, and then a reply came. Yes, D remembered and had enjoyed our brief meeting as well. She hoped I had a nice time in Ireland and at the festival. Her e-mail matched my tone of cordial formality. She signed her name at the bottom.

Then I scrolled farther down. After a large space, she had typed a simple question in an otherwise impersonal response—"Who *are* you?"

I e-mailed back, saying I would be in the west of Ireland in a month's time to do a travel story; perhaps we could meet for a coffee.

"I live in Paris," was the cryptic reply.

"Excuse me," I responded, hoping playful sarcasm reached through e-mail.

She e-mailed back. "I'll actually be only a few miles away from where you're doing your story on that weekend, at a family reunion. Coffee would be fine."

The plan was to meet for an hour at the Old Ground Hotel in

Ennis when my friend Seve would be joining me. Yet four platonic and charged days later—with my friend acting as an unintended chaperone—we were still together. I finally put her on the train east and I walked a foggy and windswept beach at Lahinch and knew that my life was about to get complicated.

I was still married to my first wife. But we were drifting. I knew she was frustrated. I felt like I had to leave 20 percent of myself outside just to walk in the door of our marriage. We had met in college, a youthful love, and had been together, on and off, for years. Twenty years after we met, we married. It seemed that instead of our marriage being the beginning of our life together, it had been the culmination. The subsequent birth of our son was its finest moment. We loved each other, but together, we were under a rock.

My meeting D had stirred a feeling that sent my wife and me into therapy, but the marriage was over. She wisely took some time to find a relationship that suited her adult self better than I did, while I rushed headlong into a relationship with D.

That was seven years ago.

We came to the decision to finally get married without drama. It was soon after we had returned from Vienna, a family trip with D's parents. She was sitting at the dining table, drinking tea. I was across the room at the desk, going through e-mail. The kids had just gone to bed.

"So should we get married?" she asked, without warning.

I stopped typing and turned toward her. She was smiling—the smile where her lips don't part and her head tilts a bit to the right. The smile she gives when she is playful and confident.

We hadn't broached the topic much in the last few years. I had proposed on a moonlit beach in the Caribbean four years earlier—six months after the birth of our daughter—after which we began to make plans that went nowhere. Date conflicts, location issues, family members' attendance—all masked an unpreparedness that we had been unable to address. The plans floundered, then so did our relationship. It took time to acknowledge how off course we were, then time to let it heal, and then here we were again.

This time, when she spoke, I looked at her face for a while. It was a moment we hadn't had before. I knew my response would lead us in one direction or the other.

"Yeah," I said, "we should."

That night I awoke at four A.M. I couldn't breathe. I got out of bed and opened the window and lay back down. It was pointless—I was done sleeping. I got up and brushed my teeth, then looked in on my sleeping children—perfect, both of them, the way children are as they sleep. I went to the kitchen and made a cup of tea. I splashed cold water on my face in the sink.

I wanted all this, I had fought to get it. I had lost a lot along the way and gained even more. I was where I felt like I should be, but something was wrong. Why was I still filled with so much doubt? Was all my resistance really just a typical male fear of intimacy? Maybe the idea of who I was, who I wanted to be, simply didn't match up with the person I had become. Was this just a midlife crisis, was I simply a walking cliché?

But this questioning and these feelings of doubt weren't new. They had been shadowing me my whole life. I simply couldn't outrun them anymore. I was tired of all the ambivalence, tired of being a slave to it.

Yet, staring out the window waiting for the dawn, I found myself reaching for my computer. I began going through story ideas, some new ones, others I had long wanted to do, places I yearned to experience and write about. Quickly, I reached out to editors, and within the space of a few short days I had assembled a string of assignments, in some of the most exotic places in the world. When I laid out the half dozen and more stories I planned to write in the time leading up to the wedding, D simply looked at me.

"Well," she said with a shrug, "I guess I'll see you at the altar."

What was it in my nature that pulled me in opposing directions with seesaw regularity, sometimes simultaneously? How many things had I walked away from in my life because I hadn't been able to commit? A teacher once implored me to jump: "You're wading in the water and it will drown you. Dive into the deep end." She was speaking of my acting, but what she said could have applied to my entire life.

I was a parent, I was in a committed relationship—I was engaged, for God's sake—but I was still fighting it, still keeping myself separate. In the middle of a family, somehow I was still going it alone. And my signature ambivalence created unease, not just in myself, but in those around me, in those I loved. It had to change. I went to cancel my writing assignments—but D stopped me.

"No," she said. "Go." As usual, she was one step ahead of me.

I went through my first marriage withholding myself—without even understanding that that was the issue—and it had doomed us. But I have two children whom I want to see grow. I am engaged to a woman I love—with whom I want to share my life. I have to move beyond this habitual position of singularity—but I've followed my own rules for so long I don't even know if any other way is possible for me. And yet I need to try to give those I love my complete self, without ambivalence, fear, and doubt.

Emotion has been the tangible currency of my life. I have made a living—both in acting and in writing—exploring my feelings, at times dredging them up, bringing them to the surface. Faced now with a decision that will deeply alter the lives of both myself and those clos-est to me, I can't afford to back away from the challenge of uncover-ing what it is that keeps me from getting where I need to go.

I stand on the precipice of the rest of my life. My constant vacil-lation has kept me dancing along that edge—I need to step back and stake turf, for D, for my kids, for myself. And so I'm going on these journeys, not to escape the commitment I recently made—but quite the opposite, I'm going to use them the way I have always used travel: to find answers. I'm setting out in order to gain the insight necessary to bring me home.

CHAPTER TWO

PATAGONIA

"I Hope You Like to Be Alone"

"You do understand that as soon as we decided to get married you're going as far away as you can get. Literally to the end of the earth," D says.

"What's your point?" I ask.

I'm already waiting by the elevator when I put down my pack and return for one last good night. I slip into the bedroom and can hear D singing to our daughter. When my eyes adjust to the dark I can see that D is lying beside our daughter in bed. She's crying softly.

"Sweetheart, what are you doing?"

"Nothing," she says, wiping her tears.

I sit on the edge of the bed and lean in to embrace her. I brush our daughter's fine blond hair back from her face, tell her I love her, and rest my hand over D's heart. Her hand moves to cover mine. The three of us sit for a while like this in the dark, with only the sound of our breathing, back and forth.

On the corner in the fading light, I search for a cab. My arm, extended out toward an approaching taxi, feels frail and insubstantial in the still-too-cold March air. I'm aware suddenly that this is my departure, the moment my trip begins. I look at my watch. I toss my backpack across the seat, climb in, and experience my first flash of excitement about the journey ahead.

"Kennedy," I shout to the driver through the Plexiglas partition. I sit back and open the window; a harsh late-winter blast burns my ear.

The day has been long and fraught with the usual strain of imminent departure. My nine-year-old son from my first marriage had to go back to his mom after lunch today. On "transition days," as we've come to call this weekly switch-off, my son and I often get into a fight. I'm upset he's going away and he's upset—about what, I'll never truly know. Usually, the fights are easily resolved and we hug and I tell him how much I love him. He says, "I love you too, Dad," and I feel I have at least one more day before our relationship deteriorates the way mine did with my own father.

We were playing soccer in Central Park. He beat me ten to nine. "Did you let me win, Dad?" he asked.

"My knee is still bad, but when it's better you're in trouble."

Then we waited on the sidewalk in front of our apartment for my former wife and her partner to pick him up on their way out of town. The switch-over usually takes place at school, where the moment of handoff is invisible and easier on everyone. Or we wait upstairs and my son's mother and her partner come in, occasionally for a cup of tea, but more often we just stand around and fill the time with casual chatter as we wait for my son to get his shoes on. But today D was working and when I suggested that my son and I wait downstairs, she kissed him good-bye and we slipped out.

My son was hugging his mom hello when her partner pulled me aside and stuck out his hand. "Congratulations," he said.

"For what?"

"Oh, well, you know . . ."

"Oh, right." Last night I told my ex-wife that D and I were finally going to get married, in August—after the nearly four-year engagement. "Well, I mean it's no big deal, at this point," I lied.

"Hey, listen," he said, "at this age—you *know*."

I nodded. My ex-wife's partner is a solid guy, and I'm sure he does know. I myself have never been able to be so sure. I thanked them and waved good-bye as they drove off.

Back upstairs, I found D silently moving around the apartment. I tried to engage her in conversation, asked how her work was going, what she was thinking.

"When you're going, I wish you would just go," she said. "You're asking me all these questions but I can feel you're already halfway to Patagonia."

She was right. Whenever I'm about to leave on a trip, I'm distracted and overcompensate. I'm too solicitous and overly interested. Morning departures are easier—I just get up while everyone's still asleep and slip away.

At Ezeiza international airport in Buenos Aires I funnel toward customs. Down a long corridor, I move quickly past people shuffling along after the ten-hour overnight flight. I didn't sleep. I never do. It has become impossible for me to relax on a plane. Once carefree in the air, flying has become the receptacle for my anxiety and fear—an obvious desire for an impossible control. The higher the levels of stress in my life, the greater my yearning for such control, thus the greater my discomfort while flying. That I can see all this does nothing to alleviate my irrational responses. Images of calamity race through my mind and even the slightest turbulence has me jumping in my seat. I decided long ago that my fear wouldn't stop me from traveling, but still, flying haunts me, even when I am nowhere near a plane.

I have a recurring dream of being in a low-flying jet as it races along, swooping down, flying beneath highway overpasses and tilting wildly to slip between buildings and trees. Often, in mid-dream, the wings are sheared off. Other times the dream starts earlier in the scenario. The plane is about to take off, I'm boarding but can't find my seat, and then we're in the air and the low, drastic maneuvering begins. Rarely am I aware of others on the plane. Only occasionally will an air hostess appear and behave as if everything is completely normal, raising my already elevated stress level. These dreams always wake me with a start and have only intensified in recent years, despite the fact that I'm a "million mile" flyer.

In the arrivals hall there's a sign in Spanish, dividing people into two lanes. I bypass the crowd struggling to read it and pick the shorter queue. The flight was two hours late, and I need to get across town to the domestic airport, to catch a three-hour flight down to the Patagonian town of El Calafate.

The line snakes slowly forward. When my turn arrives, the immigration officer flips through my passport. She's looking for something. Then she speaks in rapid and clipped Spanish. My Spanish is poor in the best of scenarios, and rusty, but in my exhaustion, I panic. I'm back in Mr. Gonzalez's tenth-grade Spanish class, the one I flunked and had to repeat.

"Do you speak English?"

"Little bit," the immigration official says, holding up her thumb and forefinger very close together. "AC/DC. And the Clash." Then she begins to sing, "Should I stay or should I go? Na-na-na-NA-na-na-na-NA." Her singing is loud. Her long, loose black hair flies as she flings her head forward and back. I wouldn't have taken her for a headbanger. I step back from the window and look around. No one is paying any attention. When she finishes singing, her face is flushed and she's smiling. "You need to pay entry fee," she says, and points me toward the back of the long line.

Heading across town I call D from the back of the taxi. She is walking around the reservoir in Central Park. She's high from exertion, happy. She sounds close yet far off.

"Are you going into town for an hour, luv?"

"No," I reply. "My flight was late, I need to get across town if I'm going to make my connection. I can get a bite at the airport."

"Airport food, yum."

I look out the window as we pass a billboard for McDonald's—DOBLE McNIFICA.

"Go into town, luv," D says. "Get a steak. You'll make the flight, you always do. God knows when you'll get a decent meal again down there at the bottom of the world."

I ask the driver his name and where I can get one of Argentina's famous steaks. Paulo's gaze shifts to the rearview mirror. He lifts his eyebrows. I nod and he swerves across two lanes, exits the highway, and heads toward Puerto Madero. Ten minutes later we pull to a stop outside a red brick converted factory.

I'm ushered through a cool dark room to a seat at the last free table on the back terrace, beside the restored canal. The tuxedoed head-waiter hurries over. I try to think of what the correct words for "rib-eye steak" might be in Spanish. Just to be sure I'm being understood, I point to my ribs and then my eye as I say them.

The headwaiter does not laugh in my face but instead nods his approval, snaps his fingers at a passing busboy, orders him to fill my water glass, spins on his heel, and is gone. I like him immensely. When my steak turns out to be the best rib eye I've ever eaten, I dub this a superb restaurant and Buenos Aires a sophisticated and welcoming city.

Then I'm back in the car with Paulo.

"Good steak?" he asks.

"Very."

"Expensive?"

"Very."

Paulo shrugs. "You're an American."

Then we're weaving along back roads, slicing between loading trucks, racing to Aeroparque Jorge Newbery. The oceanic Río de la Plata opens on our right and I'm deposited on the curb.

"Do you speak Spanish?" the ticket agent asks.

"Badly."

"What are you doing here?"

"I'm going to El Calafate."

He nods. "I hope you like to be alone."

Mery Rios is small and round and can barely see over the steering wheel of her Honda. She will be heading down to Ushuaia for the christening of her grandson next week. She and her husband came here from up north when the military transferred him to this lonely outpost twenty-five years ago.

"A long time, no?" She takes her eyes off the road and turns to beam at me, in the passenger seat beside her.

"Yes," I reply. Mery and I conduct this entire conversation in Spanish. I had no idea that I knew the word for "baptism" or "border dispute." But apparently, I do. Perhaps I speak the language better than I remember, or maybe it's a testament to Mery's clear, precise, and S-L-O-W enunciation. It gives her away as the schoolteacher she used to be, before she retired. She drives a taxi occasionally now, "to help out." There's a friendly yet distant quality about her that relaxes me. I like her.

The drive into El Calafate from the airport is over open and stark land, interrupted by jutting outcrops. There is little vegetation, apart from the occasional lenga tree struggling to survive. Far to the north, beyond the milky aqua of the sprawling Lago Argentino, jagged peaks of snowcapped mountains are buried under a shroud of dense, gray clouds. The sky is vast and dominating, by turns wildly expansive and forbidding. I try to adjust to the magnitude of the vista and am left shaking my head. I sigh heavily and open the window farther. After a checkpoint on the outskirts of town, the only road in swerves through a roundabout and funnels us toward the main drag. Suddenly there are trees, tall poplars and conifers, and more development than I anticipated.

"How many people live here now, Mery?"

"Twenty thousand," she says. "But still, it is *muy tranquila*—very calm."

My guidebook says six thousand. At first glance, I'd put the number somewhere between the two estimates.

Mery offers me a quick tour before dropping me off at my guesthouse. My first glimpse of the main drag, Avenida del Libertador General San Martin, is a shock. I had expected a dusty strip with a sloppy assortment of ramshackle dives, but instead, a tree-lined promenade bisects a wide and welcoming boulevard. It's filled with high-end outdoor-wear shops, artisanal boutiques selling handmade jewelry, wine bars, and upscale steakhouses. Tour companies offering to take people of all levels of fitness on all variety of adventure appear nearly every third shop. There's even a brand-new casino—*"Horrible!"* Mery calls out when we pass it. The town is more inviting than I expected, and prosperous in a way that makes me wish I had gotten here ten years earlier, before all the success.

An old trading post that sprang up in the early part of the twentieth century, El Calafate limped along for years, sheltering gauchos tending to the millions of sheep that gave the land purpose. No one else came this way—there was no reason. Then UNESCO named the forty-seven glaciers contained in the nearby Parque Nacional Los Glaciares a World Heritage Site in 1981. This caught the attention of a few hardy adventurers who began to make the five-hour drive over dirt roads from Río Gallegos, itself a far-flung outpost. During the next twenty years, the town grew to a few thousand, and when a local airport was opened in 2000, El Calafate became the boomtown it continues to be today.

After a dozen blocks, commerce suddenly quits and the vista is broad again and the tundra stretches. The lake is close by to our right. Mery swings into a U-turn without looking and heads back. Near the edge of town she turns and drives away from Avenida del Libertador. The pavement gives out after a block and the roads are loose gravel. We bounce farther and farther away from the center. At a corner lot on a dirt track imaginatively named Road 202, Mery stops in front of a recently constructed, redbrick, two-story house, with large windows that expose an open dining area beyond.

"We arrive." Mery beams.

She walks me to the door and I feel an urge to hug her—we shake hands instead. A bell jingles when I walk through the door. The large room I saw through the window is all blond wood, filled with half a dozen small tables. A curved, purpose-built counter is beside the door; behind it hang a half dozen keys. A black-haired and thin woman of

Asian extraction hurries through a door at the far end of the room, closes it behind her, and smiles warmly at me. She has braces on her teeth; she's in her mid-thirties.

"Andrew?" she says. Her English is heavily accented by Spanish via Japan. Her name is Maria. She is high-strung, her hands in perpetual motion. She seems both grateful and relieved I have arrived.

"Can I get you tea?"

"Uh, sure," I say.

She begins to head back through the door from which she emerged.

"Do you have any green tea?" I ask.

Maria turns back with delight. "Yes, of course. The tea we drink. I will get it for you."

"Thank you." And I fall into the chair that will, in the instant of my falling, become "Andrew's chair" for my entire visit. From now on, every time I come in, Maria, or her husband, Jorge, will offer me a green tea from their personal stash, I will feel obliged to accept, and I will sit in this spot. Jorge will then turn the channel on the television in the corner from an Argentinean *telenovela* to CNN, until the day I tell him that I prefer the Latin soap operas to the news. I will sip from the same small cup each time, emblazoned with two small bunnies and a mother rabbit on the side—Jorge and Maria have two small children. Each morning my breakfast will be set on the table before this same chair.

My room is up a flight of stairs, the first door on the left. Although there are only six guest rooms, the number on my door says 7. Inside there is a twin bed, a small desk, and a chair. A small mirror is mounted on the wall. A single bulb covered by a paper lamp provides light from above. I find the monastic simplicity of the room a relief. I stand in front of the single square window, overlooking a backyard with sparse grass and a clothesline laden with bedsheets and children's clothes. The day outside is fading without drama.

After nearly twenty-four hours of travel and ten thousand miles, I drop my pack. "Where am I?" I say aloud to the empty room. I'm wired and the small space cannot contain me—within minutes I make my way back to town.

I have a steak at one of Avenida del Libertador's trendier-looking spots, with an open grill and a robust, healthy-looking crowd that appears to contain more locals than tourists.

"This time of year it is," my very solicitous waiter, Nicolas, says. He's trim, with closely cropped hair and a well-manicured beard. Nicolas moved down from Buenos Aires a year earlier. "It's much kinder here," he tells me. So kind, in fact, that I wonder if Nicolas isn't trying to pick me up.

I go next door and buy an ice cream from the chubby teenage girl behind the counter, stagger back to my twin bed, and collapse.

The next morning I'm back on the main street. There's only a faint breeze blowing through the tops of the poplars. Nowhere in evidence is the infamous Patagonian wind that rips car doors from their hinges or sends picnic tables rolling like tumbleweeds. The sun is shining and it starts to grow warm. Then clouds roll overhead and rain falls, leaving a chill in the air, then the sun is out and I take my jacket off again—all in the space of twenty minutes. The temperate climate and endlessly changeable weather are nearly identical to D's native Ireland.

Beside the town's only taxi stand there's a storefront shop with a small chalkboard out front. Viva La Pepa has a dozen empty tables and a lone woman with prematurely graying hair and a sad face standing behind a high bar. She gives me a wary welcome; I order a smoothie and sit opposite her on a high stool. Her name is Julia, and she came to El Calafate from Rosario, up north, six years ago because she was "tired from the city."

"Is everyone here from somewhere else?"

Julia, who is cutting a mango, pauses with the fruit in her hand. "I don't know anyone who was born here."

When I mention children she smiles for the first time. She shows me pictures of her daughter on her phone; I show her pictures of my kids.

Her husband, Roberto, comes into the shop. He was just at home watching *Seinfeld*. "We love Kramer," Julia tells me, and laughs a little sadly. Roberto is a shaggy dog of a man, with long black hair and an unkempt beard. His spirit is as distantly amiable as his wife's is guardedly pleasant. He works at the new ice museum just outside of town. He doesn't know anyone who was born here either.

Julia mentions where I might get a rental car, and two blocks off the main drag I look for the house with the white metal door with no signage. Veronica Riera, who moved down from Chubut eleven years ago, eyes me from under her low-hanging hair and rents me the small Fiat sitting in her driveway. She reminds me to "park against the wind, I don't want my door coming off." And I wonder if this is Veronica's personal car; there are no others in sight.

I take the lone road west out of town, the lake to my right. Along the water's edge a dozen pink flamingos take flight from the cloudy turquoise water. I pass a brown and white horse nibbling on long yellow grass. Nearby a black dog chases three gray-crested ducks through the reeds and back into the frigid water. Little has changed about this scene since the explorer Valentine Feilberg became the first European to lay eyes on it in 1873.

When I get my Fiat up to fifty miles per hour, the steering wheel begins to vibrate, and the entire car beneath me starts to shake violently. After a solitary hour on the deserted and straight road, I come to a T-junction at the base of a large hill. There is no sign. I turn left. It starts to rain. The tarmac carries me around the hill and begins to swerve and hug the suddenly lush terrain. The road dips and curves through moss-covered trees and as I come out of a tight bend, something catches my eye—glowing, a translucent blue and white. I stop my car in the middle of the road.

"Oh my God." And then I repeat it like an idiot to the empty car, "Oh my God." Ahead, but still a good way off, is the Perito Moreno Glacier. The rain falls harder. The clouds are hanging low, the light is dim and dull, the sky is a dirty gray. Despite this, the glacier appears to be glowing—not reflecting light but emitting it, radiating it. It looks like a pulsing, living thing. The suddenness and surprise of the view has filled me with such a feeling of being alive that in this instant I tell myself it is worth any cost I have to pay to ensure the continuing possibility of such moments. Slowly, I drive on.

Perito Moreno may lay claim to being the only "drive-up" glacier on the planet. A few miles from where I first laid eyes on it, a parking lot welcomes visitors, who can hop out of their cars, march across the gravel, and come face-to-face with the three-mile-wide, twenty-story-high snout of the nineteen-mile-long glacier—just a few yards across the lake. Sheets of rain have begun to lash down. The few visitors from the single tour bus flee toward the snack shop, their thin yellow ponchos clinging to their hunched frames.

A series of walkways leads from the observation deck down toward the glacier. I follow one, then hear thunder and look to my right. A large sliver of blue ice calves off and crashes into the water, sending out a small tsunami. I walk closer. My clothes are soaked through. Eventually I'm at the end of the walk. I want to be closer still. I want to be on it.

Back in town, I walk into one of the "adventure" shops on Avenida del Libertador at random and hire a guide to take me out on the ice.

The next day, Tachi Magansco, a young and athletic blonde who moved down from Bariloche, leads me to a small boat that takes us across the narrow bay and we begin to climb up the drainage parallel to the hulking glacier. A bird I can't see makes a screeching sound I've never heard before.

"Uh-oh," Tachi says.

"What?"

"That's a *cachaña;* it always starts to screech like that when there's bad weather coming."

The sky is cloudless. We pass a forty-foot waterfall, then drop down into the ravine and sidle up to the glacier. Close up, its edges appear dirty—sediment has risen up and been expelled. Tachi hands me a set of crampons, each with ten two-inch spikes set into the bottom. Then she hands me a harness.

"In case you fall down a crevice and I need to make a rescue."

I look at her.

"Don't worry, it rarely happens." We step out onto the glacier. The brittle ice crunches beneath my feet. My first steps are tentative, as if the three-hundred-foot-thick ice won't be able to hold my weight. She leads me out over rolling and then jagged undulations on the frozen sea. We walk for an hour. The screeching *cachaña* was right; the sky begins to cloud over and the temperature drops. The farther we walk, the vaster the glacier is revealed to be. It begins to snow. Quickly, the blue ice gets a dusting of white. Then the clouds drop lower. Then lower. We're in a rolling portion of the glacier now, giant and gentle swells frozen in mid-movement. The snow dances in front of me. Then it's impossible to see where the ice ends and the sky begins. I lag back and for a few moments I'm alone, lost in a pillow of white. Above, below, and all around me everything is the same. I can see nothing. I can hear my breathing and that is all. If I didn't know I was standing I could be floating, like I used to dream about as a young man.

Before my fear of flying took hold, I used to press my nose against the window as the plane rose up into the sky; I would dream of bouncing on the banks of clouds as if they were a trampoline. I would envision myself doing flips and spins, naked, twisting and twirling in the sky, dropping deep into the clouds and then bouncing back up. I would have given anything, anything, to be allowed to do this solitary flying for a single hour.

Then the cloud lifts and I can see Tachi looking back at me. I feel caught, exposed. Embarrassed, I grin and we pick our way off the ice.

ⵊ

Back in El Calafate, I have my nightly quota of side-of-Argentinean-beef from one of the restaurants on Avenida del Libertador, buy my ice cream from the girls in the Helado Shop, and head out of town. When I step off the main drag, El Calafate instantly loses some of its more obvious charm. The roads that lead away from the center become gravel and then dirt, and then quit altogether. Small, worn, and weather-beaten houses cramp one another, close to the road, many with only a single lamp burning. I walk in the gutter along the street—there are no sidewalks—and glance into a bare window. Three generations of a family are huddled in front of a large television, their faces bathed in a bluish, flickering glow. Next door, an old man irons a shirt in the half light, sipping a bottle of beer. Dogs bark at me from the darknesss.

I've seen similar scenes in small towns in Brazil and Cambodia and even the American West—lives being lived with unself-conscious deliberateness. There's no desire, or no energy, to pretend anything. I see desperate disappointment and loneliness in such scenes of domesticity and routine. I feel far removed and want no part of them. Yet I can't look away. What hunger of theirs is being fed, when they seem to me instead like scenarios of slow decay? What is it about these scenes that I don't understand?

I walk until the road and streetlights give out, then mount a small, swinging footbridge. Someone has nailed a handwritten sign on it, PUENTE BAEZA. I cross the small stream and walk down a dirt lane; make a left at the house with the black Lab that barks at me every time I pass by; ease past a row of tall poplar trees, planted to offer protection against the fierce winds of summer, their tops only occasionally catching a breeze now; move on past the gray mare whose restraining rope is too long, allowing her to wander far enough for her hindquarters to stick out into the gravel track as she nibbles from the last grassy patch. Then I pick up the stumpy mixed-breed dog who silently escorts me one last block to Jorge and Maria's.

When I come in Jorge is waiting up for me. My teacup is already set. He hurries his stocky frame into the back room and returns with a small pot that he places in front of me. Then he flops down on the nearby couch.

"How was the glacier?"

"Big."

"I've never been."

Jorge was born in Buenos Aires, of Japanese parents. He first came down to El Calafate in 1999, liked what he saw, bought the property in 2001, built the place himself, and opened in 2004.

"It's a good place for family, quiet, safe," he tells me. "I worked in a factory for fourteen hours a day for eleven years in Okinawa. And now"—he spreads his thick hands wide—"the sky. We have the sky." There are tears in his eyes.

I'm touched by his vulnerability, his effort to connect, and his desire to please, yet I'm embarrassed by it in equal measure. As much as I enjoy Jorge's company and appreciate his desire for domestic security, I find my knee bouncing and I'm always relieved to get away.

It is just this kind of limited tolerance for social encounters that confounds a social animal like D.

I climb the stairs to my narrow room, and under the single bulb I video Skype with her back in New York. She answers quickly; her face on the screen is dim. There is only one lamp lit, over in the far corner of the room. She's sitting at the dining table back in our apartment. It's odd to see her there, to be in two places at once. Yet more and more, this duality—being both home and far-off simultaneously—has come to define my once solitary travel.

I pick up my computer and give D a tour of my room. I show her the single bed, the desk and chair.

She laughs. "Perfect for you."

"I know. Isn't it?" I smile back. Over the distance, our different needs find a way to amuse us and bring us closer.

"I found a poem by Hafiz today that reminded me of you, want to hear it? It's called 'This Place Where You Are Right Now.' 'This place where you are right now / God circled on a map for you . . .'"

As she reads I can see and hear her acceptance and appreciation for what it is I'm trying to do on the road and why it's important, not only to me but to our future. It's a generosity that will be severely tested in the coming months. When she finishes the poem, we're silent for a while, just looking at each other on-screen.

"Dani and Michael invited us up for the weekend when you get back. They're having a dinner party."

"Okay, well, let's think about it."

"I said yes."

D watches me nod my head.

"Do you ever think it's strange that you never want to go out with anyone?"

"I want to go out with you," I say.

"That doesn't count."

"I think that's all that counts."

"Hmm . . ."

"Do you ever think it's strange that you want to go out all the time?" I ask.

"No, I don't. I like to go out with people. I like people. It's normal. And fun. Your never wanting to see anyone, that's what's strange."

It's a conversation we've had many times, but the distance allows a playful, even flirtatious tension to fill our familiar words.

"And can we please go dancing when you get back? I can't believe that we never go dancing; I used to go dancing every week. I need to dance." D abandons herself while dancing—while I'm too hamstrung by self-consciousness.

"Okay, okay, we'll go dancing," I say. I have no intention of going dancing.

"So I've been thinking about the wedding, want to hear it?"

The first time we started to plan a wedding, four years earlier, we made a guest list in two columns on a yellow legal pad. D's column ran to well over four pages. Mine petered out somewhere in the middle of the first page. We decided to get married in Dublin and then we changed our minds and decided on New York, and then it was back to Dublin. We picked a date, and then changed it, and then changed it again. Time went by. D's parents wanted to know what was going on. We picked another date and then canceled it. On the surface, logistics seemed to overwhelm us, but there was an underlying tension between us that needed to be addressed. The very idea of coming together started to push us apart. D also struggled with her new life in America. The relentless drive for success that defines life in New York and supersedes time with friends confounded her.

"Is every relationship in this city a work relationship? I just want to have a cup of coffee and a chat."

She lamented the distance from her family to a degree that did not abate over time. "I would like to be able to walk over to Mum and Dad's house. I'd like to see my brothers. You live ten minutes away from half your family and you never see them. I mean it's crazy, who am I with? What is the Universe trying to tell me?"

Eventually we just stopped talking about the wedding.

I joked that it took D a year to like me again after she put on my ring. But then it stopped being a joke. By the time she had come to terms with the idea of our marrying, I had grown skittish. We struggled for power—over everything. We settled into a pattern of simmering tension, slowly escalating to open conflict, followed by a silent retreat and then tentative coming together, before a broaching of tenderness and acknowledgment of our love, and the subsequent rediscovery that there seemed to be something bigger at play holding us together than our own wills. And then the cycle would begin again. The kids also fell into a dynamic of relentless bickering.

One afternoon during this period, after a particularly bad spell, I picked up the phone, and my son, who was with his mother for the week, was on the line. He never called during the day. He was struggling not to cry.

"Hey, kiddo, what's up?" I said.

"Dad, I don't think I can come back."

"Sweetheart, why, what's going on?"

"My sister and I can't get along." His tone was very formal, very grave.

I tried to downplay their squabbling. "That's completely normal, all siblings fight. I fought with my brothers. It's totally normal."

"No, Dad, this is different. We don't get along, we never will. It's something else."

"What, sweetheart, what is it?"

"I don't know," he said with deep sadness.

But I knew. From the start, the kids mirrored D's and my relationship, absorbed it, were affected by it, and reflected it back to us—the good and the bad.

I promised I would take care of it, that it would all be okay, hung up the phone, and cried. I stared out the window, listening to the sound of drilling from the street below. After a while I walked into the bedroom, where D was on the bed, reading. I sat on the side of the bed and she put her book away. I didn't speak for a while and neither did she. "What are we doing?" I said finally, turning to look at her.

D held my gaze and then began to cry. I cried some more too. We hugged and said nothing else. Later, after a dinner in which even our normally talkative daughter was quiet, I told D about the call with my son.

She nodded. "He's a very sensitive person."

The next morning when we woke, an unspoken decision had been reached. A few days later my son returned as scheduled, everything was the same, and yet it was different. Instead of using our considerable passion for each other against one another, we returned to the baseline of support and appreciation that had somehow been turned on its head. Suddenly we were allies again, with the goal to unite, not battle to gain victory and confirm incompatibility. Our lives, all our lives, shifted.

This time, D is suggesting we simply tell our friends that we're getting married in Dublin.

"Maybe we just have it in Dartmouth Square," she says over Skype. Dartmouth Square is a small park across the street from where D lived when we first met. It's an elegant neighborhood green encircled by Georgian row houses.

I have a vivid memory of looking out D's bedroom window during a purple dusk and watching hundreds of swallows circle and dive in unison, screeching until they settled on a tree to perch for the night.

Many afternoons I pushed our daughter's stroller on the path that wraps around the park—around and around and around, trying to get her off to sleep. And when my son was four he dressed as Superman on Halloween and raced around that same path, disappearing behind the hedge, his red cape flying, until he reappeared at the next opening and then disappeared again, only to appear at the next opening.

"We'll just tell everybody who wants to come to bring along a picnic and come celebrate the afternoon with us." I watch her sip tea over Skype.

"Sounds simple," I say. "I like it."

"Mmm . . . we'll see," D says.

There's something in the way D says "We'll see," and I know that things will never be that simple.

Jorge has noticed that a fairly good-size pool of oil has formed under the engine of my Fiat. I'm grateful, because today I'm headed a few hundred miles north, to the village of El Chaltén.

On the way out of town I stop by the house with the white metal door. Veronica opens it a crack and peers out at me from under her hair. When she hears my stumbling Spanish she remembers me, and then we're both on our knees, watching oil drip slowly from the engine of the Fiat. She nods knowingly and offers me the keys to a similarly battered vehicle, same make and model, parked across the street. This one doesn't begin the death rattle until I hit seventy miles per hour. I race north over the recently paved tarmac.

After a few hours of relentless and barren earth, Lago Viedma comes into view on my left. It's the other massive, glaciated lake that anchors southern Patagonia. I turn left onto Highway 23, and within a half hour I'm approaching El Chaltén. The jagged tower of Mount Fitz Roy, one of rock climbing's crown jewels, presides over the village of one thousand—but is nowhere in sight. A dense and gray blanket of clouds is entrenched just above the tree line.

Common are stories of climbers who come halfway around the world to conquer Fitz Roy, only to leave without ever attempting it, or even seeing its famous peak, so domineering is the infamous weather. I'm not interested in scaling the mountain, but I'd like to hike its slopes and get a look at the cragged peak that graces virtually every calendar of Argentina. A light rain is falling as I cruise along Avenida San Martin, El Chaltén's wide and sleepy main drag. A skinny dog chases my car.

It's a strange little town. Nothing much existed here a decade ago, other than a ranger station, some primitive shelter for a few hard-core climbers, and the occasional gaucho passing through. Then, when the airport opened in El Calafate and tourism started to hit, a town was hastily constructed. They forgot a few things—like a bank and a gas station—and when I go into the town's only pharmacy, they're out of Band-Aids.

Maybe it was the drive, or the fact that there is no one hanging around town, but I feel unsettled, anxious. I eat with my back to the wall at a corner table in an empty restaurant and realize that I'm lonely. It's something I rarely feel, but when I do, I usually experience it as a pleasant sensation. Only occasionally does loneliness sadden me, or fill me with anxiety, and when it does, it takes me by surprise and leaves me feeling adrift, as if I have misplaced myself somehow.

I walk back out of the restaurant into the cool midafternoon breeze. The rain has stopped and I walk right out of town and up into the mountains. I focus on my steps, concentrating on the rhythm of my movement. I hike for several hours. Something in the repetition and measurable progress of walking brings me back to myself.

Lost in an insular pattern of random thought, I don't notice when the clouds lift, until I look up and suddenly see Mount Fitz Roy for the first time. The late-afternoon sun is painting its jagged spire a golden brown. I stop in my tracks.

"There you are," I say aloud.

The following morning I set out for another hike, out to Laguna Capri. The day is bright and the granite, sheer face of Fitz Roy cuts up into the sky above me. My hike is simultaneously exhilarating and grounding, the way walking over earth far from pavement is, yet when I return to town late in the day, I'm struck again with feelings of loneliness.

Everyone here in El Chaltén is just passing through or is here only to service the needs of those who are. There is a lack of the self-possessing permanence that is required to maintain solidity in so solitary a position. Unlike El Calafate, where people seem to have found a haven, El Chaltén strikes me as a way station, a stunningly beautiful one to be sure, but a way station nonetheless.

I always lose confidence when I'm in transient places like this, and feel as if there's something I don't understand, something that the others around me do. Perhaps these are the feelings that people like Jorge and his wife, and the families I saw through the windows in El Calafate, are striving so hard to avoid.

Virtually everyone I met there had a quality about them that was both independent and yet part of something bigger. I began to wonder, while hiking on Fitz Roy, if that comfortable duality I felt in El Calafate was a homegrown sensation. What was it about the town that bred some special form of independent ease? Was there something in the water that cultivated solitary yet communal characters? Or was it because everyone I met in El Calafate was a transplant from somewhere else? Was the town a magnet for loners looking for a place to fit in and belong? Whatever it was, I don't feel it here in El Chaltén.

So before the sun quits for the day, I hop in my Fiat; glance at Fitz Roy, stark against a cloudless blue sky in my rearview mirror; and beat it back to El Calafate.

Jorge and Elizabeth embarrass me with the sincerity of their warm welcome. My retreat to the safety of domesticity isn't lost on me, yet when Jorge's mother, a tiny woman who speaks no English and is visiting from Japan, insists I share some of her homemade sushi, I wish I had gone into town for dinner. My seesawing social sensitivity has always been maddening to D, and in moments like this, I can understand why.

So many times I've committed us to a function, only to be sitting at a table with strangers or standing at a cocktail party, suffering, while D whispers in my ear.

"You knew we were going out tonight, luv. It was your idea. Now you don't want to be here; what's up?" she has said to me more than once.

I decide to try to find someone, anyone, who was actually born here in El Calafate. To see if perhaps they see things differently from me. My search eventually leads me to town hall. Several men and women sit behind a long desk. When I explain what I'm after, they stare at me for a while. Then one of the vaguely friendly ladies remembers an older gentleman named Nuño, who she thinks grew up in town.

A search through the phone book is made, the number found, and a call put through. Nuño's wife says he's out, but she'll tell him when she sees him and maybe he'll come by town hall and talk to me. So I wander off, say hi to Julia at Viva La Pepa, have one of her crepes, and drift back to town hall.

Nuño is there, waiting for me. He's a small man, stocky, with tightly trimmed hair, thick glasses, and a bandana around his neck. He's wearing a black *boina*—a Patagonian beret. He looks like he could be from the Basque region of Spain. Everyone at town hall is very pleased that they could help me. Hands are shaken all around. Nuño and I walk out to speak in private.

Immediately, Nuño has difficulty deciphering my horrible Spanish—apparently it's not as good as Mery Rios led me to believe. I struggle to understand his rapid-fire, slang-filled dialect. Nuño worked on *estancias,* shearing sheep, herding cattle, and at the airport taking tickets, and thirty more jobs. He's retired now, at seventy-three, "but still working, of course," he says with a smile.

It turns out that Nuño wasn't born in El Calafate after all, but in a tiny village called Río Mitre a few miles away. When I ask him if it's true that things here used to be so dire that the government paid people to move to El Calafate, Nuño stares at me.

"*Otra vez,*" he says. I repeat the question. His eyes narrow, his square chin drops, and he launches into a long, rambling answer filled with rapid and clipped consonants. His hands begin to wave violently. His face is flushed. He is getting very worked up. Who would say such a thing? He wants to know. Not him.

I apologize, assure him I must have misunderstood, and gently touch his arm in solidarity. He shakes me off and drags me across the street, in search of someone who can translate. Nuño doesn't want to be misunderstood. I tell him I know a woman who works in a restaurant where I got some juice who speaks pretty good English. He grunts. There are no traffic lights in town yet; we almost get hit crossing Avenida del Libertador. We enter Viva La Pepa, and I wave to Julia.

"*Hola,*" she says, and smiles. She's happy to see me return. Before I can explain, Nuño launches into a tirade and Julia translates, as best she can, what Nuño has already told me. Julia's English becomes halting and fractured under the pressure of Nuño's assault. At first she looks at me with an apologetic furrow in her brow. Then her frustration begins to show. Soon, her anger at me for bringing this scene into her world of quiet reprieve cannot be hidden. I apologize and try to usher Nuño toward the door. He won't budge; he is adamant that he be understood, that things are clear. When a paying customer finally comes into the shop, Julia turns her back on us without hesitation. Out on the street, the old man is still very upset. "*Estoy preocupado,*" he says. He's worried, very worried, that I just don't understand him.

I assure Nuño that I understand—but perhaps I don't. His pride in his home, his unapologetic investment in it and attachment to it, these are things I've never experienced. What kind of solidity might these feelings have offered me if I had? He storms off without shaking my outstretched hand.

It is still dark the next morning and the wind blows hard on the bow of the *Francisco de Viedma*. The engine drones belowdecks. The predawn clouds hang close. The largest freshwater lake in Argentina looks black beneath the boat. When the sun breaks the horizon, for a few minutes light shoots up onto the low ceiling of clouds, reflecting back down onto the suddenly turquoise water, and everything is alive. The snow line is low on the mountains that meet the water's edge. The metamorphic rock glistens. The boat passes a small blue iceberg—an orphan from the Upsala Glacier. It feels too warm for snow, yet snow begins to fall. A rainbow forms on my right; an austral thrush darts past, just above the whitecapping glacier milk. I've not always had the gift to know when I'm happy in the moment, but the wind ripping across my face, the spray from the lake biting my skin, and the rapidly changing light are so exhilarating that it's difficult to breathe. I'm aware of storing the moment away, like an emergency supply of food.

Eventually, the snow turns to an icy rain and chases me inside the cabin. The sky grows lower toward the lake, and fingers of deep gray clouds reach down to only a few feet above the windswept, choppy water. My exhilaration wanes and the morning takes on a wistful mood as the boat pushes farther up into the northern arm of Lago Argentino.

The eighteenth-century Swiss author Madame de Staël once said, "Travel is one of the saddest pleasures in life." As I watch our progress through the window my thoughts follow the pace of our movement and allow a melancholy feeling of isolation and separateness to unfold like a soft blanket spreading out beneath me. I have the luxury of indulging in this state only occasionally, when I'm alone and far from home. It has no place in my relationships with my children or with D. It's a mood she has little patience for—a shadow of the child I was, not the man she shares her life with—but it's one that's been indispensable to my internal rhythm.

When I was no more than ten, possessed by the same sense of separation, I put on my winter clothes one evening and went outside. My brothers and I rarely went out after dark, but I wanted to make angels in the snow before it melted. The tail end of the afternoon storm had turned to sleet and freezing rain, so a hard sheet of ice covered the snow on the ground. My boyish weight didn't crack the crusty top layer to the fluffy snow beneath unless I stomped hard with my boots. Since angel making wasn't possible, I lay on my back, atop the hard icy shell, and looked up into the cloudless night sky. I breathed deep, again and again, to see the condensation rise. After a while the stars beyond took my attention. It was the first time I had looked up into the night sky for longer than a few seconds.

As a boy I was prone to worry and fret, but that night, as I lay still under the stars, a feeling of calm spread over me. I suddenly had a conscious realization of what it felt like to be alive. I had never considered my life, but now, in that instant, a flood of gratitude washed over me and I felt an expansiveness. Softly, the distance between the stars and me disappeared. I wasn't closer to them, or they to me, but the distance became insignificant, pliable. The size of my body swelled and I was huge—for a boy who was very small for his age, this sensation was thrilling. I was no longer bound by the rules that governed physics; size and distance became changeable, then vanished entirely. I grabbed at this feeling, in order to possess it. But in my clutching, it began to slip away. I softened my grasp and the sense of fluidity returned, I rode it like a wave. I have no idea how long this went on, but eventually my brother Peter came outside and found me. I asked him, "Do you ever feel like you're changing sizes?"

He just looked at me.

For years after that night, I had occasional, accidental moments in which my sense of size and perspective shifted and I felt like I understood something that I normally forgot. Feelings of separation dissolved, yet I was aware of my ultimate aloneness. This paradox provoked in me a sense of freedom and relief—relief that what I was always aware of on a faint, subconscious level was a strong and satisfying truth.

After nearly four hours we are deep into a narrow finger of water and the end of the lake comes clear as a thin line on the horizon. As the boat gets closer, a cluster of tall trees becomes visible, and then several low, pale yellow buildings emerge, set back a few hundred yards from the shore. Beyond, a snowcapped mountain range interrupts the vista that would otherwise continue without limit.

When I disembark, José Argento, a young Argentinean with black hair and olive skin, is there to greet me. "Welcome to Estancia Cristina."

The sudden silence after the long boat trip, coupled with the almost oppressive expanse, has left me with little to say in return. He leads me away from the shore, but after just a dozen steps I stop and look around once more.

When he speaks, José has read my mind. "You feel so small when you see all this."

"Yes," I say. Then I am grinning like a child on Christmas morning. "Yes."

The Catherine River is a few hundred yards inland. The original buildings of the *estancia* are set close to its bank, secluded in a grove of poplar and sequoia planted long ago. A restored water wheel sits on the river's edge. The stable is off to the right.

The ranch used to work huge numbers of sheep back in the early twentieth century, when fleece was known as "white gold," before the bottom fell out of the market with the invention of synthetic fiber. Like most *estancias,* it continued to run cattle for a time and now welcomes a small number of guests to help keep the doors open.

I'm led to one of the three simple and small outbuildings. The large picture window in my room contains a view across the river and the *arroyo,* up the vast golden valley, and into the snowcapped peaks of Mounts Masters and Moyano and Masón. The view is shocking in its scale, and through the window frame it looks frozen, like an Ansel Adams photograph in color.

I am unsure how to settle myself. I step outside into the fifty-four thousand acres set amid hundreds of thousands more in the national park. There are no other guests at the *estancia*. The idea thrills me. I stand awkwardly beside one of the buildings, unconsciously hovering close to the security it offers, as my ears ring with the silence around me.

I strain for even the slightest sound. There is no breeze through the poplars or the long grass. The mountains, freshly covered in snow, look like cutouts in their stillness. The horses down by the stable are far enough away to move without sound. I hear no birds call. The vista before me appears impenetrable.

Suddenly José is beside me. "Want to see some of the property?" he asks.

We bounce along a hopeless dirt track in his truck, up into the mountains. We pass through groves of beech trees, their leaves turning orange and red in the Patagonian autumn. Upland geese fly up out of an unnamed lake. Just below a ridge, the questionable road becomes impassable and we scramble to the top on foot. When we crest the ridge the Upsala Glacier confronts us, rising up and wedging itself between Mounts Cono and Agassiz.

A cloud below begins to drift up and over toward us, partially obscuring the view down into the valley. Then, as if a switch has been turned on, a gale-force wind slams into us, and I stagger back. José laughs. Then large clumps of snow are being hurled at us, horizontally. We're enveloped in the cloud. I can see only a few feet around me. Now frozen rain stings my face. I take it for as long as I'm able and then step back down off the ridge. Just a few feet below the precipice, the air is nearly still, and the snow falls in fluffy, happy clumps. José is already heading back to his truck.

"Just follow the valley back down," he shouts over his shoulder. "There's a trail most of the way."

"Where are you going?" I holler back, trying to keep the panic out of my voice.

"I have work to do, I'll see you at dinner." He slams the door, and the truck bounces away and out of sight.

I hike down into the Cañón de los Fósiles, with snow falling on my shoulders. The rock is slick underfoot. And then the weather passes. The sun pours down and I peel off a layer of clothing. Then the wind begins to swirl and it's cool and soft again. Within half an hour I experience the four distinct seasons—a typical Patagonian afternoon. I walk back down into the valley, past Lago Anita, another glaciated lake. I pass the skeletal remains of a *guanaco,* a Patagonian llama, probably killed by a puma, lying in the sun. Knotted clumps of gray fur lie beside bones that have been picked clean by the condors. Its small white skull is gleaming in the sun. This *guanaco* must have been young—its teeth are still perfectly in place. A few feet away, the bones of its intact rib cage jut toward the sky like outstretched fingers in what seems a desperate plea. A femur and hip bones lie within reach.

Cristina's yellow buildings are just dots on the valley floor below. The endless expanse I saw from my room, the valley that I looked out upon as alien, that seemed impenetrable in its vastness, becomes familiar terrain as I descend.

At the Catherine River, a three-foot salmon is facing upstream, making no progress, only the tip of its tail, barely swaying back and forth, helping it hold ground. I cross the wooden bridge to the other bank and watch. Exhausted and dying, trying to return home to spawn, the fish will make it no farther upstream; its journey will end. How long has it swum to return to its birthplace, how many hundreds, perhaps thousands of miles, to get this near to its goal and no closer?

At dinner, alone in the dining room, I see José briefly.

"Nice walk?" he asks.

"Nice walk," I reply.

After dark I step out and look up into the sky for the Southern Cross. Whenever I see it I know I am far from home and I get a childish thrill. Beside the lake, in the original sheep-shearing shed, stands the *estancia*'s "museum." The door is open. I switch on the light. The smell of livestock is still strong.

In 1914 a young English couple by the name of Joseph and Jessie Masters, who had been wandering Santa Cruz for nearly fifteen years, sailed up this northern arm of Lago Argentino and staked a claim on land that they and their son, Herbert, would live on for the next eighty years. Random items of the Masterses' family life have been preserved and are strewn about the shed in a vague semblance of display. Two photographs of the young couple in 1900 hang near the door below the corrugated iron roof—the husband with his dandy's mustache, his bride in a cameo-like profile. There is nothing about these photos that hints at the strength of character that must have enabled them to live in this remote outpost a century ago.

The night wind whistles through the gaps in the wood plank walls. A cotton press stands beside a long wood dining table. A lone black and white photo of the family, seated around the table, is propped beside it. A copy of the *Illustrated London News* dating from the sixties, milk bottles, a puma trap, all sit unadorned, without commentary. I flip through the radio logbook and land on a page from 1957. Wooden oxbows and hand plows are on display beside a ladies' purse. I'm awed by this couple and envy the kind of partnership they must have had to sustain, survive, and evidently thrive and raise children here. Their youngest daughter, for whom the *estancia* is named, died of pneumonia before they could get her to help. What must they have felt about their life choices at that moment? My own daughter has twice had pneumonia, and my fear for both my children's safety hovers over me, humming in a perpetual state of quiet alert.

My feeling isn't so much one of nostalgia for a past I never knew, it is more of an active yearning, an anxiety that these people knew something of how to live, that they possessed information that I need. I examine each object, again and again, looking for clues. I'm heartsick for people who lived a century ago.

I walk around and around, circling the room, becoming more and more desperate to take in as much as possible. I probe these touchstones, these relics of lives well lived. If I could show this to D, perhaps it would explain to her, better than I ever could, the courage and stoic harmony that I admire; perhaps she'd see in all this what I have no words to explain.

🚶

The next morning I am on a colt named Pantriste, high in the hills above the *estancia*. The horse belongs to a young cowboy named Michay Gonzalez Guerrico. He wears leather chaps and a black *boina*, pulled down over the left side of his forehead. Like their American counterparts, Patagonian gauchos tend to be impassive, insular, and extremely macho. Michay is all this.

All morning we climb higher into the mountains, the horses picking their way. Finally we arrive at an overlook and Michay dismounts. He sits on a log and peels bark off a small twig. When a condor sweeps overhead, Michay silently points up toward the sky, so I won't miss the sight. I don't know how he saw it; his eyes never left the twig in his hands. Back at the stable, when I thank him for the ride, he nods.

The following morning we're on horseback again, climbing up to a different view. When we stop, Michay tends his horses and then sits a good distance away. I turn over my shoulder to look at the hanging glacier on Mount Masters. The milky turquoise of Lake Pearson is below.

Then, for the first time in two days, Michay speaks. "The quiet," he says, "the silence," and gestures out toward the valley with his chin.

I want to laugh but stop myself. I wonder what D would make of Michay's social ease.

Later, I sit by the *estancia* in the afternoon sun, and take pictures down by the river, and watch birds picking at the grass. I can imagine myself staying here for a long time, alone and content, at the end of the world.

I have found several places in my travels where I've experienced a similar sensation—the bare and rocky Burren in the rural west of Ireland, on a remote northern coast of Brazil, in central Wyoming, and at an unlikely spot in Hawaii. Places where I felt received by the land, where my perception of the world and of my place in it fell into sync. I recognize that sense of belonging instantly.

That I didn't feel that connection in my boyhood home in suburban New Jersey is no one's fault, and that I've traveled enough to have found it on several occasions has been one of the biggest revelations in my life.

The sun sinks behind the ridge, and the air is instantly cooler. The wind picks up and I leave the river, heading back toward the main house. Smoke is coming out of the chimney. I stand on the stoop until the first stars replace the sun. I take such satisfaction and comfort in being alone like this—together with the ancient feeling of familiarity and security it brings—that I question my willingness to relinquish this sense of insular freedom, in order to open myself to D, and wonder if it could remotely supplant the satisfaction of this moment, or if it's even possible to reconcile the two.

The next morning I linger over breakfast, staring out over the valley for a long time. I revisit the museum, the stables, the river. I hike back up into the foothills of the mountains, where I can see my return boat coming across the glacier-milk lake.

Once on board, I stand on the stern and watch Cristina recede. After a long while, I go inside to sit down. Then instantly I return to the rail. Only after a long while are the buildings lost from view, and then the tall trees become indistinguishable from the land and the mountains that have dominated my world become just a few jagged ridges in a range of snowcapped peaks. I feel compelled to watch until the boat turns out of this northern arm of Lago Argentino and Cristina is gone. The light dies without event and the lake below and the sky above grow black. The wind blows hard and cold. I feel untethered, as if I have left something important behind that I may never find again.

CHAPTER THREE

THE AMAZON

"A Dirty Trick Life Plays"

"No, you didn't tell me."
"I did, sweetheart."

"I think I would have remembered you telling me that you were leaving for the Amazon on Monday." D slides her hand free from mine in the back of the cab. There have been a lot of logistical conversations lately and maybe this one slipped through the cracks.

"You just got back from Patagonia this morning," D says, and turns to look out the window. We're in gridlock on Eighth Avenue.

🚶

It started as a family trip—D, the two kids, and myself, going down the Amazon. It was D's idea, or more correctly, it was our daughter's idea. She was sitting on my lap while I looked at photos someone had sent me—an elegant, wood and steel, luxury Amazonian riverboat

THE LONGEST WAY HOME

chugging downriver under a blue sky, pink river dolphins, and large purple butterflies.

"I want to go on that boat, Daddy," my daughter said. "I want to see those dolphins."

D walked over to have a look. "Me too."

The next day when I came home, mother and daughter were looking at the photos again. And then later, when my son saw them—"Oh, yeah, Dad." I knew that the Amazon was in our future.

I obtained an assignment to write about it. Plans were set in motion. Departure was scheduled around school vacation, plane reservations made. Then someone mentioned mosquitoes. And malaria. After some intense scanning of the Internet, D ascertained that the section of Peru to which we were headed had the highest instance of malaria in the Amazon, perhaps the highest in the world. "I'm not giving the kids that medication," she declared, "it's completely toxic. It makes people insane."

There went the family trip—but by then I was committed. The plan to head upriver, deep into the Amazon with the kids, was in line with both D's and my desire to raise them to be comfortable out in the world. That there would be other travelers on the boat mattered little; I could easily imagine us carving out our own little universe on board. But the idea of going alone, trapped with a dozen strangers on a small boat, fell right into the kind of travel, and the kind of situations, I have spent a lifetime avoiding.

The week I'm home is spent digging out from things that didn't get handled while I was in Patagonia. D spends her evenings going out with friends—"When you're not here, I have to hunker down. Now I've got to go out or I'll go nuts."

On the afternoon of the third day I brush the small of her back as I walk past her in the bedroom. D turns and we look at one another. Her eyes well up. She puts her arms over my shoulders, linking her fingers behind my neck. "I know you've got to go, and that you're a travel writer and it's your job and all, but this is a lot. We need you."

D's willingness to emotionally invest in others and make herself vulnerable allows her to inhabit her humanity to a degree that still baffles me. Why would anyone who is so strong-willed, so self-sufficient, want to make herself vulnerable to someone else? D would say that what is most important in life is family, connection, and community. Loving someone, she will say, is the only thing that matters and is worth the price of relinquishing control.

"It's a dirty trick life plays," I once said to her, "what loving someone does. It's a horrible feeling, caring so much about someone. How vulnerable it makes you. I hate you for how much I love you."

"Thanks, luv. That makes me feel great."

"And the kids—all the things that could happen . . . It's completely ridiculous to love someone so much. I hate it."

"You might not want to mention that to them."

"I'm telling you, it's a dirty trick life plays. And once you're in, you can't get out."

We sit down on the edge of the bed and D tells me about the wedding plans that are taking shape in her mind.

"I think the picnic idea is fun. Dartmouth Square will work great, and whoever wants to come can just come," she says.

To believe that any social event that D is involved in planning might ever be this simple is to be willfully naïve. She grew up in a family that ran a hotel. They planned and carried off elaborate banquets, weddings, and large events on a weekly basis. D is most comfortable in a swarming and chaotic crowd. That her own wedding will be a simple picnic is an idea I greet with skepticism.

"What if it rains?"

D looks at me.

I shrug. "I mean, it *is* Ireland."

"It's not going to rain."

"Really?"

"Not if you stay positive."

"So it's up to me?"

"Kinda, yeah," she says.

"And what about the people who come from New York, how are we going to deal with them? It's a long way to bring a sandwich."

"I'll assign them each an Irish buddy, to look after them."

"So your two worlds can finally come together."

"Exactly." She leans over and kisses me. "And what do you think about Shelly marrying us?"

Shelly is a friend of D's from Ireland. She's a very funny woman, with a typically sarcastic Irish wit, but not someone who jumps to mind as the person who should, or even could, marry us.

"Shelly? Is she a priest or a minister or something?"

"No."

"Then how could she marry us?" I ask.

"It'll be a spiritual ceremony."

"What do you mean?"

"Well, we have to legally get married in the registrar's office anyway."

"We do?"

"Since you're divorced, we can't get married in a church—not that we'd want to—and in Ireland you can't get married anywhere but a church or at a civil hall."

I sense an opening. Perhaps we can simply get married in the presence of a few witnesses and get away with a small celebratory lunch. "So then why are we talking about getting married in the park with lots of people, if it doesn't count?"

"Don't say that. Of course it counts."

"But you just said—"

D glares at me. "Are you deliberately being like this?"

"Like what?"

D begins to speak very slowly. Her diction becomes very clear. "Because, I would like to have a spiritual ceremony, with our family and our friends present, to celebrate our marriage. Is that a problem?"

This is a battle I won't win. "Where is everyone going to go to the bathroom in the park, darling?"

My bag is by the door, D is on the phone, and I'm sitting in the large, overstuffed armchair in the living room. It's the most comfortable chair in our home, the one every visitor sits in when they come over. My son loves to snuggle up underneath the large cushions in the morning after he stumbles from bed. Our daughter lines up her dolls on it. I bought the chair years ago, long before D and I met. When we got together, she had it reupholstered from the ugly red pattern it had to the soft pastel green it is now. Still, she hates it and has been trying to get rid of it for years. I can't really understand why, except perhaps because it represents my world before her. Some of our other furnishings pre-date our seven-year relationship, but fewer and fewer over time.

When D gets off the phone, she squishes down into the chair beside me, something she does often. The seat is not quite large enough to accommodate both of us comfortably and I'm forced up on one hip, cramped.

"See, if we got rid of this chair then we couldn't sit all cozy like this," I say.

D groans. She has just heard about a friend of hers who is getting a divorce, and earlier in the day we learned of an acquaintance who is having an affair.

"Are you sure you want to get married?" I ask.

"We're different," she says.

"Everyone's different."

D ignores me. "I told my parents this afternoon. They wanted to call tomorrow and congratulate you, but I told them you were leaving tonight."

I nod.

"Mum was like, 'Didn't he just get back?'" Here it comes, just as I'm about to walk out the door. D goes on. "All I can say is that when I talk to you tomorrow I better hear the sound of mosquitoes buzzing around. And is malaria contagious? If you give me malaria . . ."

We sit for a while and watch it grow fully dark outside. We haven't turned on any lights; only the glow from the street fills the room. "When you get back we can tell other people." D's voice is quiet, detached.

I nod again.

"I told Lou and Karen." Louise and Karen are D's oldest friends.

"Oh, what did they say?"

D shrugs. "Lou was excited, Karen was good."

"Then why do you sound so down?"

"I don't want you to go."

"I don't want to go either."

"Don't lie. I can see that smirk on your face. It'll be amazing."

"It should be pretty cool," I confess.

"Don't," D says. "Don't talk about it. I'm truly jealous. I'm not usually jealous of your trips, but this one, my stomach is starting to churn."

"Mine too," I say. "But I think it's the malaria medication."

When I land in Lima twelve hours later I have an e-mail from D. She has attached a photo she took of a mosquito lying dead on the sheets of our bed in New York. The insect bit her during the night. It's early April; there hasn't been a mosquito in New York in six months. D has taken this mosquito's mysterious appearance as a sign that she was right in not taking the kids to the Amazon. Where others might see a curious coincidence, D will read deep meaning.

Often, I struggle to follow the chain of thoughts that leads to her conclusions, yet I try to make an effort to support her reasoning, even when it has only the most tenuous connection to the reality that I live in. But the idea that a mosquito was sent by the Universe to confirm her decision not to come to the Amazon—I get behind this immediately. I call her from the food court in the Lima airport while eating my Papa John's *quatro queso* pizza at six thirty in the morning.

"Thank God you stayed home," I shout into the phone when she answers, cheese hanging from my mouth.

"Can you believe it? I heard this buzzing in the middle of the night; I thought it was in my dream." For D, the interpretation and significance of dreams plays nearly as important a role in understanding life's directions as does the metaphorical significance of waking events, such as the mosquito's appearance.

"Well, if ever there was a sign . . . ," I say.

"Oh, shut up." She's laughing.

I can feel myself relax. I'm wired from lack of sleep and with food slowly filling my stomach, my spirits become buoyant. I love D deeply in this moment, and tell her so.

"You just love me because you're far away."

"No, I don't."

"But it's easier," she says. I can hear the smile and an acceptance in her voice that isn't always there.

Our four-year-old daughter, who has just woken up, squawks for the phone. When I tell her I'm having pizza for breakfast she tells me she wants to move to Peru.

During a very bumpy one-hour flight to Iquitos, in the heart of the Peruvian Amazon, I try to focus on an elegant brochure of the vessel I will travel on. It's an old riverboat converted for luxury cruising; up to twenty-four passengers are housed in twelve deluxe cabins with king-size beds and large picture windows that look out onto the passing river. Twenty-four attendants pamper the guests. The brochure has photos of an elegant dining area with crisp white linen tablecloths and of a glass-encased lounge with deep couches and a bar. In one photo, a captain in white uniform stands chatting with a guest while a barman mixes what must be a *pisco* sour—Peru's contribution to the world's libations. The boat is all shining metal and rich mahogany.

My examination of the brochure serves two purposes: first, it helps to distract me from the incessant turbulence, and second, I'm searching for a phone number. The prospect of such luxury has made an idiot of me. Because I knew I was simply getting on a boat and heading upriver, with all the day-to-day decisions taken out of my hands, I have done none of my usual preparations. I can't even remember what Peruvian money is called. And the thought has occurred to me that if the car arranged by the boat to pick me up at the airport isn't there, I have no idea where I need to go or who I could contact for assistance. I will be—quite literally—up the river without a paddle. The only phone number on the brochure is for reservations—it's a U.S. number. Perhaps I should have headed into the Amazon more prepared.

"Are you going on that boat?" the man across the aisle asks. He is a lean, well-tanned, and casually elegant man with dark hair and a confident manner.

"I am," I answer. As is often the case when I travel, my vulnerabil-

ity—like not knowing what the hell I'm going to do upon arrival—
makes me more open to outside interactions than I might be when
I'm at home and think I know best what needs to be done. On the
road, serendipity is given space to enter my life.

"That's my boat," he says.

"This is?" I ask, holding up the brochure.

He nods.

"Oh, good, then you can give me a ride."

"Pleasure," he says, extending his hand and smiling. His white
teeth are in a perfect line. Crow's-feet wrinkle beside his green eyes.

Francesco Galli Zugaro is a citizen of the world. The son of an
American mother and an Italian father, he grew up in Switzerland,
was educated in the U.S., married a Peruvian woman of Ecuadorian
parents, and lives in Lima, after running boats in the Galápagos for
six years. He is on his way to Iquitos to check up on his second Amazonian boat—which he has plans to put in the water in a few weeks'
time.

"Come have a look at it with me," Francesco says, "then maybe we
can eat some lunch, before your boat launches in the evening."

Iquitos is, in essence, jungle-locked. There is one road that stretches
for sixty miles into the rain forest, only to taper out at a small village.
Other than that, you need to travel upriver for three days to get anywhere that has a road leading to anywhere else. Most people arrive,
and leave, by plane. Yet when we land, I see an old DC-8 sitting just
off the lone runway, rusting badly, a not-so-subtle reminder that so
much of what takes the trouble to get into the Amazon doesn't make
it back out.

Francesco's driver is waiting for us in the stultifying heat and
humidity. On the way into town, I see few other cars on Avenida José
Abelardo Quinones. In fact, there are hardly any cars at all in Iquitos.
But there is no shortage of motorized transport. A strange hybrid

called a *motokar*—a bastardized motorcycle modified into glorified tricycle, with a bench to seat three in the back and a plastic cover to protect passengers from the afternoon showers—owns the city streets. The *motokars* produce a loud, high-pitched buzz that keeps Iquitos humming in a constant state of heat-induced laconic frenzy. Along with open-air buses, they are how most of the five hundred thousand locals maneuver around the riverfront city.

We funnel onto Avenida Grau and are engulfed in a swarming chaos of the weaving and darting *motokars*. Horns tap-tap out a thin "meee-meee," much like the sound made by the Road Runner from the Looney Tunes cartoons. Francesco says something to the driver in rapid-fire Spanish—of which I understand nothing—and we turn onto Putumayo Street.

An abandoned eight-story construction site dominates the sky. "That was supposed to be the tallest building in Iquitos, the Social Security Administration building, but the soil was sandy so it was going to be too unstable," Francesco explains. There are no plans to take down the aborted project. The rest of Iquitos has a similarly unimpressive appearance; unfinished cinder block and raw cement seem to suffice for most newer structures.

Then we approach an open green square where the buildings have a sense of permanence and a faded charm. Blue and white Portuguese tiles adorn facades of tired mansions. "This is the Plaza de Armas," Francesco turns and shouts to me over the incessant din of the *motokars*. "It's really the only sight we have in Iquitos." Then he points to a two-story silver building with a cast-iron balcony dominating the second floor. The building looks strangely familiar.

"It's from Paris," Francesco says. "It was built by Gustave Eiffel."

It turns out that during the Universal Exposition of Paris in 1889, rubber baron Anselmo del Aguila saw two structures built by the French architect—a tall tower and a two-story iron building. The tower was too large to move, but he bought the smaller building, had it dismantled piece by piece, and shipped it across the Atlantic, steamed two thousand two hundred miles up the Amazon, carried through the jungle by hundreds of men, and rebuilt beside the Plaza de Armas. It still stands, a testament to the glorious and fleeting moment of global significance Iquitos enjoyed in the late nineteenth and early twentieth centuries, when the nearby rain forest was plundered for its rubber to meet the global demand created after Charles Goodyear's invention of vulcanization. Iquitos's brief moment in the sun ended as quickly as it began when rubber seeds were snuck out of the country and orderly plantations were set up in Malaya, plunging the town back into Amazonian oblivion, where it has remained ever since.

"Our industry now is oil, illegal logging, logging, and tourism, in that order," Francesco explains as we walk the once-fashionable Malecon Tarapaca promenade, which stretches for just a couple of blocks above the river. A few more vestiges of Iquitos's glory days line Próspero Street, but there is little else to point toward any immediate appeal. Despite this, the hanging heat and dense folds of humidity, there's a shaggy-dog charm to Iquitos. There is nothing here that is remotely reminiscent of my life back home—none of the threadbare shops, or primitive advertising, or restaurants have a familiar or even recognizable feeling about them. Such an alien sensation is increasingly rare in a world heading toward homogenization. The only thing familiar in this environment is me; consequently, I am acutely aware of my own thoughts, which in moments like this run toward a feeling of possibility. I wish I were staying in town for longer, possibly much longer.

"I'm glad you see it," Francesco says when I express my immediate affection for Iquitos. "It's not always obvious. I like it, too," and then we're back in his jeep and headed out Avenida 28 de Julio to see his boat.

In short order the road is filled with puddles, and soon it is too flooded to continue. The level of the Amazon fluctuates up to thirty feet per year, depending on the rains, and a tributary of the river has begun to flood the area. We hop out and walk along planks placed just above the rising tide.

"Last year the river was the highest in recorded history, and this year the water is already higher, and the rains aren't finished yet," Francesco tells me. Several vendors have set themselves up beside the water. An old woman is grilling something on sticks over an open fire. Francesco lifts a twig off the grill that's holding half a dozen large maggots. He offers it to me. "Loaded with protein."

We climb into a long and narrow skiff and head out across the water to the boatyard. A hulking shell of steel is swarming with men. The boat is already booked full for its maiden voyage in a month's time. There is much to do. Francesco walks me through the still-raw vessel. "The toilets are from Kentucky, and I had to DHL the engine from China to get it here in time. It cost more to ship than the engine itself, but I have to be ready." It will take one hundred men and three tugboats twelve days to set the boat in the water. "If you told me twelve years ago that I'd be running boats in the Amazon, I'd have laughed in your face," Francesco says, shaking his head.

His comment makes me consider my own course over the past dozen years. Twelve years ago, I was drifting, still trying intermittently to capture a version of pop stardom I had run from when it was on offer a decade earlier. The accidental second career as a travel writer, which would revitalize my creative trajectory, was nowhere on the horizon. A dozen years ago, I had no children. Nor had I been through a divorce—and while it was one of the more amicable dissolutions of a marriage, I was still deeply grieved.

The failure of my first marriage nearly eight years ago hovered over and fatigued me for much longer than I admitted, even to myself.

That I was still mourning that relationship when I plunged deep into another one was probably ill advised. A feeling of sadness permeated the early period of discovery and excitement with D; it is a regret we share, albeit one she has been gracious enough to move beyond. Why these thoughts come to me now, while I'm walking belowdecks, looking at exposed piping, I have no idea. But travel does this: it creates space that allows thoughts and memories to intrude and assert themselves with impunity. Smells and sights, the quality of light, the honk of a horn—can all act as touchstones when least expected.

Francesco takes me to lunch on a floating island in the middle of the Amazon that looks back toward the scruffy riverbanks of Iquitos. The river is littered with all sizes and varieties of boat, transporting all shapes and types of cargo. There are long boats and squat ones, open barges and dugout canoes, most jammed full with people. One, with the name *Titanic* painted in red, sits particularly low as it chugs upriver, the faces of scores of cramped passengers peering out the small glassless portholes. Another battered boat boasts a herd of goats walking around on deck, and dozens of others, loaded with bananas or palm fronds or lumber, float past. "It is very informal on the river, people will transport anything, anywhere," Francesco tells me.

Rarely do I take the time to marvel at how fast one can get so far from home, but in this instant it's not lost on me that just last night I was eating a cheeseburger for dinner in a still-chilly New York City, and I am now sitting in the middle of the steamy Amazon River eating fresh dorado for lunch.

Francesco has to return to work and suggests I visit the manatee rescue center.

"I was thinking I'd head over to the market."

"Belen?"

"Yeah."

"I don't really recommend it for tourists. It's not that it's not safe, but you have to be very careful."

I smile at him. I'm always warned against local street markets. That they invariably reveal a town for what it is, with all its unguarded voraciousness, is something locals are often shy to expose about themselves.

𝆏

At a cluster of stalls on Calle 9 de Diciembre, small women grind up fresh fruit for juices, *chambira* and papaya, *camu-camu* and mango, and others I don't recognize. The high-pitched hum of the blenders competes with the more insistent buzz of the passing *motokars*.

I turn a corner and see an armadillo, sliced open upon a table, beside a dozen butchered turtles. Farther on there are bananas, carrots, beans and potatoes, monkey skulls and chickens, and a stall with dozens of long machetes hanging like wind chimes. A jaguar skin is stretched taut—selling for twenty dollars. Tables support scores of different types of fish, including dorado and piranha, *zungaro,* and giant *paiche.* There's an entire dusty street dedicated to charcoal, and farther on snails the size of grapefruits; butcher blocks with bloody, dripping cuts of meat; huge mounds of loose tobacco leaves; barrels filled with olives, sneakers, and pig parts; coca leaves and anaconda skins; caiman tails and *masato* (jungle beer) in glass bottles; and there is the hallucinogen ayahuasca, in plastic bags, and yucca root is everywhere. Anyone with anything to sell sells it here.

The market sprawls over a dozen city blocks and tumbles down to the river, where it continues on boats. I squeeze between the wooden homemade stalls, from one aisle to the next. Rain begins to pour down and primitive tarp roofs overhead displace water until they're too full and collapse. The rain stops as suddenly as it began and the sun comes back out and the ground steams. Then it's raining again, then the sun is out. It makes no difference; the market continues unabated.

I turn right down a narrow lane. It's quieter than most. The small stalls, one after the next, are lined with different herbs in bags or bottles. There are wooden bowls filled with roots and twigs. There's *abuta* bark, for menstrual cramps; the vine of *una del gato,* for cancer; hearts of palm root for the kidneys; cassia for hepatitis; patchouli for baldness; and a jar of cream-of-anaconda for sore muscles, as well as the aphrodisiac *maca* root, to be boiled and made into tea. *"Muy efectivo,"* the creased woman on a stool beside the display assures me.

A little farther on I come upon a man beside shelves of bottles filled with a golden-brown, syrupy liquid. ROMPA CALZONES—"underwear breaker"—the label reads. "Good for honeymooners," the small man with the wispy mustache promises. I pick up a bottle. I hold it up to the light, tilting it first one way and then the other. The thick goo oozes slowly from side to side. The small man smiles at me. He's nodding and grinning. His eyes are dancing. He knows something that I don't yet know. He wants me to have this, he wants me to be happy. I put the bottle down and thank him. He holds up a finger.

"Espera"—wait, he says.

He lifts a mostly empty bottle down from the shelf and pours half an inch into a dirty plastic cup and offers it to me.

I once drank shark-liver oil on Montserrat, in the Caribbean. It tasted like what I imagine motor oil must taste like, but this, despite the not-dissimilar texture, has a deep bouquet, an oozing, clinging, pungent quality. I have no way of knowing what's in it, all I know is that when I put down the empty cup, I want more.

"Mmmm," I say. And now we're both nodding our heads. Up and down. And grinning.

The thought of trying to explain what Rompa Calzones is to a customs officer at JFK flashes into my mind. I tell my new friend that I'm alone—*"Soy solo,"* I explain—and shrug. He nods some more, this time knowingly. He shakes my hand a little sadly, and, still nodding, he pats my back and sends me on my way.

I don't know if it's a placebo effect or if there really is something to the elixir, but my senses are now on high alert, my vision is more acute, everything is intensified. The smells around me are stronger, the colors brighter, the noises more intense. When I look at the fish laid out on tables, I not only see heads and fins and tails, but I sense what it must have been like for the fish on their journey to this spot. My feelings make no sense, yet I'm invested in them. I want to reach out and caress those fish. And the fruit I pass. It all appears so plump. I want to fondle a swollen orange, and do. I imagine the juices oozing out through the skin and onto my fingers and dripping over my hand and down my arm. I want this. I walk past a woman in a black tank top and a red apron tied snug around her thin waist. She's slowly pouring water from a blue plastic bucket over a countertop of fish, making them glisten. I don't look away as she raises her gaze toward me when I strut past. A little farther on, a buxom woman with her hair tightly pulled back is scaling a silver fish, about six inches long, that lies across her palm. She's rhythmically thrusting the knife over the fish, back and forth, again and again. The fish and her hands have a smattering of blood; her nipples are erect beneath her low-slung, gray T-shirt. A bead of sweat rolls down between her ample breasts. Whatever the reason, I haven't felt this kind of unapologetic sexual potency in some time.

As a teenager, I was the close friend and confidant when all I wanted to be was the boyfriend. It was my sudden success in movies, several years later, that gave me the sexual currency I craved. My overt sensitivity, previously not potent bait for the opposite sex, suddenly manifested as a draw and instilled in me a power I welcomed. It's unlikely that young women would have wanted to follow me into public bathrooms had I not been in the movies they were going to see, but whatever the reason, my ability to attract women became a core part of who I was to become as a man, a strong component of my identity. It fueled my self-esteem. Even as I started to be monogamous, I still maintained a flirt-first rapport with every woman I met. Only with my first marriage did I begin to make an active effort to alter my by then automatic response.

When an old man offers me a ride in his wooden plank canoe to go out into the floating portion of the market, I get on board and a thought begins to dance at the edge of my mind. My investment in my sexual desirability has always been linked with my attachment to my youthful success. From a distance, they are separate issues having nothing to do with each other, but in my experience, they were interwoven. After all, I became sexually viable because I became successful. So if I no longer seek that kind of sexual confirmation, perhaps I'm also letting go of an attachment to that success—a success that defined much of my adult life. Getting married would be an acknowledgement of who I am rather than clinging to what I had. On the other hand, I'm an accumulation of all my past, and if in getting married I leave it behind, I don't know what I take forward. If I let go of my past, I'm uncertain what I have to offer. If I'm not that person, then who am I?

While my mind struggles with this notion I'm suddenly jabbed in the back. I turn around and the old man is pointing directly in front of us. I spin back and prostrate myself just in time to duck under a very low plank, functioning as a bridge over the swollen river. Everywhere, row upon row of shanty homes have been flooded out of their first floors, and temporary walkways and bridges have been constructed from any wood that could be found. Daily life continues in this improvised, third-world Venice as we drift past.

Ahead, a dugout canoe is billowing smoke. We paddle toward it. The most beautiful woman I have yet seen in Iquitos is sitting before a small charcoal fire in a bowl in her boat, selling *juane*—a chicken and rice concoction wrapped up in a banana leaf. I smile stupidly at her as she ladles out a pile of rice and ties the bundle. Our fingers touch when I give her ten soles. I hand the banana leaf to the old man and he hands me a small plastic cup. It's only then that I notice that my feet are wet. Our canoe is filling with water. I shrug at the beautiful woman and she laughs at me as I begin to scrape the cup along the bottom of the boat and bail.

Late in the day I leave Iquitos and catch a ride sixty miles to the end of the only road out of the city, to Nauta, a bustling little river town with deeply rutted dirt lanes along the northern bank of the Río Marañón, the main tributary of Peru's Upper Amazon basin. The day is dying quickly. Francesco's 130-foot riverboat is anchored among the reeds on the far bank, several hundred yards downriver. Its clean and sleek lines stand out in contrast to the raw contours of the riverbank. The lights from the boat's large windows appear golden in the twilight and reflect off the water, giving the vessel the appearance of a hovering spacecraft in the fading light.

A small and silent man beside the river gestures out toward the boat and when I nod he points toward a wobbly skiff tied fast in the rushing current. The twenty-five-horsepower outboard grinds and we drive directly across the brown water. The current is strong and pushes us hard downstream. The small man judges the drive vs. slide of the current perfectly and we ease up abreast the larger boat. Without a word, he passes me my bag. I extend my hand in thanks, offer him a few soles, and climb aboard. There is no one there to greet me when I board. The riverboat seems deserted.

Night has fallen fast, like it always does at the equator. Only a few lights burn dimly across the river in Nauta, including the red glow of a looming cell phone tower, blinking on and off, high in the sky—a jarring totem of contemporary life in an underdeveloped backwater. Otherwise, the sky is suddenly very black.

There are no stars. The air is humid and close. Then it begins to rain. Hard. The river boils under the assault. The rain crashing into the forest is thunderous. The downpour feels violent, like it must be causing harm, although I know it isn't. I go belowdecks and come across a young man sweeping. When I tell him my name he disappears and returns a few minutes later with a key and points me to my cabin, one of three along each side of the corridor that runs the length of the boat. When I open my door I'm confronted with an almost floor-to-ceiling window. I laugh at the image reflected back at me. In my dark city clothes I look comically out of place. I have a bemused, excited, and slightly apprehensive look on my face. I strip down and jump into a lukewarm shower. The boat is listing to port, the drain is on the starboard side of the shower basin, and the water puddles at my feet. While I dry off I can hear others coming on board.

The engines start up; the boat slides into the current and begins to chug upriver. Quickly, I begin to dress. I want to run up on deck to watch our progress but hear voices in the hall and, not for the first time in my life, choose to remain alone instead. I can't see anything out my window, only my own self-conscious reflection staring back in the night.

Before the boat is out of range of the cell tower, I call D to say good-bye.

"See any mosquitoes?" she asks hopefully.

"Not yet, but it's raining, so maybe after it stops."

"What are the other people like? I bet it's a really interesting mix."

"Haven't met them yet." I groan. "Can't wait."

I can hear some of the other passengers scurrying back and forth outside my door. A message on the chalkboard on deck, written in a swirling hand with a smiley face dotting the "i," mentioned "welcome drinks" in the deck lounge. Communal meals, group adventures, bathroom breaks—the realization of the shared experience with enforced intimates settles down around me as we speak.

"That's your dream, baby," she laughs. "Surrounded by strangers, with no exit."

"Yeah. Kind of forgot about this with all our mosquito talk."

My initial reaction to nearly every social situation is to shy away. That in the end I often come out of such encounters energized and excited is something I've been slow to acknowledge. What stays with me is that I often stumble away anxious and fatigued, my internal monologue running parallel to each outward discussion. Add to this my acute barometer for shame—both my own and the one I perceive in others: when I see people behaving in ways that betray insecurity, masked with bravado, I feel embarrassed for them. I'm always shocked they don't. I judge them, harshly, and run for the exit.

In my early twenties, when I suddenly became recognizable as an actor, I was utterly unaware of how to handle the beam of attention directed toward me (unless it was sexual attention). The mask of casual disinterest I had begun to develop as a child grew into a defining personality trait of defensive aloofness.

That ambivalence about my success didn't help my reaction to it. No doubt I was masking anxiety and insecurity—part of me certainly believed that my present good fortune might be fleeting, and so I convinced myself I didn't really want it. My ambivalence guarded me against disappointment—a stable position from which to operate. A position I struggle now to shirk.

Add to this the lingering doubt I harbor as a result of my failed first marriage. My ex-wife is a doting mother and a loving woman who gave herself fully in marriage and had the right to expect the same in return. That she may have gotten less than that from me speaks to my own limitations and lack of self-knowledge at the time and not any lacking of hers. It is partly out of respect for the grief I caused her that I'm endeavoring to discover and overcome my limitations of character that might prevent me from giving myself more completely to D. The rain stops as suddenly as it began, and I finally make my way up on deck to the lounge. Most of my fellow passengers are already assembled.

An older man with an unapologetic Louisiana accent approaches me right away.

"I'm Ken. And you're from Baton Rouge," he declares, extending his hand.

"Uh, no, Ken. Actually, I've never been to Baton Rouge."

"Are you sure? Your face looks very familiar."

Two women, one stout and blond, the other tall and with chestnut hair, step up. They are cousins from Cornwall, England. The tall one, Stella, is a librarian. Catherine, the blonde, works in finance and tells me quickly that she has exiled herself to the Isle of Man, "for tax reasons." Stella arches her eyebrows at this comment.

"Oh," is all I can think to say.

While on the road I have frequently heard deep personal revelations from people I've just met, often I don't even know their names. Just a few weeks earlier, in Patagonia, I met a couple at a restaurant in El Calafate—when the man went to the bathroom, his wife confessed to me she had met another man and was going to leave her husband. She had told no one else, she said. Perhaps she was just floating the idea, seeing how it felt to say it aloud, or perhaps she really was about to act on her declaration. Her husband came back from the bathroom before I had a chance to find out. The episode did nothing to ease my mind on the subject of marriage but served to remind me that the near invisibility of the solo traveler far from home allows for exploitation in any number of ways.

The English cousins travel together often and don't like to waste time. "We did China in nine days, saw it all," Catherine says. They've been to Africa (one week) and Australia (six days), "Opera House, Great Barrier Reef, the big rock in the middle, all of it," Catherine assures me.

There are also two couples from Canada traveling together, and a pair of German ladies—travel agents, and a family of three with a gangly teenage boy. "We live in the wine country, above San Francisco," the flush-cheeked teen tells me.

Then there's a Russian couple who keep to themselves and, after a curt hello, speak to no one until the end of the trip.

A large man with black hair and dark skin, wearing a white uniform with bars on his shoulders, calls us to order. His name is Emanuel and he will be in charge of our needs during the voyage. "I will see to everything, and make sure you are comfortable," he says in thickly accented English. His manner seems brusque for a concierge, but perhaps it's just that his English is not very good. He explains a few things about the boat, and before he introduces us to the three guides who will be leading us on our daily small boat excursions to look for wildlife, Emanuel asks if there are any questions.

"I've run out of toothpaste," Ken calls out. "Can I get some?"

"We don't have that," Emanuel replies. "I will get you some bug spray."

Before Ken can protest, one of the Canadian women speaks up. "I have some you can borrow, Ken."

We retire for dinner in the stern of the boat. Beyond the glass wall, the Amazon rolls out behind us. There's a brief period of awkward shuffling of feet and chairs until people take seats in what will establish itself as a self-imposed seating map. I'm beside the cousins from Cornwall and across from one of the German travel agents, called Ruth. During the five-course tasting menu the discussion focuses mainly on travel, as the cousins and Ruth volley back and forth all the destinations they've checked off their lists.

Another person, namely D, would find this kind of ever-evolving social petri dish a fascinating study, worthy of hours of discussion, dissection, and analyzing. I find it slightly nerve-wracking, and it prevents me from more solitary pleasures. The idea of eating my next eighteen meals with these strangers fills me with dread. During dessert I slip silently away to my room.

At some point during the night, we leave the Río Marañón, join the Ucayali, and chug farther upriver. I wake before dawn and watch the day creep into being as the brown water and the dense green of the rain forest roll past my window. I'm nervous and restless this morning. I pace around my cramped cabin, unpack my bag, inspect my teeth in the mirror. I try to sit still and can't. Knowing I have no Internet connection, I check my e-mail anyway.

After breakfast we head down to the loading area, where we are split into three groups and hurried aboard twenty-four-foot skiffs with sixty-horsepower engines that will take us zipping out into black-water tributaries of the larger river. The family from Napa Valley, the cousins from Cornwall, and I are on a boat with Ricardo, one of three guides, who are all small, black haired, olive skinned, with round cherubic faces and perky demeanors.

Within minutes of leaving the larger river and entering a narrower tributary, our boat slows and we're peering into the dense foliage when Ricardo starts shouting. He is pointing, nearly jumping out of the boat.

"Shoot it! Shoot it! Shoot it!" Half a dozen spider monkeys are leaping from one tree to the next, bending branches as they leap. "Shoot it with the camera!" Everyone pulls out their cameras and begins to snap away.

Ricardo loudly kisses the back of his hand, making a sucking, snapping sound. The monkeys begin to shout back. "They're laughing at us. Ha, ha. Shoot it, shoot it, quick!"

Eventually everyone is snapped out, the monkeys disappear deeper into the jungle, the driver slams the throttle down, and we're off, looking for more.

And the pattern is set. We zip along; Ricardo stands in the back of the boat, eyeing the passing rain forest through his binoculars, and when he sees something, anything, he motions for the driver to slow and we try to spot whatever it is that has caught his eye—scarlet macaws; a massive wasp nest; a great black hawk perched high in a cecropia tree, draping his wings to appear even larger; toucans flying overhead; a crimson-crested woodpecker on the twig of an acacia. At the sight of a red howler monkey in a ficus tree, I think Ricardo might faint. "Oh my God, I'm gonna die!" he shouts. "This is unbelievable. Shoot it! Shoot it! Shoot it quick!"

As the others click away, I turn back to Ricardo and ask quietly, "When was the last time you saw one?"

He stops pointing and leans in close to me. "Two days ago," he says softly, and shrugs.

If it weren't for an innate innocence, Ricardo's hard sell might be off-putting. He comes from "five hours down the river," from a village called Indiana. "The missionary who came there last century was from Indiana. He was very proud of his home. When he died, they named the village to honor him."

A few hours later, the skiff returns to the boat. "There it is," Ricardo says when we reemerge into the main river and see the riverboat glistening in the sun, "Da cutest little boat in da Amazon." Emanuel greets everyone solemnly as we board, and when the heat of the day passes, we load up into the skiffs and do it again.

After dinner, during dessert, Ken comes over and joins our table. Ruth asks Ken to explain "what exactly is this thing called 'gumbo.'" And while everyone is living up to stereotype, I'm able to slip away once again, without having to spend too much time plotting my exit. Just when I think I've made a clean getaway, I hear Catherine say behind me, "There he goes again."

I make my way toward the bow. This is the first moment of solitude I've had on the boat without having to resort to hiding in my cabin.

The writer Paul Theroux was a great early influence on how I chose to travel, and he has always made a strong point for going alone. Only in the "lucidity of loneliness," as he calls it, can we see what we came to see and learn what it is we came to this spot to learn.

The humid air has the beginnings of a chill as the boat's movement creates a breeze that doesn't otherwise exist. The sky on the river is vast, even the night sky. Clouds gather on the horizon where lightning bursts like a cluster of flashbulbs popping. Another front is far off to my left, where distinct and jagged bolts silently slash open the sky at regular intervals. The Southern Cross hangs low to my right, and the canopy of the rain forest is a dark mass spreading out on either side of me. Occasionally the small orange glow of kerosene lamps from the dark shoreline can be seen—the only proof of villages whose names I'll never know. When the moon comes clear, the Amazon shimmers as it rolls under the boat.

The following days pass in similar fashion, two daily excursions in small boats to spot giant Aztec ant nests and three-toed sloths, and to hunt for anaconda. "Remember," Ricardo warns us, "if an anaconda attacks you, the best defense is to bite it." When we pull up close beside one of the other skiffs they are looking at a four-foot-long iguana sunning itself on the limb of a dead tree.

"I've seen them before," Ken says from the back of the other boat.

"Where?" Ricardo asks. "Costa Rica?"

"My backyard." Ken yawns.

Often, in the evenings, we go out hunting for predators. "There are thousands and thousands of eyes on us, and we don't see them," Ricardo whispers, his sense of melodrama heightened in the dark. He shines a strong spotlight along the edges of the river in the darkness. When we see a pair of shining red marbles we zero in and suddenly Ricardo is lunging over the side of the small boat, rocking us badly in the water, and comes back with a three-foot juvenile caiman in his hands. Then we head deep into a close cluster of trees until we find a goliath tarantula the size of my fist, clinging to the trunk of a cecropia.

Over dinner one evening, Catherine scolds me for always leaving early. So I make an active effort to connect more with my fellow travelers. I mention my stargazing spot on the rail and linger longer than usual at the dinner table. I chat with Ken long after the others have gone.

I've come to enjoy Ken's company; he is decidedly himself. His wife died several years ago and he has been traveling the world extensively ever since. Having never left Louisiana for the first sixty-seven years of this life, Ken has now seen all seven continents and been on all seven seas. He's lonely but content.

"There's something about the moving that I like," he says. "You know what I mean, An-drew?"

Ken says my name in a lazy southern singsong that makes it sound like two words. I know he's not really asking me a question, but I answer him anyway. "I do, Ken."

After Ken heads off to bed, I pass the lounge on the way to my spot on the rail. Suddenly one of the Canadians, a retired engineer named Bob, whom I haven't spoken to at all, corners me in a conversation on immigration. He's lamenting a Royal Canadian Mountie of Indian origins who sued the government so that he could wear the traditional garb of his homeland.

"If he's gonna come live in Canada," my traveling companion complains, "then he can act like a Canadian."

I wonder to myself what exactly that might mean.

"In the end, they let him have his turban, but they wouldn't let him carry his knife."

"Well," I say, "at least that's something."

"I guess I don't like change," Bob says, and goes to the bar for another *pisco* sour.

By the time I get to my usual spot on the rail, the ladies are already there. I curse myself for mentioning it at dinner—serves me right for trying to be social. Ruth is trying to point out the Southern Cross to Catherine and Stella. They've never seen it before and are not sure what to look for in the night sky.

"There, see?" The German woman points to a spot not far above the horizon. Because the moon is out, the constellation is not as bright as it might be, but it's clearly visible, the dominant sight in the western sky.

"No," say the cousins in unison.

"There." Ruth thrusts her finger with more authority toward the stars. "There are three bright ones, and the one at the bottom is dimmer. And there's the one on the side." The cousins still don't see it. The German woman is becoming frustrated. "There." She jabs her finger into the air again.

Eventually one of the cousins exclaims, "Oh, there it is."

The other quickly follows suit. "Oh, yes, there it is. Lovely."

Satisfied, the travel agent marches away.

"Do you see it?" the librarian whispers.

"No, I do not," the other replies.

Without contact with D—the intermittent phone calls, e-mails, and texts throughout the days that would anchor me to my familiar reality—I lose rhythm and time lunges forward through spots of deadness that would otherwise be filled with the news of life's daily micro-dramas coming across the line or over the web. I feel the void; my spirits sag. But as the days wear on, I become aware that my thoughts and observations pass without any desire on my part for communication. I pay attention only to the solitary processing of my own reaction to them. My internal world grows smaller, more self-contained and self-involved, reminiscent of my life before children.

Then, one afternoon, we're out on a tributary of the Pacaya River. We've already stopped for all the requisite monkeys and birds.

"Now we'll go to a village," Ricardo announces. A buzz comes over the skiff. A village visit, to see how the "natives" live, is one of the highlights of the trip. The three skiffs pull close together. The two couples from Canada prepare the pencils that they've brought along to give to the local children. The boats are alive with anticipation. I wish I could jump overboard.

The village we draw up to consists of ten to fifteen wooden huts with palm-frond roofs built on stilts above the river. We are days away from electricity and running water. A hole in the floor over the river serves as toilet. Despite the huts being built on stilts fifteen feet off the ground, many of the homes are flooded and empty. We float past a few deserted shacks; filthy, threadbare clothes hang from lines in the damp breeze. A lone white dog hunches on the edge of a platform, watching our progress. His coat is matted and wet and clings taut over his jutting ribs. We drift on. The skiffs are silent. We come to a platform that's nearly a foot above the still-rising water. The village has gathered here. Two dozen children and half that many adult women stand behind rows of beads laid out on display, strung together in an effort at jewelry. A few of the children hold simple carvings, offering them up to us as we arrive.

The guides all step out onto the deck. They playfully shoo the children into the dugout canoes tied nearby and invite the passengers up to get a closer look. No one moves. The self-conscious resistance and the fear of filth of my fellow travelers make me nervous, and I'm self-conscious before the humbly eager and defiant looks from the deck. I stand with a lurch. The boat rocks back and forth. I stumble over the two cousins from Cornwall and climb quickly up on the platform. I pick up the first two red and white necklaces I see, thrust twenty soles into the hand of the closest woman, and climb back into the skiff.

Soon everyone is out on the deck, trying to chat and barter, pushing pencils into the hands of children who have no paper. Everyone is happy. Both locals and travelers are laughing and smiling. The children orbit around, between and beneath the adults, smiling, playing. I remain in the back of the skiff.

To my right, alone in a dugout canoe is a young girl, facing away from the others. She's my daughter's size and build. She wears a dirty pink T-shirt and aqua sweatpants. Her hair is tied back in two braids, like my daughter often wears hers. She turns to get a peek at the goings-on. There's something sticking out of her mouth—she's eating something or sucking on something. She turns away again and then turns back once more. Whatever she is sucking on is the size of a large banana, but it's pinkish and has a black tip. Her jaw is extended as far open as it will go. And then I realize that what is sticking out of her mouth is her tongue. And the black on the end of it is a rotting infection. The mangy white dog swims over and climbs into the canoe with her, rocking her boat only slightly as he slips aboard. The girl swallows often and her swollen tongue rides only marginally in, still protruding hugely, and then juts back out completely. The girl turns her back on the proceedings.

I've seen poverty and starvation in Africa, I've been silenced by squalor in Asia, but suddenly I'm crying behind my sunglasses. The singularity of her shame punctures my detachment.

The medic who travels with the boat quietly searches for the girl's mother. He hands the exhausted-looking woman a few white pills. She receives them without comment.

When we return to the riverboat, the medic tells me the girl has a clot so the blood can't drain. The tip of her tongue has begun to rot, similar to frostbite. She can no longer eat properly. She will die soon, he tells me, without a ninety-minute operation in Lima.

I hover on deck, aimless, long after the other passengers have gone back to their cabins to shower for cocktails. I hear a splash and then voices, shouting and calling. One of the skiff drivers has fallen overboard while climbing back onto the boat. He can't swim. The current is strong in this part of the river and the boat is driving hard against it. Quickly, there is a good deal of distance between the driver and us. There's more shouting, a buoy is tossed to him, and he's able to grab it. His T-shirt and jeans cling to his body as he's hoisted back on deck, confused. Someone gives him a hand towel, the kind usually doused in cool, perfumed water and offered by Emanuel to guests returning from excursions. Nervous laughter follows, and then back-slapping, and then the half dozen men are silent. Some look out over the water, others stare at their shoes. I watch them, unseen, from the deck above, with the growing realization that life on the river is cheap.

It no longer feels like a game that I'm not in contact with D. I'm far from home, and to what end? My son and daughter are reading their bedtime stories while I am thousands of miles away, heading deeper into the Amazon. I feel foolish and selfish.

At dinner, I mention the young girl with the infection. None of the passengers had noticed her. People seem relieved when the subject is changed to the downloading and sharing of photos. Then one of the cousins from Cornwall, Stella, the librarian, asks me again about the girl. We talk quietly between ourselves, but soon the table can feel the weight of our conversation and they fall silent.

I've often kept important moments in life to myself, fearing they would be received as mere anecdotes, without the significance they held for me. As with the first time I acted, I worry that my experiences might be diluted and diminished, their import minimized. I don't know why I brought up the little girl. I'm surprised at myself but also somehow relieved that I have.

Back in my cabin, the Amazon keeps rolling past my window. I've felt alone for most of my life and never minded. I've considered it my natural state. I've longed for that solitude, sought it out, and lamented its absence. Yet it's not the life I've chosen. I have two children I love and miss; I have a partner who stirs me. They all affect me the way no solitary pleasure can, and yet I continue to leave. The push-pull of my decisions strains any kind of stability I've created.

The next few days feel much the same. We gawk at water lilies seven feet around and at a one-hundred-and-forty-pound rat. I take copious notes for the story I must report, all the while feeling increasingly detached. The joy I now take in the small boat excursions is limited to the thrill of racing along with the wind ripping loud through my ears, not in the endless stream of monkeys we stop to photograph. Only when we come upon a cluster of pink river dolphins in a tranquil pool am I brought back from my private thoughts. Their strange humped shape and peculiar color, coupled with their elusive movements, give them a prehistoric appearance and ethereal feel. I can understand my daughter's attraction to them.

"People believe the river dolphins can take on human form, your mother, your sister. For this reason, people don't hunt them," Ricardo explains.

And in a tributary of the Yanallpa River we round a bend and come upon a half dozen young men standing atop a cluster of felled mahogany trees tied together and floating downstream. They eye us with suspicion as they slowly drift past in silence.

"That didn't look very legal," I say quietly to Ricardo as the men recede.

"The farther downriver they get, the more legal it becomes."

$\text{\textdagger}$

On the last evening on the boat, dinner is an elaborate tasting menu and drags on longer than usual. Over coffee, the two Canadian men, as well as Ken, pull up their chairs beside me.

Each gives me his business card. "We want to do something for that girl you saw," Bob, one of the Canadians, tells me. No one has mentioned the girl since I spoke of her several nights prior.

"You said you met the owner of the boat, right, An-drew?" Ken says. "Yeah."

"Well, you tell him what you saw and if he can arrange the logistics, we'd like to help," Bob says, then points to his card. "That's how you find us."

Suddenly tears are burning in my eyes; quickly I excuse myself. I'm not sure if it's their concern or the feeling of unwitting connection with these strangers that has snuck up on me that has taken me so off guard.

When I return to the dining room, the two cousins from Cornwall have also written their numbers down, and as the Russians pass on their way out of the dining room, the man drops his card on the table, points at me, and nods. I didn't even know they were aware of our conversation.*

The meal breaks up and I make my way to my spot on the rail, but after just a few minutes I find myself returning to the dining room. Ken is still there, alone, finishing his coffee. He tells me that he'll spend a few days in Iquitos.

"I hear there's not much to see," he says. "I'll have to give my travel agent some hell."

I tell him of my experience and that I think he too might recognize some of Iquitos's more subtle charms.

"I am glad to hear that, An-drew. Now I'm looking forward to it." "And, Ken, when you go to Belen market, make sure you pick up a bottle of Rompa Calzones."

---

* See Note page 271.

CHAPTER FOUR

THE OSA

"People Said to Avoid This Place"

The day after I return from the Amazon, D e-mails me a sample of our wedding Evite she created. I don't respond for two days.

"Did you get my e-mail?" D asks finally.

"E-mail?"

She glares at me.

"Oh, the wedding invitation?"

"Yes, Andrew. The wedding invitation."

"I did, yeah."

"And?"

"Well, when I read it I fell down and hit my head and got amnesia and I'm just now coming to and starting to remember things, so that's why I haven't said anything."

"You're lucky you're funny."

"We're not going to have regular invitations?"

"You said you didn't want it to be a formal, big huge deal."

"I know, but . . ."

"But what?" D says.

"Do you think anyone will take us seriously with just an e-mail, 'Hey, come to Ireland for our wedding, it's in a park, and bring a picnic' invitation?"

"Is that what it looks like to you?"

On the invitation that D created, two bold peacocks flank the screen; their colorful tails hang down, framing a poem by Hafiz. The pertinent facts are placed discreetly below. It is an elegant, simple, and poetic invitation. "It's beautiful, sweetheart," I say, and kiss her.

She kisses me back. "Do you think so?"

"I do."

"Do you like the poem?"

"I love it."

"And the peacocks?"

"Love them."

"Any input?"

I'm silent for a minute. "Don't only the male peacocks have colorful feathers?"

"Yeah, I think so."

"Do you think anyone will notice that it's two males?"

*

On the morning of my departure for Costa Rica, I'm eating breakfast with D and our four-year-old daughter.

"Well, at least you were home for almost a couple of weeks this time," D says.

With a mouth full of cereal our daughter looks at me. "Do you know when I like you best, Daddy?"

"When, pumpkin?"

"When you come back from staying at the airport."

I have often wondered why certain acting jobs come my way when they do. What's the lesson to be learned aside from the obvious challenge of the work? Why, for example, am I cast as a widower while I'm in the process of getting divorced? Or in a silly comedy while I'm going through a particularly tough stretch personally? With travel writing it has been the same.

In Patagonia, I indulged my desire for solitude, and the boat up the Amazon thrust me into the heart of the group dynamic—obviously not the reasons why I first proposed these trips to my editor.

Usually I have an idea for a story I want to tell that is tied to a particular location—a place I either love or have long wanted to visit. My rationale being that I will have more to say if I have a passion and a curiosity about where it is I'm going. But Costa Rica is different. I simply said yes when my editor asked me to do a story about it. I have never had any desire to go there, or anywhere in Central America for that matter. My uninformed preconception of the region is of a swampy little bog that attracts a mangy crowd looking to do seedy things on the cheap.

The plane to San José lives down to my expectations. It's filled with squat men with thick necks and their women, wearing velour warm-up suits. Tall, skinny frat boys in yellow V-neck sweaters, probably heading down to take advantage of Costa Rica's booming sex tourism trade, slouch up the aisle. "Fishing trips" is the term I believe men use to describe these expeditions to their wives and girlfriends back home.

At Juan Santamaria airport I pass a life-size, cardboard cutout of a delicate-looking young woman propped up beside the customs desk, reminding everyone that sex with a minor is illegal and punishable by a stint in local prison. I wonder what it is exactly that I've been sent to Costa Rica to learn.

I make my way to a small hangar beside the main terminal and find an old man with tousled gray hair and a drooping mustache. He's waiting for me. Beside him stands a teenager—no more than fifteen; they both wear white, short-sleeved shirts, with blue and gold bars on their shoulders. They're standing beside a twin-engine, six-seat prop plane.

"Puerto Jiménez?" I ask, pointing at the small plane with paper-thin wings.

The old man nods.

I'm heading to the Osa Peninsula, on Costa Rica's southwestern Pacific coast. The underdeveloped Osa is far from the well-worn eco-circuit of volcanoes, zip lines through cloud forests, and surf schools along the northern coast, for which Costa Rica has become famous.

"Solo?"—am I the only one? I point to myself.

Again, the tired old man nods. I approach the plane and give the fragile-looking wing a gentle shake. The entire plane rocks badly. The old man holds up a finger of warning.

Before I climb aboard I check my e-mail. D has just sent a message. It hasn't downloaded completely, only the subject line has come through: "WARNING," it reads.

I'm hoping she hasn't had one of her dreams of premonition, but in order to buy some time for the message to download, I ask if I can go to the bathroom. The captain shrugs and points to a door in the corner of the hangar. I scamper off and lock myself in the filthy toilet. The message never comes through and eventually the young man knocks on the door. Reluctantly, I exit the pungent room, shuffle across the blistering heat on the tarmac, and climb on board. The plane is stifling; no air moves. In thickly accented English, the old man finally speaks. "I am George," he says. He then slams the door shut, locking me inside.

George trudges around to the cockpit, fires up the engines, and the high thin hum of the props rips into my ears. The plane begins to vibrate—my teeth would clatter if my jaw weren't already locked shut. We roll out toward the main runway and stop. George looks left and right.

"See anything?" he shouts over his shoulder. Is he talking to me? Without waiting for an answer he slams the throttle forward.

Once we are airborne I try to focus my attention on a small rivet on the wing, to stop my mind from wandering to images of disaster. The rivet begins to vibrate, badly. Is it coming loose? I look away and then return my focus to it a minute later. Was the rivet jutting out this far before? Should I alert the captain? I decide to focus on something else. We're between two cloud banks, cruising on a river of blue sky. Soon we're flying over the mountains of Talamanca, and the plane begins to bounce. Every time the plane jumps, I lift my feet as if I'm hopping over something. There is no need for this, and I'm not sure why I do it, but I can't stop. When we hit a particularly bad patch of turbulence, my head bangs on the ceiling six inches above me. I decide to tighten my seat belt. Then, just off to our left, a small plane, similar in size to ours, comes zipping out of the clouds. The plane buzzes past close enough that I can easily read its call letters. Did someone inside wave? At least I'm no longer worried about turbulence.

Twenty minutes later George begins to tap a circular screen in the center of the instrument panel. He does this for a while, shakes his head, and then stops. After a few minutes he taps the screen again, harder this time. Then he instructs the young man in the seat beside him to bang the panel while he steers. We sweep out over the deep blue water of the Golfo Dulce and then in an arcing dive we turn back toward the dense canopy of green. A thin ribbon of open ground sliced into the jungle comes clear directly ahead, and then a loud and piercing buzzing fills the cabin. George slaps the young man's hand away from the console. He jabs at a few buttons. We lose altitude fast. George pulls back hard on the controls. The sea below is getting very close; I can plainly see the coral beneath the now-turquoise water. Then we're inches above the trees and we bounce our way to a less than delicate landing on the small and narrow airstrip conveniently located beside a wide and crowded graveyard.

I like this place immediately.

Standing under a cashew tree beside the cemetery, I count twenty-six scarlet macaws squawking so loud from its branches that I don't hear the small, square-shouldered man with the thick glasses stepping up to shake my hand. Tom Connor lives in a simple home beside the landing strip and likes to stroll over whenever a plane lands, "just to see who's crazy enough to want to come here." An expat from Cleveland, Tom has lived in the Osa for more than twenty years. He tells me the airstrip was paved a few years ago, and that a spinning prop recently decapitated a man—it's unclear if the man was buried in the adjacent cemetery.

"How about some lunch?" Tom asks. With nowhere to go and no idea what I might do otherwise, his invitation is easy to accept.

"Want to see town first?" he asks after I climb into his pickup. We bump over a dirt road through dense vegetation, beneath palm and bamboo and acacia, and in two minutes we emerge onto the one paved road in Puerto Jiménez, the only town of any note in the Osa. The road's cement gutters are so deep to accommodate runoff during the rainy season that if Tom were to misjudge a turn and his pickup were to fall into one, his axle would be in serious danger of snapping. The three-block main drag has no name and few services.

"We've got no KFC here, no dry cleaners," Tom says in a wry tone. A man pedals a rusting bike past us, dangling a three-foot-long fish over the handlebars as he goes. We pass the medical clinic; opaque plastic sheeting is taped over the windows where glass is missing.

"They have some equipment, but no one knows how to use it. I got sick once, needed some care, and got out of here in a hurry." We pass a gas station, "the only one in the Osa," and come to the end of the town, where the obligatory soccer field is located, across from the Catholic church. There are some unfinished houses. "We have a lot of construction, but not a lot of progress."

"Is there a strong community here?"

"The main pastime is talking about other people's business. Who's dating whom."

We turn off down a dirt lane.

"Where are you staying?" Tom asks.

"Nowhere, yet." I mention the two places I read about in my guidebook.

"Stay at the cabins, they're cleaner. It's right there"—he points out the window down a short, dead-end road—"and once you've had enough of the big city, come be my guest out in the jungle." We bounce along farther and suddenly the bay opens out to our left. The unpaved road hugs the coast until we come to a shack beside a large palm-frond roof covering a patio. As we climb out of his truck I hear a thud over my shoulder.

"There's an event," Tom says lazily, "a coconut fell." It's impossible to know how Tom really feels about his adopted home. His true opinions about this, and everything else, seem locked behind a knowing and detached irony.

We take a seat out of a hot sun that's trying to burn itself through a thin layer of clouds. The humidity hangs heavy. There is no breeze under the overhang. Sweat rolls freely down my back. Tom orders a beer, I ask for a soda water. My body is disoriented and my mind disjointed from lack of sleep and jet lag.

"Not quite a dream state, but it's certainly not wakefulness," is how writer Pico Iyer describes the malady that has afflicted the traveler for only the last half century. It's a state I find myself in often and it only seems to be getting worse, never better. I've tried sleeping on arrival and staying up for twenty-four hours. I've taken melatonin and vitamin C. I've stood barefoot in a green field and watched the sunset. I've drunk gallons of water. Nothing works. I get jet lag, bad.

When I'm under jet lag's spell I often feel as if I have the clarity to see between my thoughts, a clarity that I usually lack. These insights invariably fill me with feelings of loneliness and melancholy, often accompanied by a shrugging sorrow that engulfs me. I've tried to embrace this state, but when my jet lag passes my thinking is often revealed to be deeply indulgent and sometimes just plain wrong. Consequently, I try not to take myself too seriously for a few days upon arrival at any distant locale.

But it's in this altered state that I hear Tom's story over lunch. A Peace Corps volunteer in the late sixties, Tom became a lawyer, defending large corporations. After a decade he grew disgusted, switched sides, and fought for the little guy for another ten years.

"But I just never got out of the Peace Corps mentality. So my wife and I came down here in 1990. We were looking for a third-world adventure; we wanted to contribute something. We wanted something fast moving and challenging. We had an idea to start something in ecotourism—very few were doing that then, and virtually no one in the Osa. In fact, people said to avoid this place. We were told it was full of jaguars, snakes, and no humans. When we heard that, we came here as fast as we could."

Tom and his wife built their eco-lodge—one of the most successful in the Osa. She has since returned to the States, but he never left. It's clear from the way Tom tells me this that their marriage is over—we stare out across the water in silence for a minute. He lifts his sweating bottle of beer, takes a long pull, and sets it down. He pushes his thick glasses back up his nose and wrings his hands. With his heavily creased forehead, Tom still looks very much like the lawyer he once was. I sit with his tale.

He seems content enough with his choices, and yet something about his story bothers me. I've admired similar individuals who went their own way, but in my current mood, sitting here, sweating by the sea, eating cold ceviche and drinking warm club soda, Tom's saga strikes me as quixotic, a search for an elusive freedom, only to wind up a lonely old man tilting at windmills in a small house beside an airstrip in a remote backwater.

"Do you miss anything about back home?" I ask.

Tom shrugs. "Just the conveniences."

A few tables away, over Tom's shoulder, two young women are seated with a man who keeps looking around with quick glances. One of the women has her back to me, but the other, with long, loose black hair and coffee-colored skin, wearing a red, low-cut T-shirt and black shorts, is staring directly at me and has been throughout the meal.

"I know I've only just arrived, but there are some very pretty women here," I say.

Tom looks around and sees the two women and the man at the table near us. He laughs. "*Zorras.*"

"What are *zorras?*"

"Well"—Tom shrugs—"they're not exactly prostitutes, but it's not exactly free either. My understanding is you pay a little bit."

"If you 'pay a little bit,' how is that not prostitution?"

He raises his eyebrows and lifts his bottle. "The Osa."

Tom drops me off in front of the cabins he recommended. They're not really cabins at all, rather a half dozen detached and semi-detached bungalows on the water's edge.

A trim, frail man with thinning, sandy-blond hair is standing behind the counter of the open-air lobby to greet me. John Planter is originally from Cape May, New Jersey, and came to the Osa nine years ago on vacation. "I never left." He shrugs. "Never went back for anything. There's not a lot going on here, but it does me a lot of good."

I drop my bag and John offers me a rusting bicycle. I pedal into town a few blocks away, and there really isn't much more to see than what Tom already showed me. When night falls, I park my bike and wander the streets.

On the main drag people loiter under dim streetlamps. A group of women convene and talk lazily outside the window of the Tienda de Ropa, where football jerseys and sequined T-shirts and mini-shorts are on display. At Juanita's bar, a cement box painted yellow, a few teenagers bang away at an old-fashioned pinball machine. Around the corner an open-air pool hall with three tables draws a half dozen men. I play a game of eight ball with one of them, while a pair of chickens strut around on the dirt lane out front. I let myself lose and wander off. Except for the bold stares I get from a couple of dark-eyed women hanging around in the shadows, I drift through town unnoticed. At the soccer field, I watch three generations of locals kick a ball with playful gusto under a weak yellow light. I cross the street to an open-air restaurant beside the small library and eat pizza.

This kind of aimless drifting has always been at the center of my traveling. The freedom of being a stranger in a strange place, knowing no one, needing to know no one, with no obligations, elicits deep feelings of liberation, and the farther from the beaten path I go, the quicker the attachment to any idea of how I should be treated is discarded—I'm grateful merely that my needs are met. Without an agenda, or company to distract me, I invariably feel a certain hopefulness that can appear contrary to my aimlessness. Perhaps it's just the simple joy of being alive.

Finishing my pizza, I watch a cat, walking low and hugging close to the library wall. There is little to clutter my mind. Several of the younger men who were playing soccer across the street earlier slip onto the patio and wash their hands at the sink beside my table. I make my way back into the night.

Even in the peaceful, solitary bubble of Puerto Jiménez, I can feel something tugging at me. Often, a sudden recollection of responsibilities back home falls down on me hard, like a burden I've neglected that needs my attention. Feelings of guilt and affection, resentment and love, will often vie for dominance in my suddenly addled mind, but tonight, retrieving my bicycle and pedaling along the dirt road to my bungalow by the sea under a dripping gauze of stars, thoughts of people who need me, and tasks that require my tending, only add to my general contentment as the warm breeze in the night air blows softly past.

In the 1980s, gold mining became big business in the Osa; rivers were dredged and the sides of hills hollowed out. Tougher laws came into play to protect the land from reckless plundering, but Tom told me there are still some diehards out in the hills, occasionally pulling out a big score.

"The problem with gold miners," he said in his usual laconic, teasing tone, "is that they're always broke. When they find some, they're in town, drunk, buying drinks for everyone, and when they don't, they don't eat. But go on out to El Tigre, try your luck."

With visions of golf-ball-size chunks of twenty-four-karat cash falling into my pan, the next morning I rent a jeep on main street and head out of town. Just beyond a newly installed—and wildly out of place—cement bridge, I turn onto a dirt lane cutting through a pasture filled with bone-thin cows and bounce along until I arrive at the cluster of buildings that is El Tigre. During the heyday of the rush, the gold-mining settlement was home to seven thousand souls, but that number has dwindled to a sleepy hundred.

There's a school across the dirt track from a cement hut with a corrugated iron roof. A hand-painted sign out front says PULPERIA EL TUCAN. A small Costa Rican woman named Sandra is behind the counter of the general store, selling sacks of rice and cartons of eggs, beside cans of motor oil and fishing lures.

I ask her if there is anyone around who might be willing to take me out and do a little panning.

Sandra shrugs. Then a young girl, maybe eight, walks in with a list scribbled onto a scrap of paper and hands it to Sandra. Sandra gets up reluctantly from her perch and shuffles off to a far corner of the cluttered room. She returns with a chicken in a plastic bag, a few potatoes, and then some very limp celery. The small girl pulls out a pinky-nail-size chunk of gold and puts it on the counter. Sandra reaches below the counter and comes up with a small plastic scale. She weighs the raw nugget, makes change in cash, and the little girl takes her haul and goes on her way.

"Was that gold?"

Sandra stares at me, weighing the possible responses to such an idiotic question. "Yes," she says finally.

"Could I see it?" I have never seen a piece of raw gold, direct from the ground.

Sandra slowly lifts the small, irregular-shaped chunk and holds it out to me. She then reaches under the counter again and comes up with a pistol, an old six-shooter. She places the pistol on the counter-top without a word. Her hand rests beside it. When I give the nugget back, Sandra takes it with one hand while replacing the pistol with her other.

"I hate gold," she says, and then directs me up the hill to a shack where she thinks someone might be willing to take me over to the river. I thank her and head out. But just outside, I come upon a sturdy young man.

"Edwin," he says when I ask his name. His mitt of a hand engulfs mine and he agrees to take me a short way up the El Tigre River to try my luck. Knee-deep in the rushing water, bending from the waist with a tire iron and shovel, Edwin pries large rocks free and we hurl them aside. We create a small eddy and he lays down a metal trough through which the water funnels. Without warning, a blanket of rain falls. We are drenched within seconds. Edwin doesn't say anything, doesn't look up. He doesn't seem to notice. We continue to dig and hurl rocks aside. Then, using a circular tin pan that looks suspiciously like a hubcap, he dips into the side channel we've created and begins to sift the larger stones away. His thick hands work with delicate precision. It stops raining as suddenly as it began. Eventually the grain of soil in the pan becomes fine. The sediment swirls. Tiny shimmering specks begin to appear within the muddy mix. Edwin's fingers dance over the tray, and a dusting of fine golden grains settles at the bottom. Edwin looks up at me for the first time since we arrived here. He nods. He is pleased.

He empties the dust into a small vial he produces from his pocket and shoves it into my hands. When I try to give it back, I can see that he is offended and I tuck the vial away. As I take leave of him, I put ten thousand colones—roughly twenty dollars—into his hand. He accepts it silently, with a curt nod, and I'm back in my car cutting through the field, past the skinny cows. Back in town, time passes slowly. I go to sell my gold at a shop on the main drag and am offered roughly ten dollars. I meet an Irishman with weathered skin, shaggy blond hair, and a rugged way about him ambling down the main street. His name is Pat Murphy and he's been in the Osa since the mid-nineties.

"There's no going back," he says. I think Pat has seen *Crocodile*

Dundee a few too many times, and when he offers to take me out into the rain forest for a close encounter with an alligator, he can't understand my resistance to the idea.

"Oh, yeah, gators are his thing," Tom tells me when I run into him a little later. "You might want to stay away from him."

Otherwise, life around Puerto Jiménez proceeds with laid-back regularity. I see someone else paying in gold at the El Record shoe store. At a storefront restaurant, where I'm sitting on a plastic chair eating rice and beans, I overhear one man ask another if his pig has given birth yet.

"Not for another few weeks," the friend replies.

The first man considers this and after a time says, "That's a nice pig."

I go next door to buy ice cream.

A large white plastic cooler with a hand-painted sign in English, written in a rainbow of colors and listing a dozen flavors sits on a patio in front of a door with a doctor's name on it. No one is around. With nowhere else to go, I wait.

Eventually a tall, broad-shouldered woman with long brown hair walks up from behind me and steps around the cooler. She wears a floral hippie blouse. She has hazel eyes, and her skin is deeply tanned.

"Hi." She doesn't explain her long absence.

"How's the mango flavor?"

"Sweet."

"I'll take one."

"Sure you will," the woman says with a lazy directness, like a Jersey girl who's lost her edge, which is exactly what Karen Brown is.

Karen came to the Osa from New Jersey ten years ago, met a local guy, had a child with him, and is now raising her daughter on her own with what she makes selling her homemade ice cream. The mango isn't very sweet at all and lacks any real flavor, but this is the only place in town to get ice cream and no one else seems to be buying it. And since Karen is easy company, I make it a habit of stopping by every afternoon.

"This is the world's largest open-air asylum," she says. "But hey, you can address a letter to 'Karen, Puerto Jiménez,' and it'll get to me. Can't do that back in the Garden State."

Karen, like Tom and Pat, is yet another person I meet who walked away from it all with a dream of something better than what she left behind. Whether they found it or not is the question.

I have long harbored similar notions of escape, of walking away and not looking back. It's not a fantasy that holds much relevance these days. I'm not about to go anywhere with two small children to raise. Their lives are, to a very large degree, my responsibility for another decade at least and not something I care to miss out on. And my life with D—it's just as important.

However, the secret yearning that can linger just behind each responsible action, the mental flights of fancy, the hunger for otherness, the sexual fantasies that can blossom and undermine any real intimacy, the simple dream of flight, can be nearly as fatal to a relationship as physical departure. You can't be two places at once—even mentally or emotionally.

So maybe that's what I'm doing down here in the Osa—getting a good look at those who did escape and to challenge my own propensity toward utopian fantasies that can corrode any chance at real happiness.

A few days later, when Crocodile Dundee corners me again just off the main street, I decide it's time to take Tom up on his offer. I head out over the only road that goes deeper into the Osa, past balsa and fig trees crowding the road, out toward Tom's eco-lodge. Before I get there, I see a rental car by the side of the washboard dirt track. Since I haven't seen any other cars on the trip out, I stop. A young couple, tourists, emerge from the rain forest. They're moving quickly.

"Everything all right?" I ask.

"Yeah," the man says, but I miss the rest of his sentence as they rush into their car and race off.

I park. A few feet from the road, the rain forest is dense; another ten feet in and I wouldn't be able to see the road at all. I don't see anything unusual, but I don't really know what it is I'm looking for. I take another few steps and stop, sensing something moving to my left. I turn. Two feet away, at eye level, a fifteen-foot boa constrictor is coiled around the dead limb of a tree. His head is lifted off the branch and is arching back. He is taking a good look at me, and has been for a while.

"Whooooa," I blurt out, and jump back. The snake and I stare at each other for a while. I gasp for breath and say some more useful things, like, "Jesus Christ," and "Holy shit," and then, "Why didn't you say it was a fucking boa constrictor?" Eventually the snake loses interest in me and lowers his head back down. I take out my phone and turn on the video, to show off my courage in front of the killer snake for my kids back home, and then drive on.

Tom's lodge is another five minutes down the road. It's a tasteful operation, set atop a hill looking out over the rain forest and down to the breaking surf. The lobby/dining area has a fifty-foot vaulted and thatched roof, and it's there that I find Tom, who eases his way over to me with his trademark laconic circumspection.

I mention my close encounter with the boa. "Oh, yeah?" He shrugs. "Want to eat?"

We're joined by his manager, a stocky young Costa Rican named Carlos, who has all the passion for the rain forest that Tom seems to lack. "I'll take you out for a nighttime walk," Carlos says, "and really show you some things." Once it gets dark, he does.

The night is humid and close. It needs to rain. We drive for a while down a terrible dirt track and ditch the car by the side of the road. How this particular spot differs from any other in the utter blackness is something I don't ask.

"Put these on," Carlos says, handing me a pair of tall waterproof boots. "And this." He proffers a headlamp.

In one hand he carries a long, extendable pole with a hook on the end, and in the other hand he has a long knife. A headlamp is glowing from the center of his forehead.

"What's the pole for?" I ask.

"Snakes."

We crunch over dead leaves and dense undergrowth. I jump at every sound. The trees hang heavy and cast strange and forbidding shadows as our headlamps pass over them.

"So, are there any poisonous snakes around here?" I ask.

"The only one we need to really worry about is the fer-de-lance," Carlos says. "It's unlikely you'll die from its bite, but it's not good to get bit."

"How big are they?"

"They're small, actually."

"That's good," I say.

"Not really." Carlos shrugs. "Makes them harder to see. And they're very well disguised."

"Why are we here, Carlos?"

There are frogs and spiders, columns of cutter ants marching under their heavy loads. We walk down into a stream and find large crayfish. Carlos is thrilled by the discovery of some apparently rare type of tadpole. The rain forest is alive and pungent and inviting, yet I'm strangely detached. Any real curiosity or sense of wonder is absent. Instead, mundane images of home scroll through my mind—a colorful and detailed drawing of a house and tree that my daughter made, a karate move my son has been perfecting in the living room, an image of D sipping tea from her favorite blue mug. Something large moves to our right in the blackness; I jump and we turn our lights toward the sound, but it's gone. We come upon a small bird, perched on a twig, motionless, asleep. I lean in, inches from its beak. I have never seen a sleeping bird—I've never even considered one.

We have long left the trail and for all I know we could be walking in circles.

"Turn off your flashlight," Carlos says.

"Excuse me?"

"Turn it off."

When I do, the blackness is complete. I hold my hand six inches in front of my face and can't see it. I look up and can see only a tiny patch of night sky directly overhead, through a break in the dense canopy of trees. A single star shines.

"You know, Carlos," I say, "if you have a heart attack and die, I will be lost in here for a very long time."

From a few feet away in the dark I hear his laugh. Eventually we make our way back to the car.

"I'm really sorry we didn't see any snakes," he says.

The intrepid traveler Freya Stark once said, "To awaken quite alone in a strange town is one of the pleasantest sensations in the world." The uncomplicated joy of meeting a new day with no past, with no plan, and with no one in the world knowing where I am can be compared only to waking up on Christmas morning when I was a child. It's the closest I have ever come to understanding the word "freedom."

I've never been homesick, at least since I went away to camp at age ten—save for my children. This morning, however, standing on the deck outside my room, looking out over the rain forest down to the sea below, I find myself not exactly wishing I were home but at least aware that I'm not traveling with the same sense of abandon and unencumbered ease that I experienced as recently as my trip to Patagonia.

I spend the day exploring the surf community of Matapalo, trying to rouse a little more interest in my surroundings, and once it gets dark I join Carlos and his wife, Adrianna, at a tin-roofed bar with no walls, just down the road from Tom's lodge, in the middle of the rain forest. Tibetan prayer flags hang beside mounted surfboards under colored Chinese paper lanterns and a spinning disco ball.

"Pretty much everybody comes here to Greta's on Friday nights," Carlos explains. I duck my head when I see Crocodile Dundee sipping a beer at one of the picnic tables, whispering intently to a young couple. Karen is selling her ice cream from the white cooler at the edge of the bar, where the light ends and the night begins, just under the overhang. There are a few tables selling handmade jewelry; I recognize two of the vendors from town. A young and scruffy dude in a baseball cap—the former manager of a famous rapper—who cashed in and checked out and moved to the Osa three years ago plays DJ. Small kids tumble over the two sofas by the dance floor. Just beyond the roof, in a grassy area with a bench, a group of white guys and Costa Ricans share some very potent-smelling grass. A dozen young-ish women dance to the techno music that blares out into the jungle.

"Who's Greta?" I ask.

Carlos turns to look over his shoulder. "Which one do you think?"

I follow his glance to the bar. There, sipping a beer, and staring at me, is a heavily tattooed, chain-smoking surfer chick/earth mother with long loose blond hair wearing a sleeveless black dress with a slit up the side. I nod in her direction.

"That's her," Carlos says. "Watch out, she'll either love you or hate you. You can never tell which."

I walk over to introduce myself.

"You're new," she says before I reach the bar. Her voice is raw from too many cigarettes and too much whiskey. Her skin is tan and her dark eyes glassy. Her bare arms are fleshy under her tattoos, her body lumpy beneath her clinging dress. She's self-possessed. This is her joint, and I like her instantly.

"Where are you from?"

"New York."

She nods. "Well, you're welcome here," she says, openly looking me up and down. I'm surprised she doesn't ask me to spin around so she can get a good look at my ass. We chat, the music blares. Greta came from Munich, Germany, nearly twenty years ago. "I came down for the surfing, just by luck. Figured this place needed a bar." She shrugs. "This is it."

She pulls out another cigarette and gives me matches to light it. I can't remember the last time I lit a woman's cigarette, once a nightly task back in my bar-hopping days. It says lot about someone, the way they light another person's cigarette, and the way a person receives the flame maybe says more. Greta is good. After I touch the fire to the tip of her cigarette I look up to her eyes and she is already staring at me, squinting slightly. The look holds for an instant and then she winks at me, and then we both burst out laughing. She slaps me hard on the shoulder and marches behind the bar, disappearing into the kitchen.

The techno music suddenly quits and Marvin Gaye comes out over the speakers. I wish I were uninhibited enough to simply walk onto the dance floor, especially considering it is full of a dozen women spinning and twirling and shimmying for each other. Instead I buy an ice cream from Karen and meet her daughter, a chubby, happy child.

When Carlos and his wife leave, I sit down at a picnic table across from the young couple that was talking to Crocodile Dundee earlier. Luckily, he is nowhere in sight. The couple, Tony and Kate, run a small eco-lodge in the area. He came down more than twenty years ago from Vermont; she met him here while on vacation from Colorado. They have two small kids, one whom they are homeschooling, the other still in diapers. She was an accountant and says she was glad to give up the grind. Tony goes off to the bathroom and Kate leans in toward me.

"And what about you?" she says. Her hand lands on my forearm and stays there.

"Uh, what about me?"

"What's your story?" And while it's just the two of us chatting, Kate is caressing my back. Instead of my imagination racing or plotting covert actions and rendezvous—as I might have done in the past—I simply feel bad for her husband and wonder what the hell they're doing here, living in the jungle, looking for trouble.

When Tony returns, Kate sits back and is affectionate to her husband. I ask myself if perhaps I just made that whole sexual tension up; maybe she was just being friendly. I excuse myself and head back to the bar.

Later, as I'm about to leave, one of the not-so-young women who were on the dance floor all night approaches me. She's part of a group on a yoga retreat down in the Osa.

"You seem age appropriate," she says. "You want to dance?"

Politely, I decline, not because of her age, but because she's clearly drunk.

"Oh come on, you just gonna stand at the bar acting cool?"

"No, I'm just getting ready to go. Next time. Thanks for asking," I say.

"Hey, you know what," the yogini protests, "I'm calling you out. I'm calling you out on your very uncool behavior." She turns and waves a few of her friends over for backup.

One of the women is very attractive; I had noticed her earlier on the dance floor. The ladies escort their friend away, but not before she tells me again how very uncool my behavior is.

Maybe I've been with the same woman for so long that I'm rusty on how the game is played. Maybe I'm misreading signals all over the place, or maybe I am just getting too old, but there is none of the forbidden or illicit appeal in these brief encounters that I have felt in the past. I just want to go to bed.

The next morning I head out along the only road that goes deeper into the rain forest. Fig trees drape across the dirt track and wild cotton grows in bunches. Occasionally the rain forest opens up where it was cleared for grazing and cows with protruding hips sit under acacia trees. I ford the Río Pico—this is where Carlos told me his jeep was swept away and carried downstream for a mile and deposited into the sea, with him still in it. "I didn't want to leave my jeep," he explained.

There has been no rain and the river is low; I cross without losing my car. Soon, the road fizzles at the settlement of Carate. There's nothing here really, and no one else, except for a bearded American with a foul disposition who runs a bare-bones shop in a cement hut. I've been warned to give him a wide berth.

"I found him walking on the side of the road with a large knife sticking out of his cheek, covered in blood. I picked him up and drove him to the hospital," Carlos told me. "He got blood all over my jeep, and the next time I saw him he threatened to shoot me if I came near."

I buy a bottle of water from the sour patron, attempt conversation, receive a few grunts in reply, leave my car, and head into the jungle. A short way down the trail, I come to sign welcoming me to Parque Nacional Corcovado. The trail leads me into dense vegetation, under mango trees and through strands of bamboo. I climb over the sprawling roots of massive strangler figs. Eventually the trail dumps me out onto a long stretch of deserted beach under sweltering sun. Just offshore, a bull shark, its dorsal fin clearly visible, keeps pace. A harpy eagle lands high up in a cecropia tree. Macaws, always in pairs, eat from almond trees. I see toucans, and black and white king vultures. When the trail leads me back into the jungle, I'm attacked by a swarm of stingless bees as I stop to watch an anteater have lunch. I leap around, shaking and pulling at my hair, jumping from one foot to the other, swatting, cursing, spinning. Then the branches above me begin to shake. I duck. A troupe of spider monkeys is throwing nuts at me from above. I run away. A woodpecker is rapping somewhere. Hummingbirds whiz past. I grab a fallen coconut, hack it open with my knife, and drink down its too sweet water. I pull a banana from a tree and eat it. A little farther on, a huge mammal, a cross between a horse and a giant anteater, blocks my path. Apparently this is something called a Baird's tapir—Carlos had told me I might see one. What he neglected to tell me was whether it was aggressive or not. I stand for fifteen minutes in my tracks and wait for it to finish nibbling at whatever it is it's eating and move off.

After nearly six hours of walking I come upon a river, the Río Claro. It's thirty yards wide, and since I'm only a hundred yards inland and close to the ocean, it's a tidal river, and it's rising. I've been warned of alligators in the rivers of Corcovado. And sharks, like the one I just saw out in the ocean, are known to frequent the rivers' brackish waters as well. But it is late in the afternoon, the ranger station I'm headed for can't be more than another hour away, and I'll never make it back to where I started before darkness falls.

The riverbed is slick. Quickly, I'm waist-deep in the Río Claro. I can't see into the murky brown water. With as much speed as I dare, I pick my way across, looking neither left nor right, knowing there's nothing I could do if I were to see a fin or a pair of beady eyes gliding my way. *National Geographic* has dubbed Corcovado "the most biologically intense place on earth."

I arrive at La Sirena ranger station soggy, sore, and satisfied.

𐅉

The Osa Peninsula is largely off the grid. Most places outside Puerto Jiménez operate on generators or are solar or hydro powered or some combination of the three. I've had no cell phone connection and only very occasional Internet service since I arrived. I did receive one message from D, telling me that I need to fill out forms for our wedding in Ireland. The forms need my parents' names and ages, my witness's name, the date of my previous marriage, and the date of my divorce. My signature is needed. Nothing can move forward until these forms are filled out. Because processing paperwork like this in Ireland can take several months, all this needs to be done now. Repeat, now.

This is simply D's way of saying, "Don't forget us back here, carrying the load. There's work to be done. And you are getting married, you know." What exactly she expects me to do about this at La Sirena ranger station in the middle of Corcovado National Park, miles from a proper Internet connection or even a phone, is unclear.

Accessible only by a day's walk, similar to the one I have just made, or, in an emergency, by small aircraft—which explains the long patch of low cut grass doubling as a front lawn—the ranger station is a humid oasis, a series of low-slung, plantation-style huts painted green. There are bunk beds in dormitories and communal bathrooms. The shower is an open pipe protruding from the wall. Hikers' clothes hang from lines out back in a futile attempt at drying in the near 100 percent humidity. There is no electricity here. When it gets dark, you go to bed. Yet there's an air of survivors' fellowship among the thirty or so hikers who have made it here. Somewhere, somehow, someone is playing Eddie Vedder.

In an Adirondack chair on the deck, I rub my swollen feet and prop them on the rail. I make passing conversation with a woman from Canada, and then a family of dark-haired Spaniards—a mother, a father, and their two teenage children—take seats near me. I watch their uncensored irritation and familial ease with each other.

When I was growing up, my own family never strayed very far from home. Each summer when I was still quite young, my father would take my two older brothers and me on the one-hour car ride down the Garden State Parkway to the shore, where we stayed with my uncle's family for a few days at their home on Long Beach Island. My father's brother frightened me—he was rough in a way my father was not. He had a deep scar that ran from above his right eye far down into his cheek. His hair was unruly, his manner brusque and direct. His chain-smoking and well-meaning wife had deep black rings under her eyes and drifted through the house like a specter. Their many children ran wild and struck me as peculiar. The ocean, two blocks from their house, often swarmed with jellyfish and the sandy bottom was potholed, so that I was never sure, when I stepped, how deep my steps would go.

My mother, who didn't care for either the shore or my uncle, never joined us on these trips, but she did come with us on our annual journey across New Jersey, west to the Pocono Mountains in neighboring Pennsylvania. Each winter we would load into the Country Squire station wagon with the faux wood paneling, and my brothers and I would try to spot license plates from different states to make the seemingly endless two-hour ride pass. We always went to the same lodge, high up on a hill. It was an all-in-one facility—three meals a day in the sprawling dining room. My father's chest visibly swelled when the maître d' remembered his name each year.

In the evenings before dinner my mother liked to go ice-skating. She was a solitary person, and skating revealed a playful exuberance that I rarely saw otherwise. My glimpse into this hidden side of her made me want to skate as well. She told me I was a natural, but I was never very good—though I was proud she wanted me to join her. She recognized in me a solitary quality similar to her own, and it created an unspoken bond between us. It was a closeness unique within the family—one that did not go unnoticed by my father.

My younger brother, Justin, was born when I was eight, and soon thereafter, my mother became ill. This, coupled with a new baby, essentially ended our modest travels. Except for when my father took my two older brothers and me to Bermuda—a trip designed to give my mother some much-needed rest. I was nine. None of us had ever been so far from home, and my father had never had solo care of the three of us. He juggled our divergent desires as well as could be expected given his limited day-to-day experience of our needs.

Stephen was set up at the golf course each morning and then not seen again until dinner. Peter wanted to go scuba diving and since my father couldn't leave me alone, he lied and told the instructor that I was ten. We took lessons in the hotel pool before setting out for the sea.

"Jump in and wait under the boat," the instructor told my brother as he helped me with an air tank I was not strong enough to support.

"Wait under the boat?" I remember my brother repeating, his eyes wide. Then, for half an hour, we dove in the cloudy water and I heard my own breathing with an acute regularity I never had before. Only once did I panic and dart to the surface.

But it is riding on the back of my father's rented moped that dominates my memories of that trip. I wasn't old enough to ride my own, but I was old enough to feel uncomfortable holding on to my father's midsection as we darted through the streets. He would occasionally turn his head in the breeze and say, "I love you, pal." Only as an adult did I come to realize what it was that made me uneasy about my father's declaration. What I heard was not the simple statement of his affection but the desperate need for appreciation behind his words. I didn't want my father to be desperate.

Sometimes I can feel a similar yearning for validation when I tell my own son that I love him. To place the burden of emotional bolstering on a child is unreasonable and confusing, yet my son seems to have a better sense of himself and his place in the world than I did at his age. He simply ignores me when I express my love for him from this place of need, or he dismisses my prompting with a distracted, "Okay."

One afternoon in Bermuda, my father stopped the scooter at a port and we met a man with a long and bushy black beard who said he was a captain. My father was, and still is, a gregarious man with an easy charm. He is instantly likable, and the years have softened him. But in my youth, his explosive and terrifying anger ran roughshod over our home—its potential emergence, provoked often by things of which we were unaware, hovered over every encounter. Only later did I come to realize that his anger rose from his fear—fear that he wouldn't be able to care for his family, fear that he would never be who he felt he should be as a man, fears I now understand. But that his anger did not stem from some dark and secret place made it no less terrifying.

My father chatted with the captain at the port for a long time, like he chatted with so many people, and despite my protestations he insisted I have my photograph taken with the bearded man.

It is the only time I remember him taking my picture. I was embarrassed—for myself, but also for my father. He seemed so vulnerable taking my picture, and it paralyzed me even further. In the photo, a small and skinny boy wearing a bright yellow sweatshirt that says BERMUDA on the front is standing like a stick figure, arms hanging straight down, staring at the camera without expression, beside a squatting man with a full beard and a big grin.

Sitting now, rubbing my feet and listening as the two Spanish teens say something to their parents I'm not fluent enough to decipher, but understanding exactly what they mean when they shake their heads, hunch their shoulders, and stomp away from them, I lean over and reassure the parents what a memorable thing it is that they're doing.

"Well, it's almost destroyed us," the Spanish mother says without a trace of humor. But, later, at the communal dinner, they are all laughing together, the loudest, happiest group in the room. I wonder how long it might be before my small family is up for a similar trip. Before the sun goes down, the mosquitoes descend and a girl from Colorado offers me her herbal insect repellent. I spray it on, to no effect.

Coming up the lawn, a group of ten young men stride toward one of the outbuildings with the casual assurance of a pack. I haven't seen them before. They fan out in an almost perfect pyramid behind the obvious leader. Several men are shirtless. Some wear hastily knotted ponytails. Most have tattoos and nearly all of them are sporting leather anklets or necklaces, many with small totems hanging down, obvious trophies of their rugged travel to remote destinations like this one.

I am instantly made uneasy by the gang. They are all at least ten years younger than me, but I feel childlike and inadequate in their presence. I have never traveled in or been a part of such a group—not even as a child running around my suburban neighborhood.

That I have been so strongly identified in my acting career as a member of the Brat Pack is one of the stranger ironies of my life. And that no such tightly knit unit of actors existed in reality mattered little; it was a snappy nickname and it captured both the fascination and the judgment foisted upon a group of fortunate young actors. The last thing any actor wants is to be stereotyped and pigeonholed; this, coupled with the pejorative aspect so many associated with the term at the time, made it a moniker I tried to run from. But as time has worn on, both the label and the actors branded with it have grown in my affections (although there are members of the Brat Pack with whom I purportedly spent many a wild night whom I have never met). Most have had long, varied, and in some cases very interesting careers. It's a testament to a talented cluster of actors that movies made nearly three decades ago still hold such resonance for several generations. And maybe because I know what the label felt like, and how we all struggled with it in our own ways, when I see other Brat Pack members now, in films or on television, I feel a kinship with them I feel with no other actors. Perhaps we have finally become a pack at last.

But did I become a self-reliant loner because I was never welcomed into such a tribe, or did I realize early on that my desires could never be met in the rhythm of a group? The answer is impossible to discern from the myriad adjustments I've made through life. What is certain is that the sense of vulnerability that gathers between my shoulder blades as the gang of young men stride by—unaware of my individual gaze, but very conscious of their attractiveness as a group—is that this feeling is nearly as old as I am.

Yet unlike in my youth, when this sense of insecurity could pervade my consciousness for days and weeks at a time, these phantoms of my past move through quickly, without any real power to harm. I observe myself with a slight detachment. My thoughts then veer to something my nine-year-old son said to me recently, as I was tucking him into bed for the night.

"Dad, I feel like there's a distance between me and the rest of the world." His clear insight and simple articulateness shocked me, then saddened me and made me fear for him. When my reflexive reactions subsided, I relaxed and identified with him.

"I've always felt the same way," I told him. I wasn't sure what else to say. "But it's part of what makes me me, so it's okay. You know what I mean?" I said.

My son was quiet for a moment. "Yeah," he said, and then surprised me by reaching out and hugging me close.

This sudden mood switch, the fact that the sense of isolation and inadequacy I was experiencing while I was watching the gang of young men was quickly supplanted by this memory of close connection with my son, does not slip by unnoticed. I slap a mosquito and blood splatters on my calf.

†

Screaming howler monkeys wake me before dawn, and I have a problem. I had intended to head back in the direction from which I came, but I had no cell phone reception on that side of the peninsula. It's Mother's Day. I need to make a call.

After breakfast I hustle a ride on a small supply boat that's heading north. I've been told that I might get a signal once we come around the point leading into Drake Bay, the other port of call in the Osa. Both my children would be wild with excitement at the sight of the dolphins leaping out of the water and racing just off the bow; I have other things on my mind. When I scheduled this trip I was unaware Mother's Day would fall during the time I was away, and when I realized it, and broke the news to D, I received only a frosty, "Oh, really," in reply.

From the sea, the coastline is a series of rugged, densely vegetated hills leading to jagged cliffs that occasionally open out to empty beaches. The wind begins to pick up and the water grows choppy. The bow of the boat slams down into the white-capped waves. When we come around a point and enter a large bay, the wind dies and the surface of the water settles to a glasslike reflection of the hills above. A few houses become visible among the palms. Several boats are moored not far offshore. There is life here.

Whereas Puerto Jiménez is a rough-and-ready backwater, Agujitas in Drake Bay is a banana-republic-type idyll of dirt lanes and heavy palm trees, climbing up the hill from a crescent-shaped beach (that the beach is infested with small, red, biting ants is not apparent at first glance).

I disembark and march to the top of the hill, looking for a signal. Halfway up, two bars of reception flicker onto my phone; I dial, hear it ring, and I get D's message. I force my voice into a casually upbeat tone and promise to call again.

I call my mother and leave her a message as well.

Suddenly there's a chorus of voices singing and I follow the sound to an open-air church. Hundreds of people fill it. When the singing subsides, the preacher begins to shout into a microphone, too close. His voice is distorted with static and feedback over the damaged PA system. Whenever his voice drops lower, a muffled woofing echoes out. Occasional calls of "amen" come back from the crowd as he preaches. Farther up the hill I find an open restaurant and order a pizza—but am told there is no cheese in the village.

When I finally get D on the phone, she is not happy. Not because I'm away on Mother's Day, but because my son has upset her.

"I'm trying to make a video for Mum's seventieth birthday and I'm getting people to sing to her. And he was just really rude about it."

"What did he say?"

"Nothing, it's fine, he eventually did it. It's fine."

The child/stepparent relationship is a balancing act that can leave everyone feeling in the middle and often powerless, especially the child. But it doesn't stop me from being angry with my son from afar. "What did he say?" I ask again.

"When I asked him if he'd like to be in the video, he said, 'I'm not in your family.'"

Considering the affection my son has for D's parents (he is constantly asking to go see them in Ireland), and theirs for him, and given D's attachment and commitment to family, there is nothing he could have said that would have upset her more.

This behavior reminds me of my son's reaction upon hearing that D and I were finally getting married.

"Why?" he wanted to know when we told him about the wedding. "Everything is good the way it is, why do you have to get married?"

"Everything will still be the same, nothing will change," I explained.

"So if nothing will change, then why do it?"

"Well, it will bring us even closer."

"No it won't," he protested. "I'm not gonna come."

Eventually, and after many conversations, it became clear that my son felt he would be left out of the family—after all, his sister was D's and my child, while he was merely my son—despite D's obvious love for him. ("I've always thought I came into your life because of your son," she once said to me.) As much as I've tried to comfort him and assure him that his being excluded from our family is an impossibility, his doubt obviously still lingers.

The signal during the call is patchy and strains my conversation with D further. Eventually the call drops.

I was scheduled to get back on the boat ten minutes ago. People are waiting. The call won't go through anymore. I climb to a different spot on the hill and try again, and again. Eventually, it connects.

Luckily, a photo I took of some coconuts and had sent to our daughter several days earlier has finally downloaded during the time I was trying to call again. Our daughter is delighted with the photo and D has relaxed. Soon we're chatting and she begins to laugh. I ask if the orchid I (somehow) remembered to send before I left home arrived. "It did. It's lovely, thank you," D says. "You knew you better call today, huh?" she laughs.

"Uh, yeah."

"I thought, 'He better call.' I don't care how far off the grid you are, sometimes you've got to call."

We talk some more as I begin to head down the hill to the boat. D recounts the frustrations of trying to get a delivery made. She has recently gone back to her yoga practice on a more committed basis, which has revitalized her outlook. "The best thing about doing yoga every day is that it really grounds you in yourself. It lets you slice through a lot of crap. You just don't put up with a lot of people's nonsense," she explains, and then she laughs. "It's good you're making the cut."

"I'm not sure I am," I say. "I'm just away a lot."

"Good point."

My boat ride back to the other side of the peninsula didn't wait, and I find myself a room at a rustic lodge on top of a hill looking out over the bay. Unexpected and improvised plans are the luxury of the solo traveler. When I lie down, I hear thunderous stomping on my metal roof. Monkeys are scampering around above me and sleep is a long time coming. Later, I'm woken by a ferocious rain pounding on the roof. I get up and look out my window into the dark and can make out palm fronds and banana leaves bent under the relentless assault. The heavy drops smack the leaves with machine-gun determination. Yet dawn arrives to blue skies and I hop on a supply boat headed around to Puerto Jiménez. The captain drops me near Carate to retrieve my car and I'm on my way back toward town.

At the Río Oro I see a road paralleling the river and heading up into the rain forest. I saw it on my way out—it's the only turnoff from the main road—so for no other reason, I take it.

The dirt track is worse than the washboard main road. There are deep ravines down the center, carved by runoff cascading down during the heavy rains. A few die-hard gold miners are living and working beside the river. Green plastic sheeting is stretched taut between propped-up sticks. Beneath the plastic roofing, cots are visible, as are piles of clothing. A cooking fire smolders nearby the giant Hefty-bag homes. Two rope-thin and ragged men bend low, thigh-deep, working the river. The road climbs steeply and then turns back on itself and climbs again. The rain forest is thick, the air heavy. Mist hangs in the treetops. My car struggles hard against the steep grade; at one point the incline is so severe it feels as if the car will tumble back on itself. Then there's a hand-painted wooden sign nailed to a tree: ALMOST THERE, it says. It's written in English and the first indication of any life up this road.

Suddenly the track levels and a well-manicured circular driveway welcomes me to an elegant and rustic eco-lodge. Hardwoods have been used as pillars and palm fronds thatch the roof of the expansive open-air lobby and dining area.

"How did this get here?" I say aloud.

Then a blond woman, about my age, perhaps a few years older, with ample breasts and piercing blue eyes walks toward me. She's wearing a light blue form-fitting cotton dress that's hugging just right. Her teeth are a brilliant white when she smiles at me, and her skin is lushly tanned.

"Wow," I say inadvertently.

Holly Evans came to the Osa from Boulder, Colorado, for the first time in the early eighties, then bought this chunk of rain forest in 1994 and opened her eight-bungalow lodge in 2000. "This has been my dream," she tells me, staring deep into my eyes.

"Mine too," I'm thinking.

Over a cup of tea on the deck overlooking the rain forest Holly tells me, "I broke my leg in four places and my nose twice building this place, but it had to be. Can you understand?" She is still staring deep into my eyes, and now she reaches out and touches my upper arm.

"Um, yes," I say, "I understand."

Her lover is off in San José for a few days. "He's much younger, he needs the city sometimes." She smiles at me. "Would you like a tour?"

I nod stupidly.

She shows me her favorite suite, with a large bed overlooking the jungle canopy. "Nice, isn't it?"

"Mmmm."

Back outside Holly walks in front of me up a long flight of stairs carved into the mountain; the backside of her blue cotton dress dances before my eyes as she goes. We stand on the edge of her yoga platform, gazing out over the jungle down to the sea.

"Whenever I'm confused about something, I come up here and stand on my head, and everything is all right."

It begins to rain, loudly and with force. We stand and look out in silence. Listening. Clouds and mist race before us. The air around us is charged.

In the past, several of the scenarios I encountered on this trip might have given me pause, and my failure to react to them this time left me wondering if perhaps I was past that temptation. But suddenly my senses are alert and have me reengaged in a way I haven't been recently. I'm wondering why. Then, as the rain falls down, I realize it's not Holly's beauty that attracts me to her—although it does—it is her complete inhabitation of her life. She has the confidence of a person who knows what she wants, has the courage to make the choices to reach for it, and has the satisfaction of her achievement. When she turns to me and smiles, I can only smile back.

After the rain lets up, we slowly descend the slick steps and wander in the direction of my car. I fish my keys from my pocket and we stand for a moment; Holly's blue eyes burn again into mine. The leaves of the nearby banana trees drip heavily, the birds have begun to squawk again, and the lingering mist is burning off quickly. The air is already steamy. Holly nods and then thrusts out her hand. We shake. I smile at the gesture, and then she does, and then I'm in the car, riding the brake hard, easing my way back down off this slippery slope.

I can imagine lingering images from my brief time here, images that might fester and go deep, images that have nothing to do with reality but can nonetheless assert themselves and influence and alter the reality that does exist, back home, with D.

Yet as I bounce back the way I came, I find myself thinking not of sensuous headstands over the rain forest or of large soft beds overlooking a misty sunrise, but of images of hazy light over cobblestone streets and smoky coffeehouses, images of a swarming square outside a cathedral—images of Vienna, of an earlier trip with D and her family. What happened in Vienna that is supplanting the type of fantasy I used to latch on to and cultivate and cling to and employ when my life got bumpy?

Vienna. It was soon after that trip that D and I decided to get married. What was it, what happened, what signs had I missed while I was traipsing around on the trail of the Hapsburgs?

CHAPTER FIVE

VIENNA

"Leave the Man Some Privacy"

In life there are dividing lines. These moments become a way to chart our time; they are the signposts for our lives. There was my life before acting—and then there was my life after I discovered it. There was drinking—and then life after I stopped. And more and more, it seems that there was a time before we decided to finally get married—and now there is after.

Before all of this, before Patagonia, before the Amazon and Costa Rica, before we decided to take the final step—there was Vienna. At the time it just seemed like a fraught, unwieldy family outing, nothing life-altering—at least I didn't think so at the time.

*

Moe showed me around the apartment—the master bedroom and bath, the large office that had been converted to a second bedroom for our purposes. The ground-floor loft with the wide plank floors was to be not only D's and my temporary home but our daughter's and D's parents' as well. It was a frigid February morning in Vienna, yet Moe took pains to point out the garden, which he considered a major asset of the apartment in the converted silk factory. He showed me how to slip the key into the lock. He handed me a folder with pertinent information, maps and phone numbers. He was gracious and solicitous.

"And this is how you work the stove," Moe explained. He picked up a single detachable magnetic knob, placed it on the appropriate circle corresponding to the selected ring on the sleek, black electric stove, and then turned to the desired temperature. It made no sense to me.

"Everything is in the folder?" I asked. I knew I wouldn't remember anything he had said to me in the fifteen minutes that he had been showing me around the apartment. I had just flown ten hours, overnight, not slept at all on the plane (what if the pilot needed my help?), it was my first time in Vienna, I was completely jet-lagged and disoriented. I just wanted to be left alone.

Moe showed no sign of wrapping it up so I interrupted him and thanked him and hurried him to the door. On the way there I began to worry that my rush might make him think I was engaged in some kind of shadowy activity in the apartment he had just rented me, and so, to appear casual, since he had a Middle Eastern accent, I asked where he was from.

"Oh, you noticed," he said with pride. "I am from Iran, but I have been in Vienna for ten years."

"Do you like it?" was all I could think to ask.

"I love it," he told me. I nodded, and he told me he had a friend with a video camera and if I wanted a personal tour I could get myself taped as I experienced the city.

"Let me think about that one and get back to you," I said. "Thanks, Moe."

"And where is the rest of your family?" he asked as he stepped into the doorway.

My instinct was to correct him—D's parents were not technically my family, nor, at that time, was there an imminent probability of their becoming my family—but rather than burden Moe with my personal doubts and insecurities, I felt the tightness in my throat as I said, "Oh, they'll be getting in tonight," and closed the door on him.

I had most of the day to myself before everyone arrived. I didn't know what I wanted to do or how I might accomplish it if I did. I showered and drifted out onto the street. A red and white tram was stopping on the corner, heading in the direction of what I assumed to be the center of town. I got on. Ten minutes later, the tram crossed over the Ringstrasse, I saw some imperial-looking buildings I later discovered were the Hofburg Palace, and I made my way on foot toward a tall spire, the highest point I could see in what was clearly the center of the old town. The air was biting, but the streets were full of people. The closer I got to the spire the busier and narrower the streets became. My confused mental state, coupled with no knowledge of where I was—I had neglected to take the tourist map Moe had left me—allowed me a freedom from expectation that I usually lack. Perhaps some of D's laissez-faire attitude toward organization was rubbing off on me.

The streets became pedestrian-only and funneled toward a large square surrounding the Romanesque and Gothic Stephansdom Cathedral. Solemnly dedicated in 1147, the cathedral was rebuilt and expanded over the span of centuries, and Viennese life still radiated out from its 445-foot tower, which was visible for miles. But it was the cathedral's steep roof, covered in ornate tiles that formed a mosaic of the double-headed eagle, symbol of the Hapsburg dynasty, that was its most telling feature.

The air inside was cold, but in a different way than outside. It was an old cold, the way cold feels when it has been trapped inside stone over centuries. I watched a Buddhist monk in an orange robe take photos of the high altar. I stared up at the symbols of my Catholic upbringing, uncertain, as I always am, what exactly I felt about them. These were figures that had strongly affected my family, dictated a great many of our actions, and with whom I was forced to spend a considerable amount of time in my youth, yet I didn't know them at all. I had changed a great deal since my last real contact with them but they had remained exactly as they had always been. They were strangers with whom I was deeply familiar. I lit a candle and thought of my children.

Back outside the cathedral, I saw a small sign that read MOZART'S HOUSE. The gray town house was through an archway and down a narrow cobbled street. I bought a ticket and climbed a flight of stairs, wandered through the apartment where the genius apparently lived happily for a short time and wrote *The Marriage of Figaro*. Nothing was evocative of what the place might have been like at the time he lived there. Only the view out the window, down Blutgasse, the cobblestone street below, a gas lamp attached to the wall of a nearby building, gave my imagination a start. Images of foggy nights and horse-drawn carriages and men hovering in the shadows wearing long cloaks suddenly materialized in my sleep-deprived mind.

I sought out the neo-Renaissance opera house, where much of Mozart's music premiered. Final preparations were under way for the famous Opera Ball in a few days' time—I was denied entry. I looked across the street and up at the other apartment I had considered renting and wished I had taken it, here in the bustling heart of the city, instead of the one I had rented from Moe, in a far-flung neighborhood.

Across the street from the opera house was the Hotel Sacher, Vienna's most famous lodging. D's parents, particularly her father,

Colm, were avid dessert lovers, and he had recently told me about the famous Sacher torte.

"You're going to love it, Andrew," he shouted over the phone as I packed my bag in New York. "It's worth a trip to Vienna for that alone."

The chocolate cake, filled with a layer of apricot jam, was apparently so legendary, its recipe had to be defended in court. I went in to see if I could perhaps get a slice to take away, so that it would be waiting for him on his arrival.

Conservatively dressed men held whispered conversations on red damask couches under ornate chandeliers in the small lobby. Gilt-framed mirrors hung from the walls. Ladies with stiff hair, wearing fur coats, strode regally past. Given the elegant, old-world, and buttoned-up feeling it exuded, I very much doubted the Hotel Sacher would indulge in such crass American behavior as "takeout." I was wrong.

Three hundred sixty thousand little chocolate cakes are sold every year at the designated takeaway café, each ranging in price from twenty to thirty-five euros apiece.

"Small, medium, or large," the stout woman behind the counter said to me in English before I had a chance to speak. She swiped my credit card and pressed a wooden box into my hands. I hadn't even laid eyes on one of the famous tortes and she was looking past me—"Small, medium, or large."

When I stepped out of the metro at Westbahnhof—at what I hoped was a few blocks from my new apartment—the day was nearly gone, the sky had taken on a pink and purple patina, and there was a smoky, foggy haze that struck me as what I had always thought the light in Vienna must be like. I didn't know I held this preconception until I looked up and saw the bell tower of a small local church, shrouded in a gauzy glow. This moment, this image, lodged in my mind. What is it about the brain that chooses images, seemingly at random, to hold on to and empowers them with significance? I saw more beautiful churches and prettier winter sunsets while in Vienna, but this fleeting image asserted itself as the mental postcard for my time there.

I needed to find some groceries so that everyone would have something to eat when they arrived. The Bio-Market Organics around the corner was closed, as was the Eurospar, as well as the Merkur. Apparently, on a Sunday afternoon in Vienna, everything outside the tourist-choked center is locked up tight. I was in trouble. I cursed myself again for not taking the apartment in the center. I cursed myself for not taking care of this chore earlier in the day. It was late now. Everyone would be arriving in just over an hour and I would have nothing. I could easily imagine D, with our daughter, who was battling a cold, tired in her arms, and her parents dragging far too many suitcases.

I panicked. I marched in circles around blocks I knew I had been down before. The unpronounceable German names on every closed and shuttered shop began to enrage me. I considered returning to the center of town to get something, but I could remember only clothing boutiques and Mostly Mozart souvenir shops and cafés. The burden of having to provide for these people began to swell up inside me and I wished I were there alone. I grew angry with D and her parents for needing me to take care of them. It wasn't the first time I'd decided that the burden of family was too much for me, something I didn't know how to handle or even want. I wished I had no contacts or ties. I loved my children, but the rest of them—the hell with it! I was on the verge of a full-blown tantrum.

Whereas D would find the idea of fetching groceries for the nourishment of her loved ones in a strange city a pleasurable way to express her affections, I resented it. I felt trapped, taken advantage of, and (preemptively) unappreciated.

At Europaplatz I saw the bright lights of the Westbahnhof train station—across from the metro stop I had exited an hour earlier when my hunt began. Misreading the pedestrian traffic signal, I raced across the four lanes of Neubaugürtel and was almost hit. The station was swarming with people on the fringes of life who typically haunt such transit hubs in large cities.

Down a level, in a far corner, I found a small convenience store that was open. It was packed with some of Vienna's less desirable denizens, all picking over shelves that were close to bare. I found some eggs and a loaf of white bread and some butter. I bought some yogurt for our daughter. Hardly a feast, but everyone would be able to eat something, and they would understand my difficulties in an archaic city that still shuts down on a Sunday—they would hail my ingenuity and my generosity.

Everyone arrived amid a clamor of shouts and hugs. I hadn't seen our daughter in a week and she'd grown. Whereas I had come in from New York, D and our daughter had been in Dublin, visiting her parents, which is why they were all arriving together. Unable to miss school and join us, my son was back in New York with his mother. As predicted, D's parents had to hire a second taxi to carry their luggage.

I showed everyone the apartment. D's mother, Margot, an Irish charmer of regal bearing, of keen observations, and with an eye for mischief, insisted that D and I take the master bedroom, although I had already settled us in the office/second bedroom. Eventually she relented and the subject of food was brought up. I presented my haul.

"Oh. Well . . . ," Margot said, her voice rising an octave upon seeing the eggs and white bread laid bare on the kitchen table. "Maybe we'll just go out, leave you three to catch up."

D had assured me everyone would be tired after the long trip and would not want to go out for an extended meal in a restaurant. Consequently, I hadn't scouted for any during the day. I was more or less relaxed around D's parents—they had welcomed me swiftly and without question into their world seven years earlier—but I had always been their guest, and the burden of hosting people who had spent a lifetime receiving and seeing to the needs of others was already proving too much for me. I froze.

"Come on now, Andrew," Colm hollered, "you must have seen some restaurants on your travels today." D's father was a Kerry man, from the west of Ireland. He had run hotels for most of his life; he knew people and food. "Where should we go for a nice bite to eat in this neighborhood?" he shouted—he was also hard of hearing.

"Um, I think I saw a little café that was open, just down the street to the left, on our side."

"Perfect," Margot said, and they set out.

I snuggled with our daughter, who was feeling under the weather, and then D and I put her to bed. We sat down with a cup of tea.

No matter what was happening in our relationship, seeing each other after a time apart always gave us a fresh start—one that was often needed. This time was no exception. We had been struggling with our usual power play, not as bad as it once was, but bad enough that her trip back to Dublin had come at a good time.

The following day was D's birthday and the original reason for our trip. D was born and spent the first six months of her life in Vienna, when her father was managing one of the city's biggest hotels. She had never been back and had dreamed of one day returning to her birthplace. Her wish gave me an idea that I presented to a magazine: to discover Vienna from a "local" angle.

Then she invited her parents to join us.

Sitting on the couch now, we couldn't remember what we had been arguing about when we last saw each other a week earlier. Then we heard the front door open.

"How was the restaurant, Mum?" D asked.

"Well," Margot replied, "it was just grand."

"Now, Andrew, I don't know what you call cafés in New York . . . ," Colm called out.

"Oh, no." D stood up. "What happened?"

I had sent Margot and Colm to a greasy, dirty Viennese fast-food deep-fry joint.

"How about a little chocolate cake?" I asked, pulling out my ace in the hole, the Sacher torte.

"Andrew, you've redeemed yourself," Colm roared out, and took a seat at the table. With elaborate ceremony, I presented the famous torte. Colm lifted his fork and tasted it. There was silence as we all looked on. "No." He shook his head. "It's dry."

Then Margot tasted it. "Oh, dear."

And then D. "It is a bit dry, luv."

"Not what I remember at all." D's father shook his head in final judgment, pushing the plate away.

Maybe tomorrow would be better.

§

I left a small birthday gift, a box with a bracelet, beside D for when she woke up.

"It's gorgeous," she said with a sigh, and showed it to her parents, who made a fuss while sipping their coffee.

"I'll go get us some croissants across the street," I said, looking forward to a few minutes on my own.

As I put on my coat Colm called after me, "I'll join you, Andrew. I could use the air."

There went my five minutes alone for the day.

After breakfast, D turned to me. "You go on with Mum and Dad, luv. We'll stay in this morning." Our daughter was still not feeling well.

"Are you sure? I'm happy to stay home."

"Go on, get to work."

Margot, Colm, and I headed to the local open-air Naschmarkt, to stock up on groceries. Because I was supposed to be writing a story from a local angle, I insisted we take either the metro or the tram, as often as possible, instead of simply jumping in taxis. We changed trains twice, got lost, had to walk fifteen minutes and ask four people for directions. It took us nearly an hour, but once we found the market, there were hundreds of stalls, crammed one after the next, selling fresh fish and sausage, warm breads, freshly squeezed juices, cold meats and hot coffee, flowers, cheeses, and herbs. There were thousands of olives on display, stuffed with garlic or cheese or peppers. Small Asian women stood selling sushi beside large men hawking *Palatschinken*—Austrian crepelike desserts. Turkish immigrants sliced chunks of lamb from a spit while men and women in their winter coats stood elbow to elbow at outdoor tables drinking beer and slurping oysters. For block after block along the broad Linke Wienzeile boulevard, it went on.

"Oh, Colm, look at this." Margot stopped at the fishmonger.

"Margot, try this." Colm was tasting a piece of salami on offer.

D's parents spent a long time talking to a woman named Daniela who sold vinegar at a stall she worked with her husband. With an eyedropper, D's mother and father tasted and tested a dozen types of the nearly seventy fruit vinegars before settling on currant berry. Margot could make a stone sing, and she learned Daniela's history and how she met her husband. "I was a very eager customer," Daniela confided, "very eager," and the two women laughed like sorority sisters. "But," she lamented, "vinegar is Erwin's life."

"Oh, I know," Margot told her, patting Daniela's arm in solidarity. "I know."

A little farther along, a very stout woman named Maria wielded a long machete, hacking off bits of cheese and thrusting them under Colm's nose on the tip of the long blade. She had a gleam in her blue eyes and cackled wildly. When we were about to walk away with only a few French wedges, Maria locked her eyes on me—I had been only observing the long exchange and was surprised she had even realized we were all together—and raised her machete. Margot stepped in quickly and purchased a hunk of *Bergkäse*.

We bought four different pâtés, half a dozen types of salami, and three kinds of bread—each purchase preceded by a long chat. Eventually we came to Leo Strmiska, the sauerkraut man. He stood like a carnival barker behind two large wooden barrels of fermenting white cabbage. D's father engaged him in a dialogue on the subtleties of preparation ("You must cook until translucent, and only then do you add the bacon"), then they digressed to discussing the greed of bankers, and then the conversation drifted back to Leo's childhood and the war, and as we were leaving, Leo handed me the clear plastic bag containing a pound of the stuff. "Remember," he said in a stern voice, his hand still clutching the bag, "fermentation never stops, take it out of the bag the minute you get home." I nodded, but apparently without proper solemnity. "Do you need to write it down? Pay attention, now."

"We'll take care of him, Leo," Margot told him, and ushered me away by the arm.

We sat down for an outdoor coffee, our winter coats zipped up tight. Then, as we crossed the street to head back to the metro, we passed a taxi stand. Margot opened the door and slipped into the back of a cab.

"My feet are tired, Andrew, my love."

The ride home took five minutes.

When we got back to the apartment, D scoured the unfamiliar cabinets for platters and bowls, and everything we had bought was spread out on the table. I had an idea that somehow we shouldn't do this. "We just got all this stuff," I wanted to say. "It took us hours. Shouldn't we save it?" It was a silly notion and I kept it to myself, but it spoke to my innate lack of understanding of harvest and communal bonding through food.

Meals growing up in my house were not a time of sensuous delight but more a perfunctory ritual. There was nothing wrong with our family dinners, but they certainly weren't a shared celebration of food and fellowship. For the most part, they were unremarkable. We sat most evenings, when my father was not away on business, at the large dining room table (large to me as a child). My brother Peter and I sat on one side, Stephen alone—and then later with Justin—on the other. My mother was at the end of the table near the kitchen and my father at the opposite end. It was made clear that he was at the "head" of the table. When guests came over, as they occasionally did, the table was pulled apart and a center section was added. There was a large, cut-glass chandelier overhead.

Only two meals stand out in my memory of childhood: Once when my mother told us that we were going to have a younger brother. I knew they wanted us to be happy with the news, and so in an over-compensatory fashion, I shouted, "Really, a goo-goo, ga-ga? A goo-goo, ga-ga?" I kept repeating it, over and over, very loud, until my father became irritated. And another time when my father told Peter that he wasn't getting up from the table until he ate his asparagus, at which point he promptly ate one and threw up all over his plate.

We ate to live and in no way lived to eat. This trait has followed me into adulthood—and it's yet another point of disparity between me and D. Whenever her family sat down to eat, they did so with gusto, and this time was no exception. Everything was tasted and commented upon. "This salami is delicious." "Pass me one." "Oh, my, that's extraordinary." "Oh, you must try this pâté. Just take a forkful." "These olives are unbelievable." "Wow, that's spicy!" "Can you smell that cheese?" Forks were flying all over the table. I looked over at D, our flushed daughter perched happily on her lap. She looked relaxed and confident, like she always did when she was surrounded by her family. It made me both happy to see her like this and nervous. Was I intimidated by the serene confidence I saw in her at such moments? Or did I merely feel insecure that I might never be able to provide the kind of companionship she craved and felt she needed in order for her to live a full life?

After lunch, we went into the center of town and walked the old, cobbled streets. Down by Stephansdom Cathedral we passed the Zara shop and the McDonald's. "Seem familiar, Margot?" I asked.

"Actually, no, Andrew, it doesn't." She shook her head. When we entered the great cathedral we all stood silently. "Now, this I remember," Margot said softly after a time. D had been baptized here. "In one of these side chapels. Can you remember, Colm?" she asked, and looked off, squinting into the past.

Colm looked around as well, "I'm not sure, Peg," he said, calling his wife by his pet name for her.

After an uninspired birthday dinner taken at an informal student restaurant near our apartment—so that we could keep our daughter close to home—we walked home and took off our shoes.

"What are you doing?" Margot said, putting her own feet up. "You two go on, hurry up and leave us alone." Then she pointed to D's iPad. "You just set up that machine there, and my little angel and I will watch *The Sound of Music* while you two go out for a birthday drink. I only wish our little boy were here to watch it with us."

At home it's easier to accept the pattern of togetherness and absence that divorced parenting creates, but on a family trip like this, with one member of the family absent, the occasional and unforeseen moments of melancholy were easily explained. So many times on this trip I saw things and was reminded of my son and imagined how he might have responded to them. That we had downplayed the trip with him before we left, and promised him another special trip, did little to assuage everyone's disappointment.

D and I slipped out the door, into the night. We took one of the older red and white trams, the kind with the wooden seats, and rattled toward town. We went to a modern café. Everyone in the bar was "nerd chic." All the furniture was for sale; a price tag of 533 euros hung from my chair. Our young waitress wore an orange minidress and white knee socks. She wore thick, black-framed glasses, and we got into a long conversation with her about food and sex and Freud.

We went to the Rote Bar, in the regal Volkstheater. Opened in 1889, the "people's theater" was a reaction against the constraints of the national theater, Burgtheater, down on the Ringstrasse. There, a woman in a flowing evening gown played a grand piano before a red velvet curtain under a massive chandelier. The marble floor shone beneath our feet. We sat at a cocktail table with a dripping candle and our waitress there told us of another café.

"Just follow the tram tracks, and when they turn, keep going straight. You'll see a metal, unmarked door. Knock three times."

So we did. We were admitted into a gray, dark cave, filled with arches and pillars. Henna-like tattoo patterns were projected onto every inch of the walls and ceiling. A DJ played techno music and smoke filled the crowded room. There was a projection on the wall behind the bar that read ENGLISH IST DIE GAUNERSPRACHE—"English is the language of crooks." The female bartender had black hair, wore heavy black eye shadow, and was dressed all in black. She wore a tiny silver birdcage that hung from a chain.

"I like your necklace," D told her.

"I am a caged bird," she whispered.

We went to another café, thick with smoke. D bummed a cigarette and happily puffed away.

"If you can't beat 'em . . ." She shrugged. It was yet another difference between us. The idea that that I might be able to smoke just one cigarette every now and again, the way she did, was inconceivable to me. I had been a pack-a-day smoker who had quit years ago and intended to keep it that way.

Back on the street, arm in arm, we searched for another dive. D and I had never been bar hopping together in our life. We had never courted. We never had a playful period of dating, holding hands over a late-night cappuccino, sharing silly quirks that the other would find so charming and revealing. We had never strolled home after a movie and made out on the stoop before saying good night, only to call ten minutes later and say good night again. Our coming together as a couple had been so immediate—after only three meetings—and so complete that we were sharing a home and a life before we had given the matter any real thought.

D moved in with me in New York from her home in Dublin seven years ago and was instantly cast in a stepparenting role. My then-two-and-a-half-year-old son wondered who my "special friend" was. I existed in a constant state of anxiety over what I had done to him and to my previous life. Nothing we did was well considered or advised. I tried to tell a few friends of the sudden and life-altering changes that were happening to me. They told me I was being "insane." Their advice to slow down wasn't helpful, or plausible, under the circumstances. I simply stopped talking to them. "Love will carry the day" was our motto—perhaps it should have been "Fools rush in."

Yet here we were, years later, in Vienna, and every night, after we all went out to dinner, we would leave our daughter at home with Margot and Colm eager to go back out—just the two of us. We went to old Viennese coffee shops with surly waiters, to hip, smoky joints, and to Art Deco salons; we didn't care where. We laughed and played together, night after night, like we hadn't before. We discovered we were excited in each other's company, the way we were those first few days when we met in the Irish countryside.

"I can't be in Vienna and not go to the Hofburg Palace," Colm declared.

So a few days later, when our daughter was well again, we all boarded the tram into town.

Designed to impress and awe visiting heads of state from the thirteenth century onward, the winter home of the Hapsburg dynasty—rulers of the Austro-Hungarian Empire—the Hofburg Palace is a sprawling complex of imposing buildings constructed in various architectural styles through numerous centuries and connected by massive formal gardens and plazas filled with fountains and statues of emperors and their horses. The palace withstood three major sieges, a fire, and the vagaries of taste through generations of royalty. It is home to the current president of Austria. It has twenty-six hundred rooms. It is difficult to miss.

I got us off at the wrong tram stop. We could see the rooftops of the royal buildings far off. I apologized profusely but Margot stopped me.

"It's perfect, gives us a chance to take some air," she said, leaning hard into the brogue.

We walked. And walked. Eventually we came to a side gate that led us into a large formal garden. This might have impressed D's parents, who were avid gardeners, except all the plants had been pruned and tied up tight under canvas sacks for the winter.

Finally we made our way inside the first building we came upon. I hurried ahead and bought tickets.

"Do you know what this is, luv?" D asked.

"Don't worry, it'll be great," I said, having no idea where we were. I handed all the tickets to our daughter to present to the guard.

Inside was a labyrinth of room upon room of silverware, napkin holders, and candlesticks, all behind tall glass cases.

"Oh, no," I said, gasping. I tried to guide us toward an exit and only took us deeper into the honeycomb of rooms.

I knew Margot had little tolerance for museums, and our daughter was already squirming hard. Colm tried to show some interest but couldn't keep it up for long, and then D turned up a flight of stairs.

"Come on, luv," she said.

"No, no. We don't want to go up there," I shouted after her, still looking for an exit. I could feel sweat under my heavy coat as I followed everyone up the marble steps.

We emerged into a room with an evening gown on display, and then into another with a headless mannequin filling out a massive ball gown. The girls began to *ooh* and *aah*.

We were in the imperial apartments, once the living quarters of Franz Josef the First and his wife, Empress Elisabeth—known to her loyal subjects as Sissi. Her story was full of intrigue. A free spirit and a modern woman before her time, Sissi struggled with her role in the monarchy and, much like Princess Diana a little more than a century later, was beloved by her people. Her death, by assassination, while walking along a promenade beside Lake Geneva in Switzerland, sealed her destiny as a tragic heroine.

"This should interest you, Andrew," Colm said, absorbed in reading about Sissi. "She was an avid traveler."

I chased our suddenly happy daughter through Sissi's bedroom and into her private gym. We laughed at Sissi's personal water closet. Eventually we descended the steps and reemerged into the hard bright day.

"See, not so bad." D shrugged, taking my arm.

After lunch, I had a surprise for everyone—the one event I had booked before arriving in Vienna. The famed Lipizzaner stallions of the Spanish Riding School, a local institution and a hallmark of imperial Vienna, were practicing for their twice-weekly shows in a nearby section of the palace. The shows were sold out but I had arranged for us to see the daily practice session—which is open to the public— by finagling ringside seats reserved for special guests and dignitaries. These seats were rarely occupied during practice. My daughter would be thrilled to be so close to the action, and D's parents would bask in the elegant surroundings and the tradition and pomp, to say nothing of the special treatment. D would be pleased with my family-focused initiative.

I sought out my contact. Mrs. Drabanek was a prim woman with straight blond hair and a direct manner. She told us that the session had already begun, and entrance or exit to this special section of the hall was forbidden in midaction. D's mother looked confused; her father sank his hands deeper into his pockets. D tried to console our daughter, who got the gist that there was a problem.

I took Mrs. Drabanek aside.

"Please," I begged. "I'm so sorry we're late, but my daughter has been dying to see the horses, it's all she's talked about since we came to Vienna. " In truth, we had just told her about the stallions a few minutes earlier—but she was *immediately* very excited. "And my in-laws," I said—not even choking on the words—"it's been a dream of theirs for many years." There was no truth in this either, but they were happy enough to go along.

She looked into my pleading eyes and then over my shoulder, where the family was playing their part by looking suitably bereft.

"Come," she said, and marched toward the door.

"Thank you," I whispered as we slipped into the hushed hall. I may even have said, "Bless you," I can't remember for sure.

We settled in beneath crystal chandeliers and Corinthian columns. Under the tutelage of erect riders in brown coats with hazelwood switches, six majestic white stallions were prancing and preening, accompanied by the sounds of Chopin.

Silently we slid into the front row, just a few feet from the horses, alone in the VIP section. I gave Mrs. Drabanek a large grin; she nodded curtly and exited.

Perhaps the shows themselves present a dazzling and dizzying exhibition of equine majesty, or perhaps to the educated eye, the minute steps we saw practiced over and over and over again would be a fascinating display of discipline and skill—but within minutes we were bored. My daughter began to fidget on my lap. Margot looked at her watch, while Colm folded his arms and his chin sank toward his chest. D refused to meet my eye; she struggled to keep the grin from her face. We still had forty-five minutes to go.

Then my daughter began to talk. Loud. A few discreet glances came from the riders inside the ring. Margot leaned over and said she was going for a coffee. "You're not allowed to leave," I wanted to say. She nudged her husband awake and with D following, they slid out.

"You and me will stay and watch the horses, huh, pumpkin?" I whispered to my daughter on my lap.

"Yeah," she whispered back, and snuggled closer. Twenty seconds later, "I want a hot chocolate, Daddy," she said in her normal voice.

"Shh. Soon, pumpkin, soon."

"Where's Mommy?" she called out.

When I raced past a shocked Mrs. Drabanek in the lobby, I couldn't bring myself to meet her glare as I whispered a hurried, "My daughter's sick," and lunged for the exit.

Outside, a white carriage hitched to a white horse was standing by the curb. D and her parents were already inside, waiting. She swung the door open wide for us.

"I knew you wouldn't last long, luv," D said. My daughter climbed in, thrilled—this was her kind of horse action. She sat up tall on her granny's lap, a blanket tucked high up under her chin. Her blue eyes were wide and both she and her granny looked out with pride as we rolled over cobblestone streets.

I have no such rosy memories of my own grandparents. My mother's father died before I was born, and her mother, a small, creased woman who insisted we call her Grandmom, lived in our town, a half dozen blocks away. She would occasionally come over to babysit in the evenings. She was constantly turning off lights around the house, and my memories of time spent with her are always dimly lit.

One evening, while babysitting, she tripped over one of our dogs and fell. I heard the crash from the den and went running into the dining room. My grandmother was on the floor, disentangling herself from Duchess, our Airedale. I loved Duchess; she had an independent streak and a slightly disinterested manner that I appreciated.

"I tripped over Duchess," my grandmother said when I rushed in. Her wig was askew, and she was struggling to straighten it. From the sound of her voice I could tell that she was shaken. Duchess, who had been roused from sleep, was merely looking at her.

In Bermuda, age nine.

at pompano M. 25

When we woke up it was cloudy out. I went swimming with dad before breakfast and for breakfast I had french toast. The fishing yesterday was realy *bad*. And now the surprise I have told you about, Peter and dad are going *scuba diving*. Stephen is going golfing he shot an 82. me and Peter first went snorkeling in the pool and then out on the

The first travel story—a page from the journal I kept on that exotic trip to Bermuda.

The "ah-ha" moment, as The Artful Dodger. My first and finest performance.

On the set of *Class,* my first movie. Nervous and thrilled.

Wary and apprehensive, as usual, watching filming of the prom scene during *Pretty in Pink*. Producer Lauren Schuler, left, and James Spader, far right.

© Paramount Pictures

Seve and I, footloose
in Ireland back in the day.

On the ice of Perito Moreno Glacier, in Patagonia, southern Argentina.

About to be slammed by a sudden storm on a ridge above Estancia Cristina, in Patagonia— with the Upsala Glacier behind.

In the Belén market in Iquitos, Peru, right after drinking down the "elixir."

Corcovado National Park in Costa Rica, before the sharks and alligators and bees.

Margot and Colm,
peeling away the years
at a Heuriger
in Vienna.

At the old ballyard in Baltimore.

Near the summit of Kilimanjaro at dawn, stopping to take notes.

Atop Kilimanjaro—then it got difficult.

The big moment in Dublin.

Finally, dancing a jig.

"She's okay, Grandmom," I said without thinking, and began to stroke Duchess's fur.

"No, not the dog, me!" my grandmother shouted. "I fell and hurt myself." On the floor in the dark of the dining room my allegiances had been exposed.

And I was no closer to my father's parents. I saw them only once a year, on Thanksgiving. They terrified me. My grandmother I remember as a hard, stout woman with a stern voice. I steered clear of her as much as I could in her cramped apartment on Thirty-fifth Street in Union City, New Jersey. She and my grandfather lived on the ground floor while my more welcoming aunt and uncle lived up the flight of stairs with their daughter and two great mastiffs—dogs far too large to be comfortable in the small apartment.

I have only one distinct memory of my paternal grandfather, who was an intimidating and remote man with a thick head of white hair. It was shortly before he died, when I was around ten. It was nowhere near Thanksgiving, and we had made a special trip to Union City to see him. The end was near and he was bedridden. My father led me into the old man's room, "to say good-bye," I was told. It was very hot, and I remember my grandfather lying in a single bed under a heavy burgundy blanket. It was the middle of the day and the shade was pulled down; only a thin stream of light entered the room below it. My grandfather seemed barely conscious and was looking straight up at the ceiling. I could feel my father behind me.

"Pop, you remember Andrew," my dad said. "He wanted to say hello." I don't remember if I spoke or not, and I recall nothing of what my grandfather might have said. Even at the time I felt like there was some kind of protocol that we all needed to follow, yet none of us seemed to know what that protocol was or how we should follow it. My eyes stayed focused on the dust motes drifting across the thin beam of light that fell over the bed. After a few minutes I was led out of the room and I asked my father if I had done all right.

"You did just fine," he said, but it didn't feel fine. I felt like I had failed somehow. I walked upstairs to my aunt's to pet one of her giant dogs.

🚶

Our days in Vienna fell into a rhythm centered around late-morning coffee and afternoon tea. These were not ten-minute refueling stops but, rather, long sessions at some of Vienna's more famous cafés— Demel with its elegant salons and dessert-filled trays, its glass-walled kitchen where my daughter and I watched chocolate bunnies being poured, filled, and sculpted by a dozen bakers in tall white hats; Café Sperl, where scores of newspapers in a dozen languages were strewn across the carambole billiards tables beneath crystal chandeliers; and even the smoky Café Alt Wien, with its protest posters lining the walls while students at small wooden tables hunched over loose paperbacks and nursed espressos. Everywhere we went, Colm ordered extravagant pastries and desserts. Plates and forks were passed around, judgments made and then reevaluated. More coffee was drunk. Often my daughter and I grew bored and would wander off together. One afternoon before walking into yet another café, Margot turned to me.

"Andrew, my love, you don't like all these desserts, why don't you go take some time to yourself?"

I knew exactly where I would go.

Down a flight of dingy red-carpeted steps off Karlsplatz and into the Burg Kino, across a lobby heavy with the smell of burned popcorn, through a chipped burgundy door, and into a sparsely filled dark room late on that blustery Tuesday afternoon, I first heard the famous line—"I was a friend of Harry Lime."

"Everyone ought to be careful in a city like this," and noir classics like "You were born to be murdered," "Leave death to the professionals," and a classic Graham Greene theme, "Humanity is a duty," were uttered from the scratchy black and white print of the 1949 Carol Reed film.

Few movies are so identified with a particular city as *The Third Man* is with Vienna. Shot while the city was still under the rubble of the Second World War and divided into four quadrants controlled by U.S., French, British, and Soviet forces, Graham Greene's script is a classic cat-and-mouse tale of deception, a study of loneliness and duplicity. Anton Karas's score, played on a zither, infiltrates the proceedings, adding to the discomfort, and has come to define the genre. I had never seen it before.

As a child, I hadn't gone to the movies often, and I had never seen a movie alone until I went off to college. But as a student in New York, I joined the last generation of moviegoers who frequented the half dozen revival houses that would soon disappear with the advent of home video and cable TV. At the Eighth Street Playhouse I first saw *On the Waterfront* and *The Wild One* in a Marlon Brando double bill. At the Hollywood on Eighth Avenue and Forty-seventh Street I watched *Midnight Cowboy,* and way uptown on Ninety-fifth Street at the Thalia I was introduced to James Dean and Buster Keaton, and the films of Antonioni and Godard. I would go to the movies in the afternoon, by myself, while the world I knew carried on in my absence outside. It was my first real experience of travel—solo excursions to places that were so alien. And as I would soon discover on the road, powers of observation were rewarded, my imagination was fired, and this encouraged still further exploration. I discovered the neorealistic films of De Sica and the playfully amoral world of Chabrol. The things I saw on-screen made sense in a way that felt deeply familiar, and as with the first time I acted, I innately understood my place in it. Alone in the dark, I located myself.

In Vienna, sitting in that scrappy cinema, my two universes converged. When I walked back out into the early evening, onto the same streets where I had just seen Joseph Cotten pursue Orson Welles, I felt I understood something about Vienna and myself that I hadn't before. I possessed a sense of belonging I had lacked just a few hours earlier. When I walked past number 5 Josefsplatz, across from the statue of Emperor Josef II on his horse, and saw the statue of four maidens supporting the portico of the building where Harry Lime was supposedly killed at the start of the film, I felt like a member of some kind of a secret society, in possession of a certain knowledge and its resulting confidence. But as I walked farther, a thought began to play in my mind: perhaps this feeling of confidence and comfort wasn't just the result of having seen a movie.

D's family had accepted me from the moment she and her mother picked me up at the airport in Dublin for the first time seven years earlier. Driving back to their home to serve me a full Irish breakfast, Margo kept up a steady patter and began an active embracing of who I am that has not abated. That I have seen more of D's family in the past seven years than I have of my own in the last thirty speaks to both the active closeness of D's family and the casual distance of mine. Perhaps my mood of confidence and security that night on the Vienna streets was more reflective of my beginning to feel a part of something bigger, something I wasn't yet ready to reconcile.

Or perhaps, I thought, my feelings of familial inclusion and cinematic belonging were all of my own creation; perhaps it was just some neurotic need looking to be filled.

So the next day, I headed to Vienna resident Sigmund Freud's house on Berggasse. Perhaps a visit to the home of the great psychoanalyst would help clarify these conflicting impulses.

Colm was eager to join me. We hopped the number 2 tram, which I thought would circle the Ringstrasse. Instead, it turned off on Alser Strasse and headed in the wrong direction. Colm was patient with yet another of my navigational mistakes and eventually we righted ourselves and saw the large red sign with FREUD in bold block letters.

At the top of a flight of stairs, we were greeted by a small, trim man with a deliberate manner and precise movements, dressed entirely in black. With a watchful expression, he directed us toward a door across the hall. It was in these half-dozen rooms that Freud lived and worked for forty-seven years. His walking stick, suitcase, a few hats, and a personalized flask were behind Plexiglas in the cramped entryway lit by the filtered light of a single leaded glass window. To the right was the waiting room, still laid out as it was in Freud's time. Glass cabinets contained many of his more than three thousand Greek, Roman, Chinese, and Egyptian objects—tiny statues and fragments. (The good doctor had a bit of an obsession.) A red damask couch lined one wall; above it were four copperplate engravings depicting the four elements, earth, water, fire, and air—love and strife, Eros and destruction, vying for dominance. Opposite was the entrance to the room where the doctor listened with "evenly poised attention" to the complaints of his patients. The famous couch was conspicuously absent, having gone with Freud to London when he fled the Nazis in 1938. Instead, the chamber was left nearly empty.

Large black and white photos depicting how the room once looked covered the bottom half of the walls, while personal letters and photos adorned the top. I could only imagine what Freud might have thought, looking out the single window, beside which he used to listen and take notes (and according to his own reports, occasionally doze off during sessions). The room beyond was his inner sanctum, where Freud wrote and smoked his beloved cigars. Above a desk and between windows that looked out onto a courtyard hung a mirror where he often inspected the results of the thirty operations he underwent for jaw cancer. "Since I can no longer smoke freely," he once lamented, "I no longer wish to write." His books lined one wall. The rooms revealed a decidedly human man of great insight, large ego, prescience, vanity, clarity, and obsession.

Despite rumors of an affair with his sister-in-law, Freud's personal life was typically conservative, with a long and successful marriage that produced six children. And while his family life offered no insight into my own evolving notions on the subject, copious evidence of his obviously contradictory nature provided relief and encouraged some empathy in me for my own vacillating ways.

Reassured in my conflicted humanity, I found Colm patiently waiting by the door. As we descended the marble stairs I tried to remember if I had ever done anything like this with my own father.

The last time I had seen my dad was when D and I took the kids up to visit him and his wife a few summers earlier. My parents had divorced several years after I went to college; my father then met a woman, married her, and resettled in rural Maine, effectively vanishing from our lives, with only occasional phone calls and rumored visits to New York that rarely transpired.

My kids mentioned they were eager to see their grandfather—my son had met him only once, our daughter never had. The last time I had seen my father was when D was heavily pregnant. We headed to Maine.

We pulled into his driveway and my father and his wife were waiting on the stoop. They greeted us warmly, fawned over the kids, and showed us their home on a hill a few blocks from the water. "An old captain's house," my father called it. I recognized various furnishings from my childhood that I hadn't seen in years, a coffee table, a bookcase, a few paintings. It was odd to see them there, these relics of my childhood that I hadn't thought of since I left home as a teenager. I felt possessive of them; what were they doing here, in this strange house so far from home?

My father and his wife had prepared lunch for us, but he was nervous and couldn't eat. He kept up a steady patter with the kids. They adored him.

That evening it poured. My father bragged that there was a place not far away that served the best ice cream in the world. I put the two kids in the back of my father's Oldsmobile and drove as he sat beside me. The speedometer in the car didn't work, and only one headlamp would light. The rain was lashing down. We drove along the two-lane highway for a long time. I squinted to see in the dark.

"Maybe we passed it," my father said.

"Turn around, Dad," my son called from the back.

Then it appeared on the right, a purpose-built, Swiss chalet–like structure with two take-out windows. We huddled under the narrow eave of the roof out of the rain and ordered. On the way back to the house my father finished his ice cream sundae before either of the kids. I had no idea my father loved ice cream.

The next day was bright, and my father's wife suggested we go for a walk out on a nearby breakwater to a lighthouse. A soft breeze blew and sailboats floated in the shimmering sea. The stone breakwater was much longer than I had expected—nearly a mile out to the lighthouse. There were wide and deep crevices between the unevenly spaced rocks. It was difficult to get a rhythm walking, particularly for the kids. But they raced ahead anyway, with D and my father's wife trying to catch up. I fell back with my dad.

His walking seemed labored and slow. I thought he was merely taking care of where he was putting his feet, but that kind of caution seemed uncharacteristic of the man I used to know. He asked after my mother, the way he always did when we spoke on those rare occasions over the phone—"How's your mama?"

When we were growing up he never referred to her as "your mama," but it is the term he has always used when asking about her over the past twenty-five years.

When we got to the lighthouse it was locked up tight. We started back. My son began to hang back with my father; soon the distance between us was getting greater and greater. I kept looking over my shoulder. Then a woman came running up. "The man back there, is he with you? He fell." I went racing back.

My father was up on his feet; two women were helping him. He was walking slowly, but he seemed confused, and he was beginning to arch his back, putting his weight on his heels. D and I took over for the women and walked with him. My father's arching became more pronounced and we called an ambulance. We sent my son running down the long breakwater to wait for the paramedics. We were still nearly a half mile out on the rocks.

Soon my father's back was completely stiff, the arching even more severe. If we hadn't been holding him up he would have fallen straight back. With his full weight pushing back on our arms, he was extremely heavy. A man came and took over for D, who went to try to calm my father's wife while simultaneously holding on to our daughter so she wouldn't fall into the deep spaces between the rocks. As our progress slowed, my father's head cleared and he kept up a strangely upbeat conversation with the man helping us. It was typical of him; he was having what I assumed to be a stroke, and yet he was chatting away to a stranger about where the man was from, and who my father knew from that part of Pennsylvania, and what the man did for a living. I've often wondered if my reticence with strangers grew out of a reaction to my father's more gregarious efforts, efforts that to me as a child seemed so at odds with the more volatile man I knew at home.

He tried hard to appear completely normal as we struggled along the breakwater, unaware that his body was arching drastically back.

His hips had begun to lock and his already awkward steps had become even more labored. It became more and more difficult to keep him moving toward help. Eventually we sat him down on a small step. Then my eight-year-old son arrived with the paramedics.

We followed behind the ambulance to the hospital and spent several hours waiting while various tests were performed. No cause was immediately evident, and my father began to regain normal movements and clarity. The doctor said that it was perhaps a TIA—a transient ischemic attack—a kind of mini-stroke, but that he couldn't be sure.

I had to be back in New York for work the next day. If this had been D's father, there would have been no question that she would have stayed, no matter the consequences. But it spoke to the distance and lack of pull that had grown to define our relationship that after consulting the doctors and his wife several times, we ultimately left my father at the hospital, where they were to keep him overnight and then send him home.

When I went to say good-bye, I pulled back the curtain in the hospital room and he sprang up in bed, like a jack-in-the-box. He broke into a wide and startling grin. It was a desperate smile, a salesman's smile. It was so typical of him, and it broke my heart and made me love him. If either of us could have acknowledged the fear of the moment out on the jetty, or the bizarre intimacy it had created between us and cast over the visit, perhaps there would have been an opening to move closer. But instead, my self-conscious withholding and his mask of bravado left me shaking my head, at both of us.

We spoke a few times in the days immediately after, to make sure everything was all right with his health and to relive the more pleasurable aspects of our visit. Sometime later he called and said that he and his wife would be coming to New York and would love to see the kids, and us, but their trip never materialized and we haven't made it back to Maine.

As D's father and I stepped out of Dr. Freud's house and onto Schwarzspanierstrasse, the sky had begun to cloud over, and there was a sting in the winter wind. I wondered how much transference Freud might have detected in the mixture of deference and offhanded impatience with which I treated Colm as we squabbled over which direction to head to catch the tram.

On our last full day in Vienna, I woke before dawn and while everyone slept, I walked out. In the deserted gardens of Maria-Theresien-Platz, I saw a lone man standing up in a pruned tree, posing like a statue. I wanted to speak to him, to ask what he was doing, and how long had he been up there, but I didn't. I watched him for some time, until finally he moved his arm. I wandered down to Stephansdom Cathedral and walked in on the dawn Mass, being said in the first side chapel, beside the main entry. I passed Mozart's house again and walked into a baroque church where I sat for a few silent minutes, alone in the last pew. Outside, I passed Kleines Café, where D and I had had coffee the night before.

It was when we had left there that we strolled into the Hotel Sacher. While D ordered a drink in the Blaue Bar, I excused myself to the bathroom but went instead to the front desk to get us a room. I walked back into the bar and dropped the key on the table, and D followed me up to the third floor. We made love with the glow of the opera house shining a golden light over us.

When I walked back in the apartment after my early-morning stroll, everyone was at the breakfast table.

"Where have you been, luv?" D asked.

"Never you mind," Margot broke in. "Leave the man some privacy, he's had enough of us all by now."

Surprisingly, she wasn't correct in her analysis, but I appreciated not having to explain myself.

"Now, Andrew," Colm started, "I don't know what you've got planned for today, but tonight I am taking us all out to a Heuriger." Colm had been trying to drag us to one of Vienna's traditional—and tourist-infested—wineries up in the hills on the edge of the Vienna woods for the entire trip.

"Now, there's no use arguing, Andrew, my love." Margot shook her head. "He has his mind made up and we are going to go. And we'll just enjoy it as best we can," she said, patting my arm.

I studied the public transportation map, and when night fell, we headed on our usual tram toward the center of town. We switched at the Volkstheater to the same tram that had led Colm and me astray on our way to Freud's house, and we began to climb the hills out of town. The tram was crowded with late rush-hour commuters heading home. Then an announcement was made over the loudspeaker. Our tram was being taken out of service. People grumbled, and we were deposited on the side of a dark road on a steep incline.

"Perhaps we should have taken a taxi," Margot said quietly, "just this once."

Ten minutes later another tram arrived and we climbed aboard. After a while, Colm discreetly asked a fellow passenger which was the stop for the famous Heuriger.

"This next stop," the woman replied.

As the station approached everyone began to rise and squeeze toward the door.

When the tram stopped I heard myself say, "No," in a clear, strong voice. "It's not this stop. We need to go two more."

"Are you sure, luv?" D asked.

"Yes," I said.

Margot looked at me, then at her husband.

D' sat down, so did our daughter, and then Margot. Colm bit his tongue. The tram went on, up the hill. No one spoke.

"This is it," I said when we arrived at an unlit corner across from a gas station. We were the only ones to get off the tram. "It's two blocks up that hill."

And to all our great relief, it was.

"That a boy, Andrew!" Colm shouted, patting me on the back. "Never doubted you for a second." He of course had no belief in my navigational abilities at this point, but he had remained silent and demonstrated faith nonetheless.

Through a cobblestone courtyard, under a vine-covered trestle above, we entered a low and long room with blond-wood-paneled walls and hard wooden booths. There was a man playing an accordion by the fireplace, at the far end of the room. There was no busload of tourists, as I had feared. Only a few of the tables were filled, with locals. A waitress dressed in a traditional Austrian dirndl came over and Colm ordered a few different carafes of the fresh wine from the most recent harvest that is the Heuriger's specialty. D's parents tasted and commented on the bouquet and flavor. The man playing the accordion took frequent breaks and visited the tables of the other patrons. He drank copious amounts of wine, moving slowly, with great and deliberate care, back and forth to the bar to refill his glass.

We went across the courtyard and ordered from the small women behind the buffet counter—traditional cold cuts and pickled cabbages. We ate several kinds of salami that my son would have devoured.

Eventually Colm got up to invite the accordion player to come over and sing us a song. For a long time the man didn't come and we assumed that in his drunkenness, he had forgotten. But then there he was, on a stool at the end of our booth. Close up he looked like a bloated Robert Goulet, with a thick dark mustache and watery eyes. He spoke only German, but even in a language I didn't understand,

I could tell his words were formed with the extravagant care of a drunkard.

Margot requested "Edelweiss," from *The Sound of Music*. I wanted to crawl under the table.

When the man began to sing, his voice was as rich and clear as it was thick and clouded when he spoke. My daughter, who was wearing her authentic Austrian dirndl bought by her granny and had begun to drift off to sleep with her head on my lap, now suddenly sat up.

"Mommy, how does he know this song?" she asked in wonder, and stared at the musician as he pushed and pulled his accordion, closed his eyes, and emptied himself into a song he must have sung every night of his life.

D's parents swayed back and forth in unison and then began to sing along. Colm put his arm around his wife and she leaned into her husband, their eyes burning with unapologetic happiness.

I took out my phone and snapped a photo of them across the table. It is slightly out of focus, but their eyes are clear. They're sharing a look of such unguarded joy in each other. It's a look that trumps all of the baggage that I know they carry after fifty years of marriage, and all the baggage that I don't know about. At that moment, in their togetherness, they rose above all that life does to weigh people down.

I looked at D and she smiled at me and tilted her head toward her parents, as if to say, "See that? It's all worth it, this feeling right now, it's worth it, isn't it?" I smiled at her and looked down at the table. She touched my cheek, in acceptance of my awkwardness. I looked at her again and took her hand.

CHAPTER SIX

BALTIMORE

"The Best Thing That You Could Do Is Show Up"

Something had indeed happened in Vienna. My attitude toward the notion of family began to shift. Perhaps I was simply ready to see it, or experience it, differently.

As with so many important emotional events in my life, there was no "aha" moment. It was something that happened gradually, without my knowledge, over time, but with a seeping certainty. The change that had silently begun in Vienna had manifested one day in my consciousness, and announced its presence, while I was down in Costa Rica, where I had the space and silence to hear its not-so-confident whisper of arrival. Perhaps I was indeed finally ready to take the plunge and commit to family and all it might offer besides responsibility and strain.

Yet as I sat with the idea, there was still a voice in me, still a resistance, an ambivalence that flashed like a yellow light of warning just at the edge of my consciousness. But if it wasn't the resistance to the idea of family, then what was it?

This newly uncovered reluctance—which had been cloaked beneath my obvious misgivings—felt darker, more pervasive in my character, more embedded in who I was, than my more obvious and garden-variety resistance that I had been aware of up to now, no matter how difficult it had been to overcome. It felt like something I'd need help with, something this traveler couldn't do on his own. Which explains why I'm on Amtrak's Northeast Corridor line, heading south.

When I press the black plastic button that says "push," the silver metal door snaps open, slides across, and I see Seve standing two-thirds of the way down the aisle, holding on to the back of his seat as the train gathers speed and bounces from side to side down the track. He's grinning, that Seve grin. We haven't seen each other in nearly a year.

We high-five, hug, and settle down. I begin to criticize his choice of seat, the time of day of our travel, the hotel he's booked us into. This kind of snapping, caustic judgment I am engaging in is not an unusual way for us to begin; it's the sort of childish behavior I am free to indulge in only with Seve. Usually he ignores me.

"So who'd you invite?" He cuts right to the topic he knows I'm avoiding.

"No one yet."

"Isn't it about that time?"

"I guess."

"Who are you going to invite?"

"I don't know."

"Well, how many?"

"I don't really want anyone to come."

"Great," he says.

"Not many anyway." I am looking past him, out the window at the back of small and run-down houses on the outskirts of Philadelphia. We roll past empty lots, garbage, stray dogs. I was in Philadelphia talking to a bunch of students about travel writing—they weren't interested in what I had to say—and Seve was in Boston, where he had been on business. We are on our way to his hometown of Baltimore, Maryland.

"Well, from the sound of it, this wedding is going to be a lot of fun."

D has identified a subgroup of my friends, of whom Seve is the closest—men who are usually physically larger than me, often older than I am, and have a protective nature. "Your bodyguards," she calls them. I had never noticed the pattern until she pointed it out. Perhaps I'm trying to re-create my relationship with my older brother—who was all those things for me growing up, before we drifted off into our own lives. I do know that I relax when I'm with any one of my "bodyguards" in a way I don't with my other friends.

Seve and I met not long after I moved to New York, when I lived in a top-floor apartment of a five-story walk-up on Bank Street in the West Village with an unobstructed view of the Empire State Building from my bedroom. I would often lie awake at night, waiting for the colored lights that lit the upper floors of the great building to snap off at midnight.

I came of age in the year I lived on Bank Street. I had my first real girlfriend in that apartment. I got my first acting job while living there. And I began a pattern of drinking during that year—just a few blocks away at the Corner Bistro on Jane Street—that would soon grow to haunt me. I can't walk past my old building without looking up and recalling the sense of wonder I knew at the time, when I felt like my life was just beginning.

Seve's girlfriend lived in the apartment across the hall from me, and he was a frequent visitor. We began to play tennis together and would sometimes go out to the racetrack at the Meadowlands or down to Atlantic City on a late-night whim. We drank a lot in the local bars. Occasionally we played golf. It was on the golf course that

Seve got his nickname. A terrible golfer, he once hit what was for him a superb shot. Our playing partner, another good friend, called out, "Nice shot, Seve!" referring to the great Spanish golfer Seve Ballesteros, whose charismatic style was dominating the golf world at the time. The nickname stuck. Over the years I've introduced Seve to scores of people who have no idea that Seve isn't his real name—no one has ever questioned why a fair-skinned, blue-eyed Irish-American would have a name like Seve.

And it was with Seve that I first went to Ireland, back in the mid-eighties, establishing a relationship with a place that would first influence and then change my life. And it was on that first trip to Ireland that I initiated the impulsive, serendipitous, and intuitive pattern of travel that would take me out into the wider world. We roamed around the west, drinking, getting lost, occasionally playing golf. We found a spot by the Burren that I still return to every few years.

At some point Seve moved away for business, first to Los Angeles and then to Denver. I went through my dark times with drink, while he went through some searching of his own—we saw little of each other and spoke rarely. Eventually we found our way more regularly back into each other's lives, but when he couldn't come to my first wedding because of a dental convention, I never missed an opportunity to remind him of his failure to show up. I have told him that his being my best man in my marriage to D is his one shot at redemption.

"I'm only getting married so you can set the past right, dude."

"Will you stop being an asshole?"

Seve has booked us into a large, generic chain hotel downtown. I find such buildings soul-crushing in their lack of individuality, while he likes the transient invisibility of the herd that such places offer. He justifies this by saying they're convenient.

"Convenient to what?" Our train crosses the bridge over the

Susquehanna River. "It's downtown in a nothing neighborhood, with a bunch of conventioneers."

"Where do you want to go, Mr. Cheerful?"

"What about Fells Point? I heard that was a good neighborhood." While in Baltimore, I am supposed to be writing about the hidden charms of an overlooked American gem, a city on the rise.

"Oh, yeah, that's a nice area," Seve says.

"What about this hotel?" I point to a picture in my guidebook.

"You have a guidebook, to Baltimore?"

"Obviously I can't depend on you to show me what I need to see."

He pulls out his cell phone to try to change our hotel reservation. "I really thought you'd be better at handling this whole wedding thing this time around." Seve shakes his head as he dials.

"Go to hell."

We end up in Fells Point. The inn we check into is just off the water. Built in the late eighteenth century, it has a nautical theme; framed drawings and photos of sailing vessels of days long gone line the walls. A ghost reputedly haunts the halls. The bumpy streets outside are paved with stones originally used as ballast in the holds of sailing cargo ships. The brick-covered Fells Point Square is out my window. A tugboat is tied up at the old Recreation Pier. One of the small white water taxis that ply the harbor is docked nearby. This used to be a rough-and-tumble neighborhood. You would never know it today. Like much of Baltimore, Fells Point has had a facelift. Now a camera-ready nook comprised of narrow and crooked lanes down by the waterfront, filled with art galleries and ice cream parlors, where local bars anchor corners, it is a poster child of urban renewal. We head just down the block, to Duda's Tavern. There are brass lamps affixed to the bar and a life preserver ring mounted behind it, above the rows of whiskey bottles. The walls are covered with black and white photos of old Baltimore and sailing ships. Stevie Wonder's album *Songs in the Key of Life* plays from the stereo.

Our waitress comes over and introduces herself. Suzy is in her fifties, blond, stout, wearing no makeup and a loose green T-shirt, pleated black shorts, and sensible shoes. She's friendly, not casual. Her manner is direct and uncomplicated. She takes our drink order and walks away. I take my napkin from the plastic tablecloth that is emblazoned all over with the black and orange symbol of the local baseball team, the Orioles.

"How are the O's doing, still suck?"

"Hey, hey, we're rebuilding."

"We should go to a game while we're here."

"Planning on it."

Suzy returns and plunks down our drinks. "Ready?"

"How are the crab cakes?" Seve asks.

Suzy glares at him. "The best."

"I'll take 'em. I'm from Baltimore, so I'll know," he says, and raises a finger of warning.

"You won't be disappointed." She stares him down and then turns to me. "What about you, hon?" It's the first time I've heard the famous Baltimore salutation.

"How's the steak?"

Suzy shrugs, almost imperceptibly. "Good."

"I'll have the cheeseburger, medium."

"Better," she says, jabs her pen behind her ear, and pivots away.

Seve nods after Suzy. "That's Baltimore."

"Ordinary Pain" fades out and Stevie Wonder segues into "Isn't She Lovely?"

"So how did this come up—that you're finally getting married?"

I tell him the story of my son calling me on the phone to say he didn't want to come back home to us and how it acted as the needle that punctured D's and my balloon of habitual conflict, and that since our trip to Vienna, we have been getting closer.

172

"One moment can just change everything, can't it?" He's reacting to my story, but I know he's also talking about his own relationship that recently ended. "I just never saw it coming. I walk in and she says, 'It's over.' I was just totally blindsided."

I was never a big fan of Seve's recent ex. "Well, it'll give you a chance to be alone for while."

"No one really wants to be alone," he retorts, and then looks across at me. "Well, almost no one."

Our food arrives. The burger is huge and good.

"I've always wanted to ask this," Seve says. "The moment you met, what happened? Was there a moment when you said, 'I'm not in control here'?"

"Are you kidding me? I wasn't in control for six months. I'm still not in control."

Seve has always idealized my relationship with D—the notion that love can just slam into a person and there's nothing to do but follow it. As if love were something that happened to you and not a thing that requires the work we both know it does. But that Seve seems to recognize some nugget in my relationship with D that he holds in special regard always triggers in me a gratitude that D and I found each other. And it helps keep me moving forward.

Later, when the check arrives, I give Suzy my credit card.

"You know, when I heard you on the phone, when you told me, there was a real excitement in your voice," Seve says. "I'm not saying you accept this whole marriage thing yet, but you actually seem to be embracing it."

I resist the impulse to push back at his assessment and simply nod instead. "Well, I mean it's going to happen."

"And how do you feel about it?"

I shrug. "Yeah."

"Let's try that again. How do you feel about it?"

Again, I shrug. "I mean, I love her. And I think it's the right thing to do. And a good thing to do."

"But?"

"There's no 'but,' I just—" Suzy returns with my card and I sign the receipt with a pen she gives me advertising "Big Boys Bail Bonds—3 locations in Baltimore."

"Oh, how were the crab cakes?" I ask Seve.

"Disappointing."

"Too late, I already overtipped her."

Just down the street from Duda's we come upon a man in a plaid shirt and glasses, with tufts of unruly gray hair flying in the breeze. He's standing beside a large blue telescope that's pointed up into the night sky.

"Have a gander, fellas," the man says.

"What are you looking at?" Seve asks.

"Right now, Saturn."

I peek into the eight-inch Schmidt-cassegrain reflector telescope and there is what must be Saturn with what must be rings around it.

Herman Heyn has been standing on this spot for approximately 2,255 nights—"That's within a night or two," he says, correcting himself. "I first came down on November 13, 1987."

I resist asking the obvious question of why. Herman is a Baltimore native from Waverly, a few miles north; he was a concrete inspector on the Baltimore Harbor Tunnel, among other jobs, before he retired and started hanging out on street corners with his telescope. Beside him is his lady friend, Phyllis. They met under the stars, only recently, 118 nights ago, and have been hanging out together since. They're tender with each other and have a humble, contented air about them, as if they understand something that Seve and I don't. We drop a dollar in their bucket and cross the street.

Seve returns to the subject of his ex.

"But, Seve—is it ego, confidence, or heart that's been hurt?"

"I was totally blindsided."

"That doesn't answer the question."

He's silent a minute. "What's the difference?"

"It wasn't your last best chance."

"I don't know that."

"Hey, look at Herman and Phyllis," I say. "You just need a good telescope."

We wander past a building with a self-congratulatory plaque out front, proclaiming that it was this very building where television history was made with the show *Homicide*. "My mother used to do marionette shows here when she was a teenager," Seve tells me. Just up the street, the comforting smell of baking bread grows strong. Through an open back door we see a lone man in white apron and hat, baking in the kitchen of Bonaparte Breads. Out on the waterfront, the red neon of the Domino Sugar sign glows across the harbor. Our amble is without purpose; we say very little.

Later, I call D.

"I need your list, we need to get these invites out."

"Well, how many people are we going to have? You need to decide," I say.

"My family is at least a hundred and fifty, before friends."

"I thought you were going to have like eighty or ninety."

"I don't know how I can't invite my cousins, but what I was thinking is that maybe . . ."

This goes on for a while, different permutations and possibilities. D agrees that maybe all the cousins are too many; maybe we can keep it to two rings of extended family. But then how could she face her relations down in Cork? They had invited her to a christening.

Eventually I give up. "I mean, these conversations are ridiculous, because you know you're just going to go back to the original idea because it's all you can do, which is why you came up with it first."

"Which is?"

"Invite everybody. Throw it against the wall and hope it works out."

"Aw, thanks, baby!"

"So, are we going to go to Mozambique?" I have a potential writing assignment there, and we've been talking about its doubling as a honeymoon.

"Well, what's the deal with malaria?"

"I don't know," I reply. "I mean, they got it. We should just take Malarone."

"I'm not taking that poison, and neither should you."

"Well, it's better than the other option."

"Which is?"

"Dying."

"Let's just go," she says. "It'll be an adventure."

"Done. Amazing, something actually got decided."

"Oh, shut up, it's going be a great wedding. Are you inviting your uncle Hank?"

"I'm going to bed."

"We're actually in the same time zone, aren't we? That's so weird."

🏃

I'm sitting on a bench across from our hotel, waiting for Seve. BALTI-MORE: THE GREATEST CITY IN AMERICA is stenciled in large block letters on the back of the bench. There's an empty Paul Masson brandy bottle carefully placed beside it. It's 8:39 in the morning, and already the temperature is in the nineties. And it's humid. I send D a text, "Did I miss you?" wondering if she has left the house for the day.

Seve comes out of the hotel and we walk across the square to Jimmy's Diner. We take a seat at the Formica counter. "My family used to come here on Sundays when I was a kid," he says, looking around the large, fluorescent-lit room. A waitress slides two plastic glasses filled with water across the counter.

"Two coffees?" she asks, and is already turning away to get the pot.

"I'll take a tea," I call after her.

The waitress stops, turns back, gives me a good long look. "Course you will, hon."

Seve starts right in. "You meet any beautiful women on any of your trips lately?"

"Don't."

"So?"

To satisfy his need for a thrill I tell him about Holly, the woman I met down in the Osa who ran the remote lodge deep in the rain forest. I describe her blond hair, her blue dress, and her solid knowledge of her beauty.

"So how'd that end?"

"It didn't even start."

"There's a rule, you know, the Mississippi rule. Anything beyond the Mississippi doesn't count," he says.

"Don't be an asshole."

"I'm just saying."

"Yeah, right. I would just finish having sex and I'd get a text from my beloved fiancée, 'Did you enjoy that?'"

"My fear would be bringing something home," Seve says.

"I can't talk about this anymore." Then my phone beeps; it's a text from D in response to the question that I sent while waiting for Seve, asking if I missed her. D's text reads, "I don't know, do you??"

We head downtown, toward the Inner Harbor. "When I was a kid, I couldn't get anyone to go downtown with me," Seve says. "Now, my nieces and nephews, no one wants to be anywhere else." The port of Baltimore was created at Locust Point in 1709 to support the tobacco trade. It grew quickly as a granary for sugar-producing colonies in the West Indies and was hugely important in colonial times. There were riots in Baltimore during the Civil War and a great fire in 1904. There were riots again when Martin Luther King Jr. was assassinated, and by the 1970s Baltimore was entrenched in hard times. The harbor area was cluttered with derelict warehouses and seedy bars. But as we walk along the redbrick promenade, sweating in the morning sun, past swarming young families heading to the aquarium and the restaurants and shopping malls, all this is just a story of the past. So much of Baltimore's life now takes place along the waterfront that a large number of visitors never see anything else.

We make our way a few blocks inland, over to the house where baseball legend Babe Ruth was born. It was my ex-wife who first introduced me to the "home as micro-museum." We were in Stockholm, Sweden, when she dragged me to the apartment of August Strindberg. What I feared would be a dreary and dull hour proved to be a fascinating look inside the writer's life. His desk and chair, his pens and notebooks and letters, his eyeglasses and walking stick, relics of his life, proved fascinating. I have sought out "home museums" ever since. The Bambino's home is on Emory Street, a narrow lane of red brick row houses tucked just off the six lanes of throbbing traffic on Martin Luther King Jr. Boulevard—and a two-minute walk to Camden Yards baseball field.

Inside, an old man rises to greet us from behind a counter.

"Gentlemen," he calls out. "Welcome." We are the only visitors and our host is eager for company. I leave Seve to make small talk and head inside.

There are uniforms, and bats, even a wooden chair that was used in the box seats at Yankee Stadium, and there's a video of the old *Biography* television show, hosted by a very young Mike Wallace, telling all about "the Babe's" improbable life. Yet there's something lacking; the museum is nearly all memorabilia. There are very few personal things that hint at the lonely boy, discarded by his parents, who grew up to be the hero of a nation. I'm looking for something. Perhaps that's why I turn to Seve—"Let's go out to your house," I tell him.

"Huh?"

"Let's go out to where you grew up. How long since you've been there?"

"To the house I grew up in? Uh, I don't know. Thirty years?"

"How far away is it?"

Seve shrugs. "Fifteen minutes."

"You grew up fifteen minutes from here and you haven't been back in thirty years?"

"When we moved, we moved."

"How far did you move?"

"Another twenty minutes out."

"Let's go."

Seve wavers.

"Why is this like pulling teeth? Come on. It's too damn hot to walk around. Let's get a cab and go."

The air conditioner of the taxi we get into is broken, and the windows in the back won't go down. The driver is upset when, after a block, we switch cabs. The next car we get into is cool, and the driver is an easygoing young guy from Nigeria called Paul. Juju music plays softly on his radio. We head west.

Just fifteen minutes from downtown are a series of small, freestanding, identical-looking brick houses with aluminum awnings and small, fenced-in lawns. Like most American cities, today's Baltimore is an outgrowth of the suburbanization of the country in the 1950s. Seve's parents were part of that great migration away from the inner cities. Seve's mother has since moved even farther out.

"That's St. Bonaventure's," he announces as we pass a yellow brick church. "I was an altar boy there. Turn left."

Paul cuts through the parking lot. "Where to now?" he asks.

We turn right and farther on a ball field opens out beside us. "I hit my first home run right there." Seve points. "I remember it like it was yesterday." We drive on. Seve leans forward in his seat, squinting through the windshield, looking for his youth. "Make your next left, my friend," Seve says softly.

Paul slows the car and eases onto Knollwood Drive. These are no longer single-family homes but a series of two-story apartment buildings that line the left side of the road across from a park.

"A little bit farther," Seve directs him. We glide on. "That's it." And we stop out in front of number 4105. It's much more humble than I had anticipated.

We ask Paul to wait.

"You take your time," he says slowly, and lowers his window to rest his elbow and watch our progress.

There's a short, steep incline that leads up to the apartment building's metal storm door. Seve stops halfway up the hill. "I knocked my brother out right here." He pulls on the door; it's open. Up a flight, Seve stands in front of a red door with a number 1 on it. He has a quizzical expression on his face. He wants to go in, or to knock, something. Then he shrugs.

"I was always ashamed—all my friends lived in houses, and we lived in an apartment." I can feel his shame again now.

I want to turn away. "Stand by the door, let me take your picture," I say instead.

"Yeah," he says, and a silly grin comes onto his face. He looks befuddled and awkward, in a way I've never seen him look. He looks decidedly vulnerable and human.

"Nice," I say when I snap the shot.

Although Seve lives out in Denver now, his work has asked him to consider a move back east. He decides that maybe he ought to look at a few apartments while we're here. We head back to town and Paul insists on shaking our hands when he drops us in front of a sterile-looking glass tower. We have no appointment. We simply walk in, but an on-site agent is only too eager to help. The building and the apartments in it are so new, geometric, and without history, so strange in comparison to the worn, memory-filled halls we've just been to, that we are both left baffled and speechless. After the third apartment Seve says, "I don't want to have a place, I just want to leave Denver and keep moving around."

What I hear behind Seve's words is a sense of transience to which I know he is attracted—to a large degree it is the reason he doesn't have a family. It's a sentiment I understand and one that could easily be mistaken for my own wanderlust. But my travels are driven by a force that is quite the opposite. Impermanence is not what I crave and never has been. That I've traveled in order to feel at home in myself is a paradox that has helped me to create that feeling while in my familiar surroundings—I desire a feeling of "at-home-ness" everywhere, quite the opposite to Seve's desire for transience.

"Let's get out on the water," Seve suggests, and we quit the apartment hunting and hop on the first water taxi that comes to the Fells Point Landing. It's headed to Fort McHenry, the old military base made famous during a battle in the War of 1812, after which, upon seeing the American flag still flying, Francis Scott Key wrote "The Star-Spangled Banner" and set it to the tune of an old English drinking song. The entire fort and interactive displays are dedicated to this song, including a brief movie intended to stir feelings of patriotism and moisten the eyes. At the climax of the film, the screen drops away and through the glass wall behind it, we gaze out upon the actual banner yet waving, o'er the land of the free.

When the lights come up, the crowd seems more confused by the jingoistic assault than moved by patriotism. I find Seve leaning against a wall, shaking his head.

"When did patriotism become so agressive?" he asks.

"September eleventh," I mutter in return.

We wait down by the dock for the boat back, and then the wind blows through us on the bow of the water taxi. "Where to, tour guide?" I ask my friend.

"Let's go up to Mount Vernon."

Once home to the blue-blooded gentry and captains of industry during Baltimore's rise, Mount Vernon is filled with formidable nineteenth-century marble homes, radiating out from the nation's first monument to its first president. It was the hub of town before the Inner Harbor was restored and sucked life back toward the water. On the corner of Biddle and Morton, Seve stops in his tracks.

"I bought my first car right here, on this corner," he says. "I was dating a girl and her father was putting a For Sale sign in the window when I walked up—a Chevy Biscayne."

We walk on. Perhaps it is because of the oppressive late-afternoon heat, but the streets here are deserted and lifeless. I see a formidable beaux-arts building.

"What's that?"

"Good idea," Seve says, and we're through the revolving doors of the old Belvedere Hotel. We slide into the Owl Bar at the back of the lobby. There's not much life in here either, but at least it's cool. With its stained glass windows, red tile floors, and a heavy wooden bar backed by a beveled mirror, the Owl has the comfortable feel of the speakeasy it was in the 1920s. "This was always old Baltimore to me," Seve says, looking around the deserted room.

Perched high above the bar is a replica of an owl. Legend has it that the owl's eyes would wink when the booze was flowing and the Feds were scarce, and if the bird's gaze was fixed, it meant there was trouble afoot and mum was the word. Etched into several of the stained-glass windows flanking the owl is a children's nursery rhyme.

A wise old owl sat on an oak.
The more he saw, the less he spoke.
The less he spoke the more he heard,
Why aren't we like that wise old bird?

I've often thought that Seve applied the old owl's wisdom to my relationship with D. He was there nearly from the start. After D's and my first, brief encounter in a hotel lobby in Galway, and after our subsequent exchange of e-mails, Seve was with us a few months later to witness our casual one-hour coffee swell into four days of intensity.

"That's lightning," was all Seve said to me when we were alone in my room, just down the hall from the one D had taken. "Do you know what you're doing?"

I had no idea what I was doing or what I was getting myself into. "Yeah," I bluffed, "don't worry about it."

Over the next four dizzying days the three of us traveled the west of Ireland, with Seve acting as chaperone. He and D got on immediately, with the bickering banter of siblings. What might have been an awkward triangle quickly evolved into a playful trio.

"You deal in facts," D said to Seve, summing up their relationship, "I deal in feelings."

When she finally got on a train and returned to Dublin, I walked for hours alone along the misty and windswept beach in Lahinch and wondered what implications those few days had for the rest of my life. Seve said very little. He listened as I explained with certainty how my path had just taken a turn I had to follow. He gently wondered what this would mean for my life back in New York. Another friend would have strongly advised me to walk away—take my infatuation, head home, and let it pass. It would have been the prudent counsel. And yet he didn't; having seen what he saw and experienced what he did between D and me, Seve simply stood by my side and said, "Be careful, my friend."

And that there was someone who understood what it was I was moving toward, without my having to say anything, was invaluable to me as my life began to unravel and then slowly put itself back together.

It's 104 degrees when Boog Powell, a slugger I remember from very early in my youth, throws out the ceremonial first pitch at 7:01 in the evening. The humidity is resting steady at 94 percent. Because the Orioles are struggling so badly—as they perennially do—tickets were easy to come by. We just stand out by the front gate of Camden Yards, and people come running at us to unload their extra seats. The baseball stadium was built in the retro ballpark style that launched a trend and helped spearhead the revitalization of Baltimore when it opened in 1992; I've always wanted to see it.

A skinny guy with bright red hair promises us his tickets are right behind the dugout and offers them at less than face value. Buying tickets on the street outside a venue was something I used to do often.

Reading a scalper's pitch and potential for scam is an art form, but this is an Orioles game in Baltimore, not a Bruce Springsteen concert in New Jersey, and the urgency and potential for being ripped off are minimal. Still, I walk away and let Seve handle it.

"Deal, Seve. They just better be good."

And they are. In fact, they're the best seats in the house, front row, right behind the Orioles dugout—as promised.

"Who would have thought, someone told the truth."

"Baltimore, baby," Seve says.

A vendor comes down the aisle, shouting, "Ice-cold water. Tasty beer!" His face is pouring sweat. The first few innings roll past with little action. Neither the Orioles nor the Angels get a man on base. The normal rhythm of the game—practice tosses, warm-up swings, and covert signals—asserts itself. From the sparse crowd around us come halfhearted encouragements. "We'll get 'em next time, J.J.," and "Get wood on it, baby," and after a called third strike comes a baseball favorite, "That's bullshit!" echoing out onto the field. I haven't been to a baseball game in several years, and although I've never before set foot in Camden Yards, I feel as comfortable here as in my living room.

When my brothers and I were kids, my father occasionally took us to Yankee Stadium, and it is my fondest memory of childhood—even then, it was how I thought a childhood ought to be. I can remember, as a very small boy, sitting behind a large pillar and leaning over to see when my father said, "Look now. That's Mickey Mantle, he's one of the best ever, this will be the last time you'll ever see him." And I watched as the small figure far away struck out and hobbled back to the dugout. Another time we went to Fenway Park in Boston; we sat far out in right field and I couldn't see anything over the other patrons except second base. When a fast runner got on with a single, and I complained I couldn't see, my father said, "Just keep your eye on second, he's gonna steal." And when he did, and my eye was glued to second, I felt like my dad knew everything there was to know.

Yet this was the same man who, several years after the Boston game, took my Little League buddy and me to Yankee Stadium. I hadn't seen much of my friend since we moved several towns away, and when my mother suggested I invite him to go to the game, I was excited. My father had recently bought a used, battered Jaguar sports car. It only had room for two passengers, except for a tiny jump seat in the back, and my father insisted on taking it to the Bronx. I let my friend sit up front and I squeezed into the back. As we set out, our spirits were high.

Driving through Harlem in upper Manhattan, the Jaguar overheated and broke down. This was not unusual; the car had constant problems. But this was in the 1970s, when Harlem was a very different place than it is today. Quickly, my father grew tense. A man approached us and, trying to help, suggested, "I wouldn't leave that car here." We looked for a nearby gas station. My friend proposed calling his father, who might be able to help. It was then that my father snapped at him, suddenly and ferociously. My friend was shocked; I could see him fight back tears. I was mortified, and my father busied himself with getting us out of there. We never made it to the game, and I never saw my friend again, so deep was my teenage shame.

🚶

In the bottom of the fifth, the Orioles break the no-hitter and the meager crowd has something to cheer about. That baseball unfolds in its own time, at its own pace, and isn't subject to any clock is something that makes the game increasingly attractive in our multitasking world. Meandering conversation is as much a part of the experience as the game itself. Our exchange rambles from batting helmets and rosin bags, to the name of that hotel in Galway we stayed at years ago, to Patti Smith and John McEnroe, to the two marines who were killed in Afghanistan the day before. A foul ball is hit high in the air and drifts our way. We rise. As it begins to fall it is coming straight for us. I can see the laces of the spinning ball. When it lands two rows behind us I'm relieved—I didn't want my hands burning from a catch I knew I would try to make. The Angels score two runs in the seventh inning, and the O's come back with one in the eighth. With a bit of cunning, a base runner takes an extra base in what is one of the more intangible aspects of the game. "There's just something about watching someone run the bases well," I comment to Seve.

"You have a keen instinct for someone who does something well," my friend says.

I turn to him. One of the nicer things about Seve is his ability to compliment or criticize with insight and without ownership, as if he's talking about a simple fact that is worth noting. And in doing so, he is able to elevate the discussion to a higher significance than that of the mere observation being made.

"I do?"

"You do," he says, "and you know you can trust it."

"Which? Trust my instinct or trust what the person is doing well?"

"Both." Seve is quiet a minute and then he goes on. "I never heard you say you wanted to be a world traveler." It's an odd segue, and I'm not sure what to say. "It's not that you consciously started traveling to learn to trust people, but I think you wanted to trust people and inherently you don't. And in your travel you've learned to trust yourself, and if you can trust yourself, then you can trust others. You took your son to the Sahara because you could trust yourself in that situation. And you need to know that. And if you could trust people there, with your son's life . . ." The Angels come up and quickly load

the bases, and Seve continues. "That's what's so good about you getting married to who you're getting married to. She recognizes and
embraces humanity; you're just the opposite. To learn the things you
had to learn, you had to go out and deal with people, and I know
that's not something you easily do. It's something that's difficult for
you, but travel helps you in that."

I nod, taking this on board. The Angels' Vernon Wells steps to
the plate and hits the first pitch on offer deep into the bleachers for a
grand slam. The bulk of the already dwindling crowd heads for the
exits.

We linger to the bitter end and are among the few remaining fans
when the final out is recorded. By the time we are on the street, the
area around the ballpark is nearly deserted.

A few blocks away we find the crowd, down at the Inner Harbor.
The long promenade by the water is jammed with families, couples,
and swarming teens. A band is performing on a temporary stage. The
patios of the waterfront restaurants overflow. The USS *Constellation*,
the last surviving Civil War–era vessel, built in 1854, sits at anchor, its
tall rigging motionless in the heavy air.

"Can we get out of here?" I ask.

A water taxi is just getting ready to push off.

"Where you headed?" Seve calls to the older man untying the lead.

"Canton," the man shouts back.

Seve turns to me. "Let's go see if my sister is around."

"Do we have to?"

"Do you *try* to be a complete jerk?"

We climb on board.

Drifting away from the pulsing mass, we pass the aquarium and
a former power plant, now a Hard Rock Café, and chug past pier
five and the Seven Foot Knoll lighthouse. On the wrought-iron balcony that encircles the red building, a solitary couple is dancing in the

humid night. I am reminded of a recent conversation with D—while we were preparing dinner.

"I just don't know whether the *ceili* should be Saturday night before the ceremony or Sunday, after," she said.

"The what?"

"The *ceili?*"

"We're having Irish dancing?"

"You didn't think I was going to get married without dancing, did you?"

I took an onion out of the bowl on the counter and began to slice it.

"Would you get out the feta and pass me the olive oil?"

I reached deep into the refrigerator and handed D the cheese and slid over the bottle of oil. "And where is this *ceili* going to be?"

"That's what we need to decide. We could do it at the hotel next door to my folks' house, or in their backyard, but if they're going to have the dinner on Saturday night, it would be a lot for them to have a *ceili* there too, especially on the same night."

I stopped cutting. "Your parents are having a dinner? For who?"

"For everyone coming in. Are you going to chop that onion, luv?"

"Everyone? How is everyone going to fit into your parents' living room?"

"Well, not everyone, just the relations coming up to Dublin. You can't expect my parents not to do something for their brothers and sisters. And the Americans who are coming, we need to do something with them for the weekend. We can't just give them a 'welcome drink' cocktail party at the Shelbourne on Friday and say, 'See you Sunday morning.' They'll have come a long way and we'll need to—"

"Whoa—whoa, we're giving them a 'welcome drink' party at the Shelbourne Hotel? When did we decide all this?"

"Nothing is decided for sure, that's what we need to do. I've just been talking to Mum and Dad. Now, Dad is insisting he make dinner for the family, so that's done. If you don't want to do that, then you call him. But he's planning the menu and he's going to do it."

"But if he's going to have the dinner on Saturday, then the *ceili* has to be on Sunday."

"Perfect. That's what I thought too."

"Wait a minute. What happened to the picnic idea?"

"We're having that, too."

"But—"

"I need that onion, luv. Are you going to chop it?"

"Here, you do it, before I start crying."

The water taxi drops us at the Canton Waterfront Park. Seve's sister lives just up the hill from the water. Once a run-down neighborhood of shuttered canneries, this part of the city has become one of Baltimore's trendier places to live, with a buzzing bar and restaurant scene. Seve's sister is out and we walk two blocks farther on to O'Donnell Square, a narrow strip of green anchored by the Messiah Lutheran Church on one end and a firehouse on the other.

"I used to come here to play basketball in the CYO league," Seve says. We circle the square, looking in a few of the crammed bars playing loud music to see if his sister is around. We walk past a storefront shop that looks more like the living room of a college student. The folding glass-paneled front door is wide open to the heavy night and Middle Eastern techno music blares. Couches line the exposed brick walls and low tables are scattered around under dim lighting. A Marilyn Monroe poster hangs beside one of Manchester United soccer club. It's deserted, except for a young guy sitting behind a counter in the back, deep in the shadows.

"What's this joint, Seve?"

"Never seen it before."

The young guy hops up when we cross the threshold. "Welcome," he says with a thick accent. He has dark olive skin and jet-black hair.

"Hi, what is this?" I ask—it comes out in a worse way than I intended.

"This is my place, Anubis Hookah Lounge. Have you ever smoked the hookah?"

"No," and "Sure," Seve and I say simultaneously. Seve turns to me. "When did you smoke a hookah?"

"In Qatar, dude."

"Please," our young host says, spreading his arms, "sit. You are most welcome here." And we take the front couch, looking out past the hood of a Dodge Ram pickup truck and up into the trees lining the square and the suddenly low-hanging night sky.

Our host is an Egyptian named Karim Kamel who came to America several years ago and just recently opened his hookah lounge. Karim lists a dozen flavored tobaccos for us to choose from. "You come at a good time. Once the bars close, we are slammed." I smile at his American vernacular, spoken in a thick Egyptian accent. "Why do you laugh?" Karim asks.

"I'm not laughing," I protest. "You're great. I'll take the mango."

"Apple," Seve says. And Karim hurries away. The wind begins to pick up and blows strongly through the trees outside. Then we hear distant thunder. "A place like this would absolutely not have been possible here twenty years ago," he says.

Once we are puffing away at our hookahs, Seve leans back and closes his eyes. We smoke in contented silence for a while. The whipping wind is blowing in on us now, moving the hot air, and the thunder is closer. And then, as if we were in midconversation, Seve speaks again. "I assume her parents are very excited." Seve spent Christmas in Dublin with us a few years ago and D's parents, particularly her mother, fell for his charm.

"Oh, yeah."

"So I know you're not exactly sure who's coming yet," he says gingerly, "but how's the wedding shaping up? All set?"

THE LONGEST WAY HOME

"Nothing's set."

"What do you mean?"

"Yeah, just that, what I said."

"Oh, well. I'm sure it'll be an amazing day."

"Nothing is decided. There are a bunch of ideas, including a *ceili*, but nothing is decided."

"Irish dancing? Great."

"Well, if it happens, it'll all be done the day before."

Perhaps it's the result of running their own hotel for so long, but D's family operates in crisis-management mode as normal procedure. It is something they have passed down to their daughter. D's ability to create last-minute magic out of chaos is as impressive as it is maddening.

"I'm just glad it's in Ireland. I'm just going to show up," I say.

Seve moves from treading lightly to his usual more matter-of-fact tone. "Dude, you never just show up." He means I always have a lot to say about what happens in my own life and how it happens. Then Seve looks at me for a minute, puffing away on his hookah pipe.

"What?" I ask.

"Let me tell you something, my friend." He blows a big puff of apple-scented smoke and continues very slowly. "The best thing that you could do is show up."

And Seve has put his finger on it.

Once again, he has tapped into something bigger than the mere topic at hand. My hesitation. My remaining ambivalence. It all centers around this. Can I show up? Not literally—of course I'll be there, on the appropriate date. That is not the issue and never has been. But can I bring all of myself to this marriage? Am I strong enough to be the kind of person that I know I want to be, the kind of man I've felt myself to be at certain moments—when self-interest is left behind for investment in others, when responsibility usurps blame, and humor diffuses tension, instead of fearful ego asserting itself for dominance? Am I willing to live in a generous way? Can I be patient with my kids, encouraging them to go out into the world but ensuring their backs are covered, so they have the security and confidence to reach for big things, knowing that someone is there to catch them if they fall short? Am I willing to be interested?

Isn't that what marriage is, a commitment to become the best version of ourselves, a pledge to continually grow toward that ideal, on a daily basis? And then recommitting again when I fail, owning that failure, yet not living in it, but moving through it and stepping farther into partnership. That's what I've been afraid of all these years, that level of investment. Suddenly there is a loud crack of thunder, and then it's pouring. The rain is bouncing off the hood of the pickup truck outside and we watch people running back and forth on the sidewalk, scurrying for cover. The pressure that has been building all day is suddenly and mercifully released. The temperature drops noticeably and the air has a welcome coolness as the clouds free their burden. Just show up. Be the best version of myself every day for the rest of my life. That's what I'm committing to. Easy.

CHAPTER SEVEN

KILIMANJARO

"What Do You Say We Get the Hell Off This Rock?"

A very quick scan of the Internet reveals hundreds of mountain-climbing quotes, many heavy with metaphor. From the likes of Sir Edmund Hillary, the first man to reach the summit of Mount Everest ("It is not the mountain we conquer, but ourselves") to German philosopher Friedrich Nietzsche ("On the mountains of truth you can never climb in vain") and even Theodor Geisel—a.k.a. Dr. Seuss ("Today is your day! Your mountain is waiting. So . . . get on your way"), scaling a mountain has always been synonymous with man's struggle and need to overcome obstacles, both physical and emotional.

My own struggle in coming to terms with this marriage has been long, my progress often elusive, traveling two steps forward, only to fall one step back—sometimes more. As Seve so astutely pointed out, I need to be able to "show up." Yet there is a lingering doubt—one I wouldn't even discuss with him—a doubt that's easy to deflect and blame on circumstances, or a partner, or on work, a doubt that looks for blame anywhere but where it belongs. This insistent nagging is telling me I lack the internal strength required to make marriage work. Perhaps it's the failure of my first marriage, and my inability to be fully present in it, that still hangs over me. Perhaps this doubt in my own strength stems from having too close a relationship with my mother when I was very young, or from being physically small for my age as a boy, or because I was late to enter puberty, or maybe the sensitivity I traded on in Hollywood somehow stunted me, or not knowing how to change the oil in a car engine—whatever the reason, it's here, and it lingers, and I need to get over it.

While climbing a mountain may not solve all my issues, there is no denying that it takes a certain strength, both physical and mental, to get to the top. And I need to test myself, to prove myself; I need an achievement I can point to, something that reflects my abilities and willingness to persevere. I need something I can hold on to as I move forward toward the big day and beyond.

While Mount Kilimanjaro, at 19,336 feet, is no Everest, it is still the highest mountain in Africa. My pack is by the door; I'll leave in the morning.

When D and I come home after dinner, my mother, who has been babysitting, walks in from the living room. She's been watching the news.

"You know, there are thousands of refugees fleeing Libya and flooding into Tanzania. It's very unstable," she says. Then she drives her point home. "If you die, your children's life will never be the same."

"Actually, Mom, it's Tunisia they're flooding into, not Tanzania. But thanks for your concern, that's very helpful. Come on, let me get you a cab. Do you have a coat?"

"No, it's a hundred degrees. I don't have a coat. And why is your air conditioner blowing hot air?"

When I return from putting my mother in a taxi, D is in the kitchen. The sight of my waiting backpack, coupled with my mother's remarks, has triggered her anxiety. She's a different person than she was just a few minutes ago.

"You're always coming and going, leaving and coming, you have no time to love me," she blurts out. "We can't even get more than an hour. We never spend any real time together." We have just returned from a long, romantic dinner, after having spent the afternoon together.

"Well it doesn't seem as if you like me that much, that you'd even want to spend time with me anyway," I say, trying to tease out a smile and counter this sudden mood shift.

"True," she replies without a trace of a grin. And now the tears come.

We go back and forth and eventually I promise not to fall off the mountain and die. Like she always does, D responds instantly when I am able to pinpoint the fear that has been motivating her reactions, and her mood softens.

"And when I get back, we have to get our rings," I remind her.

"I don't think so, luv."

"What?"

"Yeah, I don't think so." And she's back in charge of herself.

"No rings?"

"I don't really want to wear one; you don't want to wear a ring, do you? Although you'd look good in a ring."

"Oh, well, okay, no rings. That was easy."

"I was thinking we should tie the knot," she says.

"What knot?"

"The old pagan tradition. That's where the saying comes from. Our hands are tied together and then something happens, a blessing or something, I don't remember what."

"Sure, sounds good. We'll tie the knot," I say in agreement. "We need to figure out how we do it."

"Yeah, yeah." D dismisses my practical concern. She's already on to the next topic. "Should we have some music?"

"Yeah, that would be helpful, I guess."

"Not 'Yeah, that would be helpful,' like it's some chore. We're talking about our wedding. Where's the romance?"

"That's what I mean. Music will be good."

"Uilleann pipes?"

"Really?"

"Yeah, they're beautiful."

"Aren't they kind of shrill? Do you know someone who plays them?"

"I do. Although he's a liar and a cheater," D says.

"Not one of your exes?"

"No, not one of my exes. And my brother's going to roast a lamb on a spit."

"He is?"

"Yeah."

"He's going to dig a hole in the park and roast a lamb on a spit?" I ask.

"He's not, but he's going to get someone to do it."

"Do we need an extra permit for that?"

"We don't have a permit."

"We don't have a permit to get married in the park? What if they kick us out?"

"They're not going to kick us out, they won't even know we're there."

"There are going to be a few hundred people."

"You're right, maybe we should have a second lamb. He was going do a pig, but I'm not having pig at my wedding."

"I thought everyone was just going to bring a picnic," I remind her. "We weren't going to feed them, remember?"

She continues, ignoring me. "I don't know what the vegetarians are going to do."

I open the refrigerator and swig some grapefruit juice. "Maybe I will fall off the mountain after all," I say.

"Look, you shouldn't even be going, not with your knee. What are you going to do if it gives out halfway up? Are they going to send a helicopter?"

"Don't laugh, I think Martina Navratilova recently had to be carried off Kilimanjaro."

"She's in very good shape," D warns.

"I know."

"Seriously, luv. You've been hobbling around for six months. And how are you going to dance at our wedding? Because you *are* dancing at our wedding."

I ignore this second threat and concentrate on the first. "It's Kilimanjaro, not K2. I'll be fine."

But I have no idea if I'll be fine. The thought of not making it to the top occupies a prominent place in my mind with every hobbling step I take. I tore my knee up over the winter while skiing—or rather, falling. I should have gone to an orthopedist right away, had the surgery, and been done. I didn't. Instead I went to an osteopath, who had helped other injuries I'd had over the years. He made great progress with my knee over several months but admitted finally, "There's no doubt you tore the meniscus, it's just a matter of how little healing can you live with." The knee is better, to a large degree; it's just not the same as it was. And it's not trustworthy.

"But it's very interesting," my osteopath said, "that you hurt your left knee as you were about to get married. There are some people who would associate the knees with ego and commitment and relationships."

"What are you trying to say, that I don't have the flexibility and strength for the relationship?"

"I'm just pointing out the correlation, what some people say. It's for you to decide what it means."

Since my skiing accident, I've hiked over the tundra in Patagonia and through the jungle of Costa Rica without incident, but there is no way of knowing when my knee will go. Just a few weeks ago, in Baltimore with Seve, I stepped off a curb and heard a pop that set my healing progress back a few months. When he saw me limp down a steep incline, Seve asked, "What the hell happened to you? I've never seen you move like that. If you were a horse I'd shoot you."

"Headaches are normal. So are gas, diarrhea, and nausea. Vomiting is common. And pulmonary edema can happen very quickly. The fluid can build up in your lungs and in twenty minutes, if you don't descend, you could be dead." The man telling me and five others this in a garden, under an African tulip tree at a hotel outside Arusha in Tanzania, is the one responsible for getting us to the top of Kilimanjaro and back down in one piece. His name is Zadock Mosha, and he's thirty-three, with chocolate-brown skin and a round, shaved head. A member of the Chagga tribe, he grew up in the shadow of the "white mountain" and has been to its summit 161 times. So I guess he knows what he's talking about.

Still, I think he's overselling the danger. After all, thousands have gotten to the top of Kilimanjaro. I've always possessed a silent confidence in my physical agility that isn't immediately obvious—I often adopt the position that I don't really know how to do anything physically strenuous, only to step into whatever it is, from stunt fighting in movies to white-water kayaking, and manage fairly easily. But this knee worries me. And Zadock isn't helping. His attitude is off-handed—almost hostile. He regards us with slight contempt as he pulls out what will become the bane of my hike up the mountain—his pulse oximeter, which measures pulse and oxygen-saturation levels in the blood.

"You want your blood oxygen level over ninety and your pulse below it," Zadock tells us, and then he tosses me the small black contraption that clips onto the end of a finger. "Let's just get a baseline on everyone."

My blood oxygen level is ninety-five and my pulse is sixty-four. I announce my numbers to Zadock with detached casualness and pass the meter to the lone woman in our group, a neurosurgeon from India who now lives in Virginia. She's in her mid to late thirties and has an open, fleshy face with a mole on her cheek and long black hair. Her name is Eila. She sits quietly and is motionless until Zadock removes the device from her finger and tosses it to the youngest member of our group, a soft-bodied, chatty college student named Tim, who is here through the largesse of a wealthy uncle. Then Roberto and Bob, a father-and-son team from Puerto Rico, each clip the pulse oximeter on for a minute. Finally, a hard-toned mortgage broker and Ironman triathlete named Hank knocks out a number right at a hundred and flips the oximeter back to our leader.

Zadock shows us our route up the mountain on a tourist map, but the red line on the paper means nothing to me. All the map really shows is that Kilimanjaro sits in north central Tanzania, not far from the border with Kenya. A visit—if not an attempt at the summit—is often included in itineraries to some of Tanzania's other "greatest hits," like the Serengeti or the Ngorongoro Crater. I first became aware of Kilimanjaro when I was a child. My oldest brother brought home a book from school, Hemingway's famous *The Snows of Kili-*

manjaro. On the cover was a painting of the famous, snowcapped conical mountain.

"Where's that?" I asked my brother.

"Africa," he told me.

"I'm going to go there," I declared. I don't know why I said it, and I don't remember what my brother said in reply, but the idea stuck. Over the years, whenever I heard Kilimanjaro mentioned, I knew that one day I would go—this is a date I've had with myself since I was ten.

When the meeting breaks up, the itinerary says we're to have a welcome dinner, but when no one mentions it, I slip off to the dining room at the hotel and eat alone.

While I'm finishing up, Eila comes in and sits across from me.

I ask if she found Zadock's talk of all the potential dangers stressful.

"'Stress.' 'Depression.' I don't understand these terms. I never heard them till I came to America. I don't believe in them. Then you people take pills for it. You're stressed about something, but why, what are you feeling? If you're upset about something, do something about it. You people take pills for everything."

What Eila says makes good sense, and I agree with her, but something in the way she says it is disquieting. She pours her tea and looks off dreamily. There's a strange detachment to both her words and actions. Her lack of investment in what she's saying makes me question her conviction, and her vague physicality makes me wonder if perhaps she's not heavily medicated herself. I drink my tea.

"Do you do a lot of hiking?" I ask.

"One day before."

"One day?"

"I was in Patagonia—in Chile—at a conference and I went hiking for a day. I liked it, so I came here next." I'm glad she's not operating on my brain.

The father-and-son team from Puerto Rico comes into the dining room. Roberto, an estate lawyer with rounded shoulders and a heavy walk, is close to sixty; his son, Bob, in his late twenties, works at a hedge fund in New York. He looks like his father must have before thirty extra years of life burdened him. They wave as they take seats in the corner and talk softly between themselves.

In the middle of the night, jet lag wakes me and I call D. When she answers, she is surrounded by so much noise I can hardly hear her.

"I'm at Dean's birthday, in Brooklyn. I'm totally in the wrong outfit," she shouts into the phone. "I should have borrowed one of your checked shirts and be wearing big disc earrings. But who knew?" She sounds happy, carefree. "And you, my love, I'm sure you're probably dealing with something very similar in the heart of Africa."

"Just talking brain hemorrhages and blisters."

"See? I knew it."

I tell her that Zadock said I should have cell service all the way up the mountain, so we'll talk soon.

"Really? You'll have cell service on Kilimanjaro? That's weird."

The next morning I have an e-mail from D suggesting we move to Williamsburg. "You'll fit right in. You can wear plaid 24/7."

🚶

We've been driving for over an hour and I'm in a jet-lagged daze, staring out the window. Tall men swing long machetes in high grass. Women stride along the side of the road carrying containers of water or baskets on their heads. Occasionally someone pedals by on a rusting bicycle, hauling charcoal.

Tim, the college student, has been pestering Zadock with questions, about people we see, trees, and weather cycles. Eila is listening to music on her headphones. Hank, the triathlete, is bouncing his knee up and down, while Bob and Roberto occasionally whisper to each other. The midmorning African light is bright but hazy. We come out of a bend in the road and suddenly there are murmurs from the front of the van.

"There it is," I hear Tim say.

To my right, through the glare I see a sprawling expanse, covering much of the horizon. The iconic flattop, snowcapped summit is lost in the clouds. The sight is impressive, but not the awe-inspiring vista I have long imagined. Then something far above the clouds shimmers and catches my eye.

My focus shifts and perspective alters. The upper outline of the mountain comes clear—twice as high as I first perceived it to be. The glimmer I had seen was the sun reflecting off the dwindling glaciers at the summit, towering far above the clouds that hug the mountain's midsection.

"Holy shit," I whisper.

It's a monster.

We drive on and turn onto a hard-packed dirt road where long yellow grass yields to a field of sunflowers. In the distance, across a vast expanse, a group of women in brightly colored clothes with long flowing skirts carry heavy loads. Where they are coming from or how far they're going in this open savanna is impossible to say. We pass a truck loaded high with men clinging to the sides, sitting on top of the cabin, hanging off the back—thirty or forty of them holding on. In a field of corn a cart is piled high and a sagging beast of burden strains under a wooden yoke. Farther on, a tall man in a light blue shirt strides toward the road between rows in a well-ordered field, munching on a carrot. We pass into a forest of pine and then cypress. This land is not the parched and dusty Africa, it is a lush and generous earth created by Kilimanjaro, big enough and

tall enough to form its own ecosystem, catching the rain and fertil-
izing rich soil.

The road narrows and then we're in a trench so deep, the sides of
the van are scraped by the thicket. We bounce through potholes and
crevasses. There is nowhere to turn and as the road gets worse, we
can only continue on. Around a bend a jeep comes in the other direction. The two vehicles pull forward and stop inches apart, headlamp
to headlamp. The driver of the jeep gets out and climbs over the hood
of his car to our driver's window. The two exchange words in Swahili.
Voices are raised. The other driver returns to his jeep and shuts off
his engine. We sit.

I'm reminded once again of Dr. Seuss and a story I often read
to my children. Two Zax, one walking north, one walking south,
encounter each other neither one yields. Ever. Highways and towns
are built up around them as they remain stubbornly entrenched and
life passes them by.

Eventually, Zadock gets out and goes to negotiate. Quickly, he and
the other driver are shouting. Fingers are pointed, first down the road
and then at each other. Zadock stomps back to our van and pokes his
head through the window.

"We're walking," he says.

We all pile out into the thicket, scratching our arms and legs. As
we hoist up our backpacks, suddenly the jeep in front of us starts up
and reverses back around the bend. We pile back into our van. Fifty
feet beyond the curve, the other jeep is parked off to the side at an
easy pull out. Laughter and happy waves are exchanged between the
vehicles and we bounce past.

I knew I wasn't going to have a solitary man-vs.-mountain experience, but I'm in no way prepared for the scene at the trailhead. Fifty
porters are packing our gear and tents and scrambling to assemble
our provisions—to support six hikers. In addition, there are three

other parties of equal size setting out at the same time. A not insubstantial village is mobilizing toward nineteen thousand feet.

"We're going *poli-poli*—slowly-slowly," Zadock says. "Stay in my tracks." We set out and Bob falls in tight behind Zadock, Tim is next, then Roberto, Hank, Eila, and I bring up the rear. The pace is excruciatingly slow, a quarter my usual walking speed, and I find it impossible to find a rhythm. On the trail, porters wearing flip-flops and torn shorts, each lugging forty pounds of gear on his back or head, hurry past us in our hiking boots and polypro tops, carrying only small daypacks.

"It will take us four to six hours to get to the first camp," Zadock tells us. Tim is asking Zadock the meaning of various words in Swahili and the names of plants. Hank quickly nicknames him "Timmy-pedia." We climb through a forest of African rose and holly and brittle wood. Eila drops back and I close in behind Hank, who is very much the young hotshot. He asks Bob where he went to school.

"Harvard?" Bob answers, his voice rising to a question at the end of the word. It's the first he has spoken to anyone other than his father all day.

"Harvard," Hank says, "where's that?"

Bob begins to answer.

"Joke, Bob. That was a joke." Hank looks back at me and rolls his eyes.

After less than three hours we arrive at a level area swarming with tents under yellowwood trees. Day one of six on our way to the summit has been a simple stroll through the forest with a thousand-foot elevation gain. Our individual tents are already set up and we assemble for dinner. Zadock passes around the pulse oximeter, then he begins what will become a nightly ritual—telling us all the things that can go wrong and all the people who have failed in their attempt to reach the summit.

Before I climb into my tent I try to call D but have no cell reception. That night I dream that D and I get married, to each other, but on different days in separate ceremonies in different locations. The sensation during the dream is pleasant and makes complete sense while it is happening.

🚶

By midmorning on the second day we're climbing through a forest of dense and gnarled trees covered in thick strands of hanging moss. The sun dapples through the trees, and the silver-gray moss takes on a bluish tinge. We stop for a rest on a fallen stump. Timmy-pedia has been bombarding Zadock on what kind of people make the trek to the top—who has the best success rate and who has the worst. Zadock laments taking honeymooners up Kilimanjaro.

"Do you get a lot of people on their honeymoon?" I ask. It seems a strange choice for newlyweds.

"Too many," he replies. "And it's always a problem. They don't listen. The men think it's just walking and always try to take care of the women and ignore their own problems, and the women want to listen to the men and then the guys are always the ones who get in trouble. Always. And then the women don't know what to do about that, because often they're able to get to the top and their husbands can't and it's a problem. We try to keep them separated on the trail."

I try to consider what this metaphor might mean for my own life and settle for knowing that D would never want to climb Kilimanjaro anyway.

Zadock continues. "Old women are the best to guide. They listen, they go slow, and they nearly always make it to the top. I had an eighty-two-year-old last year. She was great."

At just below ten thousand feet we crest a rise, break out of the forest, and drop into one of the three calderas that make up the mountain, entering into what is called the heather zone. Low scrub for as far as we can see. Around a bend in the trail we get our first full view of the iconic conical and glacier-clad flattop peak—although the last few decades have seen nearly 90 percent of the snow vanish. The mountain looks strangely bare.

Our pace is still painfully slow. The younger guys in the group can't slow down, so they're forced to stop every few strides for a beat before marching a few more steps and then stop again. I hang back and begin to count my steps in a rhythm of four. One-two-three-four. Left-right-left-right. Then again. One-two-three-four. Left-right-left-right. And again. My breathing slows. Then I'm playing a game with myself, keeping score, trying to lift my foot only enough off the ground to move it in front of me, and then the next. When I scuff the dirt I lose points. A long time passes in this way as we walk through waist-high heather. At close to eleven thousand feet, the air has a coolness just beneath the sun's efforts.

Eila begins to lag behind and when we get into camp I hear her complaining to Zadock about the distances we have to walk.

"What the hell did she think this was?" Hank says as we settle into the dinner tent. I resist telling him about her one previous day of hiking experience.

They stuff us with pasta again and Zadock launches into his nightly harrowing tales of people who died trying to summit, and then he passes around his torture device—the pulse oximeter. Immediately Timmy-pedia closes his eyes and begins a type of late-stage Lamaze breathing. His blood oxygen level has been low and Zadock has warned that anyone who cannot maintain a level of at least ninety will not be allowed to attempt the summit.

My blood oxygen is ninety-three and I toss the device back to

Zadock. I have begun to resent this testing, the way I resent anyone having power over me. Eila's rate is in the low eighties and her pulse is high. Zadock makes her breathe deeply until she gets her number up. The stress that she doesn't believe in has begun to show on her face. Roberto's chin has sunk to his chest, like it does each night at dinner. I gently nudge his arm and rouse him awake to clip the device on his finger.

"I hate this thing, Andy," he whispers to me. I generally don't like it when people call me Andy, but there's something in Roberto that is so benign and his attempt to reach the summit feels so fragile that I don't want to set him back in any way by challenging him.

Hank never has any issues with the pulse oximeter. He knocks out a number in the high nineties consistently and as he lofts the monitor across the tent to Bob—who has been quietly breathing with his hands placed on his knees, eyes closed—Hank tells us how the American people should be grateful to his company because they have paid back the government's loan with 50 percent interest. They were, in fact, the good guys in the financial crisis.

Though I've come to like him—Hank reminds me of the uncomplicated, athletics-based male friendships I have drifted away from and would be well served to rekindle—I'm infuriated by his hubris.

"You're still the devil, though. You know that, right?" I tell him.

"Oh, yeah." He shrugs.

I wake up in the middle of the night—I've stopped breathing. A disturbance to the rhythm of oxygen and carbon dioxide entering and exiting the blood that occurs at this altitude can cause breathing to temporarily cease. It's a harmless occurrence but the first time it happens it's an odd sensation. I lie awake, and anxious thoughts fill my oxygen-challenged brain.

I wonder if my knee will hold out. I wonder if my son's recent difficulty at school is symptomatic of a larger problem. I wonder if my father will die soon. And I wonder if I really am at peace with him, or at least as much as I can be, before he passes. After all my fear of his anger in my youth, and the resentment, and the judgment and disapproval of him in my twenties, and the subsequent dissolution of our relationship, and then the amicable distance that now defines it, what remains—in the middle of the night in my tent on the side of Kilimanjaro—is simply a feeling of disappointment and one of waste.

Because of both my desire for independence and my natural tendencies toward separation, more than most people I know, I would have benefited from the wisdom of a mentor. Since I have allowed myself little access to any kind of group consciousness, or the benefit of its shared experience, a single trusted person who had come before would have been ideal for me and might have saved me a great deal of trouble along the way—someone to offer up occasional insights or act as a fallback when I needed respite. In my few experiences with some form of limited mentorship, I have felt relief from a void that has long yearned to be filled. Perhaps it is one of the reasons I often seek the "bodyguards" D talks about. The self-reliance that was born of my lack of camaraderie has created a justification for a solitary way of living that is not useful in partnership. It is what D has most struggled with over the years; "I'm right here, I need you to come to me," she's often said. It has taken me a long time to even understand what she means by that.

If I can offer mentorship to my children, so they feel its presence and avail themselves of it if they wish to, I will consider myself a success as a parent.

I unzip my tent and go out to stare up at the hulking black mass of Kilimanjaro's peak, the nearly full moon shining down on the glaciers, and my thoughts are brought back to the present and the task ahead. There is something in the challenge—no matter how difficult it might be to reach the summit—that is a relief in its simplicity. The night is cold. I shiver and hurry back in, but as I zipper into my sleeping bag my anxious thoughts return.

I wonder what would happen if D were unfaithful to me. I try to shake the image from my mind and pick up my book. Unimaginatively, I have brought along Hemingway's collection of stories *The Snows of Kilimanjaro*—the book that first inspired this trip, so many years ago. I open it to a tale called "The Short Happy Life of Francis Macomber." In it, a wife is cheating on her ineffectual husband with their game-hunter guide while on safari. When the husband discovers her infidelity, she mocks him and he withers. Then, in the course of a hunt, he steps into his manhood, and when the wife sees this she knows that her husband will leave her. In a moment of panic she shoots and kills her husband, perhaps accidentally.

I should have brought a different book.

𐀠

We set out across moorland scattered with volcanic rock that yields to an alpine-like desert. We're working our way east to west around the mountain, slowly gaining some of the twelve thousand feet we'll climb while covering a little more than forty-two miles in the six days to the summit. My legs feel heavy today. To distract my weary mind, I play a game with Hank. We pick a spot in the far distance over the lunar-like landscape and guess how long it will take us to reach it. At first our estimates are hugely exaggerated. What we suspect will take us two hours ends up taking twenty minutes—but soon we're judging distances within a minute or two. Porters hurry past us in an endless stream, their loads on their heads or shoulders.

"How come some of the porters carry stuff on their heads and some don't?" Timmy-pedia asks Zadock.

"It depends where they grew up," Zadock tells him. "How far they were from the water source. Kids who grew up in the city didn't need to carry water so they use their shoulders to carry things, but if you lived in a village you were maybe a long way from water. It's the women who fetch the water, and the little kids are always chasing behind their mothers and want to carry water too."

"How much do they carry?" Timmy-pedia presses.

"When you're about five you can carry a three-liter can on your head, then at ten you can carry ten liters, and then at twelve, twenty liters. Then you are a teenager and don't want to do it anymore."

We camp above thirteen thousand feet. I still have no cell service on my phone. Timmy-pedia has a satellite messaging device that allows single letters to be scrolled and typed from a center joystick. At the dinner table it takes me twenty minutes to scroll and type a few words to D—"no cell service. halfway up mountain. knee is holding. X."

"God," Hank says from across the table, "I'm trying to think who I'd even e-mail. My father maybe."

I look over at him and am brought up short. Trying to carve out space for myself, often traveling to the ends of the earth to achieve it, wishing I had no responsibility, yearning for total freedom, and here is someone with just that, unattached, with endless space surrounding him, and my feeling isn't one of envy or even wistfulness. I don't yearn for what he doesn't have—and the realization shocks me.

Outside the mess tent, fog has shrouded our campsite.

The Lava Tower sits at just over fifteen thousand feet. It's a large out-crop jutting three hundred and fifty feet up into the sky, and we can see it from far off across the relentlessly rocky trail. Hank and I both judge it to be forty minutes away—it takes us nearly an hour and a half. By the time we arrive I have a ferocious headache. It is my first serious effect of the altitude. It feels as if a metal band has been placed around my skull beneath the skin at my temples and is being ratch-eted tighter and tighter. I try to breathe, slowly and deeply. I can feel my heart racing while I'm at rest. My chest is very, very tight. Panic rises. This is only fifteen thousand feet; the summit is at nearly twenty. The stagnant air inside our red mess tent makes me nauseous and I can't eat the zucchini soup on offer. Then Zadock goes to retrieve his pulse oximeter, and while he's gone, I lose it.

"This is bullshit. This is a total misuse of technology. This constant testing and judging. It's totally screwed up. All it does is add stress and pressure and ruins the trip. It doesn't prove anything. I'm not fucking doing it anymore."

My rant wakes Roberto. His chin rises from his chest and he looks at me with weary eyes from under his Yankees baseball cap.

"Why would you let this stress you?" the Indian neurosurgeon asks softly.

The others stare at their soup. Zadock returns and tosses the meter to Timmy-pedia, who doesn't see it because his eyes are closed and his heavy breathing indicates that he is in the late stages of giving birth. The contraption falls to the ground and I storm out of the tent.

Once we drop off the ridge after lunch my headache quickly vanishes. Clouds hang low and engulf us; we can't see more than a few feet in any direction as we walk. A stream rolls down to our left and supports life like we haven't seen in a few days. Strange cactus-palm-like plants jut up, small yellow flowers clustered at their trunks. We have come farther around to the south side of the mountain and the snow above us is thicker now. We camp below a high cliff and the next day Zadock issues a new walking order. Eila will go first, behind him. Roberto will be second, "and then the rest of you," he explains.

There is one tense moment beside a precarious drop on the Great Barranco Wall and then the landscape opens out into the strangely soothing desolate expanse of the Western Breach. The air now is thin and cool under the bright sun. There is a feeling of gathering expectation as several of the trails up the mountain converge and the path becomes more crowded. I have strength in my legs today and my eyes keep lifting to the summit directly above us. I'm relaxed in a way I haven't been until now. My thoughts are light, and the day feels full of possibility. There is a lot of banter on the trail, even as Eila falls back.

At one point I hear a porter up ahead shout. He's listening to a radio and for an instant I fear he's heard news of a tragedy coming over the airwaves. Images of a disaster like September 11 flash into my mind. The first moment of real relaxation I experience on the hike has left me open for panic to come flooding in. It turns out the porter was simply shouting to his friend farther down on the trail. Perhaps D is right when she says that I'm just not comfortable when things are too good.

Farther on, Hank blows his nose and blood begins to rush out. At the high altitude and with the blood-thinning Diamox that he's taking to prevent altitude sickness, the flow is not easy to quell. We stop and sit beside mounds of shirred rock next to a dozen porters on a break, all smoking.

"Do many porters smoke?" Timmy-pedia asks.

"I'd say about seventy-five percent," Zadock answers.

Once the Ironman's nose stops bleeding and he reties his Merrell boots, the porters squish their cigarette butts under their flip-flops and we all march on.

Roberto drops back and I slow to walk with him. His head is hanging low, his eyes on his shoes.

"You okay, Roberto?"

"I'm tired, Andy," he says.

"We're almost there, just up on that ridge ahead."

Roberto lifts his head, registers the distance to where the tents are visible, then drops his chin again.

"Whose idea was it to do this, yours or Bob's?" I ask, hoping to distract him.

"His." Roberto lifts his head toward his son before dropping it again.

We say very little, and once our movement stops each day, there is an awkwardness to our silence, yet I enjoy his company—my affection for him is an unexpected pleasure.

When we arrive at camp, the tents are up, crowded along an uneven, rocky ledge. The last four-thousand-foot push to the summit will begin here before dawn. The clouds below clear and Mount Meru, Kilimanjaro's "sister" mountain, is visible; farther off is Mount Longido and the flat top of Kitumbeine. To the west, the active volcano Ol Doinyo Lengai rises from the Great Rift Valley. I can see far into Kenya to the north.

Timmy-pedia finds me. "You have an e-mail."

I take his satellite device. D has replied to my e-mail of the other day. "I can feel you from here, big style."

𝅏

I have a friend who climbed Kilimanjaro once and described it as "several pleasant days of walking uphill, followed by one day of hell." Other than the looming question of whether the summit will be achieved, the hike to this point has been a fine amble in an exotic locale—altitude sickness and my wobbly knee being the only question marks. My knee is holding up, although with every step I take I am careful not to twist in midstride but keep it pivoting forward and back in a straight and clean arc. If someone calls me or I want to look off toward a far peak to my left, I stop and turn my entire body. It is a level of vigilance that wears on my mind and creates constant low-level stress—whatever Eila might say. As for altitude sickness, it seems that apart from taking Diamox, there is nothing else to do but take the time to acclimatize on the way up. Physical condition appears to have little or no relationship to how altitude affects you, and apart from my panic at Lava Tower, I have been largely spared.

But everything up to now has been merely getting to the starting line.

A light shines through my tent at three A.M. "It's time," Zadock says.

He didn't need to wake me. I've been staring at my watch every twenty minutes since twelve thirty, when I went out to look up at the summit under the bright moon, one day on the wane and reflecting light off the glaciers above.

I'm happy to get out of my summer-weight sleeping bag. At 15,091 feet, I slept cold during the little sleep I did get. We straggle into the mess tent and are presented with yet another bowl of runny porridge. I choke down a piece of stale white bread with peanut butter and go put on another layer of clothing. At four fifteen we organize at the trailhead. I can see a thin, speckled trail of the headlamps of hikers who left before us, dotting a curving line, like glowing gnats.

"The first hour is the most difficult," Zadock explains. "There is a lot of tight, steep scrambling over jagged rock. Eila, you're behind me, Roberto, you're next. Let's go."

There is no sound except our breathing and boots hitting, scuffing, scraping the rocks as we climb. My headlamp shines down on Hank's heels in front of me. I need to use my hands on the cold stone to pull myself up in a few steep sections. In some places footholds have been worn into the stone. We need to squeeze into the face of a rock wall as we inch past a man on his way back down from his aborted attempt, doubled over and vomiting, the altitude having gotten the best of him.

Eila's pace is even slower than the one that Zadock has set. Behind her, every few steps we stop, wait, and then start again. I begin to get angry at this herky-jerky progress. Then I'm nauseous. For a second time on the trip, panic rises. My anger swells. My fear-induced rage won't help me, and I let Hank get several strides in front of me and slow my already crawling pace further so I can keep a consistent speed.

I begin to count my strides again, one-two-three-four, one-two-three-four, one-two-three-four. My anger begins to soften and my nausea abates. I gather myself and keep climbing.

We reach a level plateau where the trail opens out and then the incline begins again over loose rock that slides underfoot. We pass several more people being led back down in the dark—the altitude or the steep grade too much for them.

For another hour we climb in silence. Again I feel nausea coming on but quickly breathe through it. Then off to our right the horizon begins to soften, first to violet, then pink, and then a thin blue. And the sun is up and we're taking photos, laughing, swilling water. Zadock hands out chocolate. I take a seat on a large volcanic rock and eat a Three Musketeers bar. I'm reminded of a camping trip I took my son on to the Catskills. For breakfast he ate sardines and M&M's—he still describes it as his favorite meal.

I peel off a layer of clothing and we continue up. We break single-file formation and fan out. Our long shadows spread across the rocky terrain, bathed in a golden early light. Soon Eila has fallen behind; two porters flank her. Zadock looks back every few strides. When I turn, Eila is sitting on a rock far below us, staring off into the distance, her hands on her knees.

Zadock whispers over the walkie-talkie to the porters with her. He nods at something he hears in return. "Okay," he says.

Eila will climb no farther. For days we had all doubted whether she would make it, but no one mentioned it aloud, not wanting to jinx their own attempts.

There's greater confidence in the group now, and we climb on. I peel off another layer of clothing. There is playfully boasting conversation, then talk of the receding glaciers we walk beside, and then suddenly Roberto is struggling; his movements are heavy. He leans hard into his walking poles with each step. His son whispers encouragement, and Roberto nods. After another hour we can feel we're close. Just above, the sky becomes vast. We reach Stella Point, on the rim of the crater, nineteen thousand feet above sea level. It's as if the mountaintop has been waiting for us all this time, wondering where we were. The air here is cold and hard under a cloudless sky. A natural bench is carved into the side of the rim, and several porters are sitting, smoking, laughing. Roberto falls onto the bench as porters make room. The receding glaciers are scattered on the caldera floor before us.

Bob is digging for something in his pack when his father tries to get up. I'm closer so I lean down and grab Roberto's arm to pull him to his feet. "Push me, Andy," he murmurs, "help me get there." He says this with such unguarded vulnerability that tears burn into my eyes.

"We'll make it, Roberto," I say. "We're there now."

We set out and the trail from here is a gentle amble, sweeping around and up another forty minutes toward the top. The Decken and Kersten glaciers are off to our left. Ahead, a wooden sign is silhouetted again the sun—Uhuru Peak, the top of one of the world's Seven Summits.

Before Zadock implemented a different set order, Bob, Roberto's son, was always in first position behind Zadock since we first set out six days earlier. He's there again now. I slide up next to him from my usual position in the back.

"Bob," I whisper, "why don't you let your dad be the first to get to the top?"

Bob turns to me. He seems confused for an instant, then nods and calls out.

"Pop," he says, turning back toward his father. "Come on, lead us to the top."

Roberto lifts his eyes from his shoelaces and the beginning of a smile passes over his exhausted face. He gives it all he has left and marches to the front of the group. Zadock hangs back and Roberto strides the last fifty yards to the top, and he may as well be the first man ever to reach the summit of Kilimanjaro. He leans his weight against the post holding the sign welcoming us to the highest point in Africa, pumps his fist, and falls into his son's embrace.

Watching them, I miss my own father—and realize that I always have.

"O! The Joy!" I scroll into Timmy-pedia's satellite contraption and send the message to D. It's a quote from Captain William Clark's diary describing his feelings when he and his partner Meriwether Lewis and their Corps of Discovery laid eyes on the Pacific Ocean in 1805. I read it first years ago, and since, D and I have co-opted the phrase and made it our own, employing it more often than not in sarcasm— usually to capture the utter and constant joy of parenthood.

"How are the kids doing?" I've often asked over the phone from a distant shore.

"O! The Joy!" frequently comes as the weary reply, letting me know that the day has been long and selfless, filled with scattershot moments of resenting my absence, interspersed with a few laughs and ultimately enough good spirits to make it okay. But I send this message now with nothing but complete sincerity.

My unqualified joy is short-lived. After the hugs, and the photos, and taking in the vista, we slide down a steep slope of scree, four hundred feet to the floor of the crater. Here we are scheduled to camp, at 18,832 feet.

The crater is stark, desolate. After the thrill of the summit subsides, it is cold, even under the hanging sun.

"Most people have had enough by now," Zadock informs us, "and want to head back down."

My head has begun to feel the contraction and intense pressure again.

"How cold does it get at night?" Timmy-pedia asks.

"The second that sun drops, it is very, very cold," Zadock warns him.

"I got what I came for," Hank says.

"Let's get out of here," I agree.

"Good." Zadock nods.

We go to rehoist our packs.

"I want to stay," Timmy-pedia announces.

We all turn to him.

"The itinerary says we get to camp in the crater," he says insistently. "I want to stay."

We all look at Zadock. He shrugs. "It's in the trip description, and if someone wants to stay, and no one is injured . . ."

"Do people usually stay?" I ask.

"Only once."

"Can whoever wants to go back down to the camp below?" I ask.

"I'll go down, too," Hank says. "Bob? Roberto?"

Bob shrugs; Roberto has fallen asleep by a rock.

"There is no one to lead you down," Zadock says. "The others are with Eila."

We stand, slack-jawed.

"Lunch will be ready in a few minutes," Zadock says.

Inside the mess tent the air is stagnant; an artificial heat burns through the nylon. It is oppressive. Hank and I work on Timmy-pedia to try to change his mind. He sits, staring at his hands in his lap.

"You have no idea how cold it's going to get here, Tim. People die from exposure."

"That's okay, I want to camp in the crater," he retorts.

"We have warm clothes, but the porters are in T-shirts," Hank says.

"They do it all the time," Timmy-pedia says in protest.

"No." I correct him. "Everyone always goes back down. You heard Zadock." Nearly every year there are accounts of porters dying from exposure on Kilimanjaro.

"Well, I want to stay," he says.

My head is searing through with pain and anger. I step outside and walk off toward the glaciers that until a few years ago covered this land. The knifing in my skull abates only slightly in the fresh air. My fury grows.

When the sun goes below the rim of the volcano, it is noticeably colder, and when darkness falls the temperature plummets. I can't eat dinner for the pain in my head and my simmering anger. The joy of the morning is long gone.

I put on literally every piece of clothing I have, seven layers on top and three below, and climb into my summer-weight sleeping bag. I'm screaming at Timmy-pedia in my mind. My anger consumes me. I'm aware, even in the midst of my fury, that I'm trying to regain some of the power that was plucked from me the instant Timmy-pedia stamped his foot and dictated our movements. After the satisfying feeling of strength I experienced upon reaching the summit, the sting of emasculation and disempowerment cuts deep.

My anger is also a way of whistling in the dark, giving me a sense of control in a situation that is so completely beyond my ability to alter, namely, the caprice of nature.

Years ago, I participated in an outdoor education course in the Absaroka Mountains in northwest Wyoming because I wanted to learn to take care of myself in the wilderness: to read a topographical map and find my way, to be comfortable building a fire in the outdoors, to know how and where to pitch a tent.

We were twenty-six days into the month-long course when a student pressured a young girl on the course into doing something we had all advised them not to do. Instead of hiking a few hours to a safe crossing, this one student convinced the others to bend to his will and cross a raging river at the very spot we had warned against. The result was fatal, the young girl died. We spent several days and nights guarding her body from grizzly bears, until a helicopter could get in to take her out. Sitting beside the girl alongside the river, I remember thinking that the worst thing in the world that could have happened just happened, and yet everything went on: the water still raced past, the sky was still full of stars, everything was the same, even as it was now entirely different for us. A strange feeling of gratitude descended on me as I sat beside her body in the dark. I felt lucky to be there; I had never felt so distinctly alive. But I also knew that none of it was necessary. It should never have happened. Someone unfamiliar with the disinterested ways of nature had made an ill-informed, youthful decision. Timmy-pedia's choice at the frigid summit feels the same.

To soften my mind, I pick up my Hemingway book and read the title story, "The Snows of Kilimanjaro." In it, a man waits for a plane to rescue him as he lies dying from an infection in the African bush. He laments not using his talents to the fullest. As the end is near, he has a dream that the plane arrives and carries him up and over the snowcapped peak of Kilimanjaro to redemption. I feel no such redemption on the icy summit. I regret my anger and my inability, or unwillingness, to release it. I regret that I feel so strongly the need to be heard. Why is it that I need so much to be right? I regret my lack of compassion for someone I can identify with, namely Tim. I can understand his youthful desire to have this notch on his belt— yet my identification does nothing to diminish my fury.

My anger is not something to which I've always had easy access. Perhaps because I was familiar with the effects of rage growing up with a father who had a "short fuse," as my mother called it, I rarely lost my temper. A few years after I stopped drinking, all that changed, and my long-suppressed anger rose up and found voice. My temper has never ruled me the way my father's presided over him, but when I get angry at my children and see that look of shock on their faces, I imagine my own youthful image looking back at me and both curse myself and understand my father in equal measure.

🚶

Sleep is difficult to come by, and I wake every half hour through the night, always covered in goose bumps. Then I begin to shiver in earnest. When dawn is near and I reach for my water bottle, it is frozen solid.

At the mess tent, still shivering, I'm forcing down tepid porridge beside Hank, Bob, and Roberto when Timmy-pedia enters.

"Boy, two pairs of socks weren't enough last night, were they?" It takes all my strength not to turn the table over on him and pummel his face. Everyone gets up and exits the tent, leaving him alone.

It's the first morning the porters rush us to pack, and we're out.

"How cold was it last night?" Timmy-pedia asks as we walk, oblivious to everyone's rage and misery.

"Minus twenty-three degrees," Zadock barks over his shoulder.

"Fahrenheit or Celsius?" Timmy-pedia asks.

Zadock stops, turns, and for an instant I think he may actually punch him. "Celsius."

Within a half hour we are at Stella Point again. Without ceremony or a glance back, we drop off the ridge and then we're skidding, sliding, giant-stepping down the scree, peeling off layers of clothing as we go. Hank rockets far ahead. I struggle to stay close. Timmy-pedia tries to keep up and when he takes a tumble, no one goes to his aid. It takes us an hour to cover what took seven hours to climb and we're back at the lower camp. Eila is waiting, sheepish.

I slide up to Hank, who is untying his boots. "What do you say we get the hell off this rock?"

"What do you mean?"

"We've only got two or three more hours down to Mweka Camp, where we're sleeping tonight. Then it's only another three hours tomorrow and we're out."

He looks at me. Suddenly there is an urgency to get clear off the mountain we fought so hard to get up.

"Let's get out of here today," he says in agreement.

"That's what I was thinking."

We bring the idea to Zadock and he tells us that everyone in the party has to agree. They quickly do. We retie our boots and continue down. Instead of the gradual traverse around the mountain and incremental elevation gain that took us six days, we head directly down, through the dense montane forest. Six hours and twelve thousand feet later, my thighs are seizing up, both my knees are aching, and my toenails are coming off.

At the trailhead, the truck to take us back to Arusha is waiting. A bottle of champagne is opened and paper cups are filled on the hood. I toast with the others and hand my full cup back to Zadock.

"Do you not drink?"

"I've had my share," I say, and we load in and bounce over the dirt track, down the southern slope of Kilimanjaro. Soon we pass through the village of Mweka, where many of our porters live with their families. There is a workaday bustle to the village of mud huts and cement shacks with corrugated metal roofs. The village has no running water. Children run free in the dirt road. A filthy sign advertising beer (IT'S KILI TIME—MAKE THE MOST OF IT) hangs in front of a bar made of simple wood and mud construction.

In Hemingway's story "The Snows of Kilimanjaro," there is an epigraph that reads in part:

> Close to the western summit [of Kilimanjaro] there is the dried and frozen carcass of a leopard. No one has explained what the leopard was seeking at that altitude.

The same lack of explanation may apply to my own journey to the top. I came to Africa to see if I could, as Seve said, "show up" for myself, to try to capture something I felt was missing. I had hoped to come down with a sense of completeness, but instead I'm left with a feeling of detachment. What was all that about? What was the point? Nothing was really achieved. No good was created. Nothing changed. Yes, I have a feeling of satisfaction and accomplishment. I am glad I made it to the top—having to deal with the irrational metaphors associated with failure would have been an obstacle I'm grateful I don't need to work through. Yet I feel no great change or release, no greater strength or feelings of manliness I previously lacked.

The acute sense of longing I felt toward my father at the summit and the realization of the place that longing has always occupied in my body is a discovery not to be minimized, and in some ways, it is a relief. In acknowledging that emptiness, I'm released further into my own life. What more can we ask of our parents than that they teach us what they have to teach and then release us into the world?

The village gives way to rolling hills and then flattens out. A cluster of activity crowds a crossroads where a large mound of scrap metal is piled out in front of a small shack. An old woman sits beside mounds of figs spread out on a dirty sheet while a man is sanding a coffin as three men watch—half a dozen other coffins are stacked nearby. We drive on. The time capsule of the last week releases me back into the world and thoughts of unattended errands, calls that need to be made and e-mails sent, flood into my mind. I wonder what further wedding plans D has hatched in my absence.

A river joins our progress by the side of the road, and something about it reminds me of the Catherine River in Patagonia, which ran through the property at Estancia Cristina. I felt so comfortable there in my solitude and wondered how I might ever move from that place of contented isolation to this forward-leaning desire I feel right now toward getting to Ireland and the wedding.

How many people will make the trip to Dublin, how much of D's family will be there? I find myself hoping many more will come than I previously admitted. The idea of welcoming a large number of people is a long way from my trying to escape the mere dozen on the bow of a riverboat in the Amazon.

And as the wind rips in through the open windows of the van, it occurs to me that I desire no secret life; I have no need to flee to Costa Rica, to leave my past behind and live out some idea of an existence. I want to be close to my children, to D, and feel that sense of inclusion I felt in Vienna.

Maybe a lot more happened on that mountain—and along the way during these last months—than I first thought.

Far off, across a field of long and golden grass, I see a lone Masai, tall and thin, wearing the traditional red *shuka* of his tribe. He carries a long walking stick. It's miles from the last settlement of any kind, and there are no buildings on the horizon. He is erect; his stride has purpose. Suddenly I have the sensation of being out in that field, of the hard cracked earth under my feet, of the late-day sun over my shoulder, of the slight breeze blowing across my arms. My walk also has purpose and my stride has rhythm and power and grace. And then I'm back in the van. I crane my head and look off until the Masai is out of sight.

Around me, the others are chatting, but their words go past me. My thoughts are now with D. I picture her face, her eyes squinting at me—suppressing a grin and shaking her head as I protest her ever-growing wedding agenda. I can't wait to be with her, to get to Ireland. Over the thousands of miles that separate us I feel a closeness to her and an excitement about our future, together. I realize that in this sensation, in this desire for unity, I feel like myself—and it's all I ever wanted.

On the outskirts of Arusha, I pull out my phone. It finally has service. I text D—"Off the Mtn. Remember me?"

A few minutes later, my phone pings. "Who *are* you, anyway?"

I'm reminded of her first e-mail to me, years ago, when she asked the same question. Now I have the answer. I text back:

"The man coming to marry you."

CHAPTER EIGHT

DUBLIN

"Everything You Ever Dreamed Of?"

Five weeks before the wedding there are still no firm plans. Nothing has been decided regarding the ceremony. No musicians have been booked. There is no contingency plan for weather—no umbrellas ordered in case of rain. I have not asked about the lamb on a spit. In addition, there is no certainty that the Irish government will even allow the wedding since we didn't turn in my divorce papers on time or my previous marriage certificate. And the documents we do have aren't properly apostilled—I don't even know what "apostilled" means.

A pleasant-sounding woman named Patricia from the General Register Office in Dublin, has been e-mailing with regularity, reminding us in the most charming way possible of the urgency to get the documents in because "it can take months," she writes, for the paperwork to be filed, and there will be "nothing we can do" if everything is not in order.

"You need to get your divorce decree," D keeps saying to me.

I have no idea where this is or if I ever even had a copy. I finally ask my ex-wife, who graciously says she will look in her safe-deposit box at her bank. The next day she calls with good news.

"I have it here," she says.

"Great. You don't by any chance happen to have a copy of our marriage certificate, do you?"

There's a pause on the line. "In my safe-deposit box. At the bank. Where I just was," she says patiently. "I'll go back tomorrow."

I call and ask my mother if she has a copy of my birth certificate.

"Well, I might," she replies, "but if I do it's up in a box at the back of the closet. I can't reach it. I'll ask the doorman if he can come up and pull it down. When do you need it?"

"A month ago."

Half an hour later she calls back.

"Well, you're in luck . . ."

When D sees it, she informs me that it's not correct. "We need the long form."

"There's a long form?"

The day after my daughter's fifth birthday, and exactly a month from the wedding day, I head to Los Angeles to direct a television show. Before I get back, D will have finished directing a play, met her writing deadline, and left with our daughter for Dublin.

On her way out of town, D stops to pick up her wedding dress. From the airport she calls me in Los Angeles. "It got rained on on the way home."

"Let's hope it's the only time it gets rained on."

Three weeks before the wedding there are still no firm plans.

Two weeks and two days before we are scheduled to get married, I am in Burbank, directing a scene in which a man is trapped under a piece of farm equipment; his left arm is broken just above his wrist and is gushing blood. For reasons I don't understand, I am unusually tense while directing this scene. At a break in the filming, I check the messages on my phone. I have a missed call from my son's gymnastics camp; the message asks me to please call back as soon as possible.

My son has broken his left arm, just above the wrist—in the exact spot as the man in the scene I am directing. An ambulance has taken my son to the hospital, his mother cannot be found, D is in Ireland. I am three thousand miles away.

Soon enough, my son's mother joins him at the hospital, and after twelve hours and multiple doses of morphine, and the subsequent bouts of vomiting, he is sent home with a blue cast from his hand to his shoulder. In the photo my ex-wife sends me, my son looks small, pale, and defenseless.

In the week before I can get home, my mind is easily distracted. Perhaps I'm misplacing anxiety about the wedding onto my son, but I am preoccupied about his condition. I call his mother often to check on him. I have driven the streets of Los Angeles for nearly thirty years, but twice I take wrong turns on roads I have driven hundreds of times and find myself lost. One afternoon after work, on the way back to my friend's home, where I am staying, I pull off to the side of the road and dial my phone.

"Hey, pal," my father shouts over the line, the way he always does.

"Hey, Dad," I choke out back to him.

He asks after D and the kids—I don't mention my son's arm. I ask after his wife. Then I ask if he is going to be able to come to the wedding. He had alerted D earlier that he had a scheduling conflict—it's his wife's birthday that weekend and they have already planned a cruise with some other members of her family. But it feels important to ask him myself.

"We'd—I'd, love to have you there, if you can make it," I hear myself say.

"I'm still trying, pal, but the cruise is paid for. I tried calling the general manager, and I'm waiting to get a call back. But I'm trying."

When we hang up I sit watching the cars roll past along Montana Avenue. I'm not sure if I'm disappointed or feel a sense of absolution. I had expected no other response, and it was pleasant to hear his voice. I turn and look over at my reflection in the window of a nearby cosmetics store.

Back in New York, nine days before we are scheduled to be married, the morning my son and I are supposed to leave for Ireland, his mother and I take him to the orthopedic surgeon. The doctor is a big man with an outsized personality. His glasses perch on the very tip of his nose. He inspects my son's cast and quickly decides to change it.

"They did fine at the hospital, but let's set this thing correctly, shall we?" While we wait for results from the new X-ray to come back, I broach the topic.

"So, doctor . . . we're scheduled to get on a plane tonight, to Ireland—"

"What?" He glares at me.

"Yeah, I'm supposed to be getting mar—"

"No." He interrupts me, his head shaking side to side. "No, no, no, no, no, no, no. This arm is not flying today. Not with this swelling and this fracture. Remember what happened to Serena Williams? She had a broken bone in her foot and flew to Hawaii and ended up with a blood clot in her lung. Almost died, and she's a pro athlete. No, this boy isn't flying for weeks. Not for several weeks."

I am speechless.

My ex-wife steps in to help me out. "He's getting married in Ireland next week."

The doctor tilts his large head and lifts his hands in a "well, nothing we can do" gesture. The X-ray comes back and the doctor shows us the multiple fracture. The break is not clean; the bone has splintered.

"And there's a chip in the wrist that they didn't see at the hospital." The doctor points to a spot on the black and white film. I sit glued to the small stool in the corner. I am numb. The doctor molds a new cast, assisted by his very young and very blond nurse. After a new cast is set, the doctor turns to me.

"Come here," he says, and hurries out into the hall.

I follow.

"When's your drop-dead date?"

While the doctor has been tending to my son, I have been asking myself that exact question. Today is Tuesday, August 16. My son and I were to fly to Galway, in the west of Ireland, tonight, and spend several days together. A father and son trip. D and our daughter were to join us there and we would all travel together for a few days, including a visit to the hotel where D and I first met. We had intended to come full circle, as a family, just before the wedding. Then we would all drive across the country to Dublin on Tuesday the twenty-third; get married in the registrar's office on Wednesday the twenty-fourth, with D's immediate family and a few friends present; and then on Sunday, August 28, have the more public wedding and celebration in the park.

"Next Monday, the twenty-second," I say to the doctor—trying to convey in those few words the urgency I feel.

The doctor nods. "Okay." He holds out his hands in a "stop" gesture. "Let me see what I can do. If the arm doesn't slip and the swelling goes down, maybe we can make it work. Maybe. No guarantees. It's a bad break, and with the air pressure in the plane—"

"I know, doctor," I say, interrupting him. "But unless you can tell me he's going to die on the plane, we've got to fly."

The doctor laughs, and I wonder if I'm joking—knowing at the same time that if there was any risk at all, I would be getting married without my son. And I don't know if I can do that. He is already worried about being left out of our family—not being in attendance on the wedding day could only exacerbate those feelings. What my son needs to do is be there in person, be a part of it and feel the love that surrounds him, rather than four thousand miles away, having to hear about it for the rest of his life.

I was not in attendance at my father's second marriage—it is a history I am not interested in repeating. I was not speaking much with my father at the time when he remarried. I have always imagined that he—wrongly—assumed I wouldn't have attended had I been invited. For that reason alone, I was never particularly hurt by the omission, but it certainly added further distance to an already remote relationship. My son has to be at my wedding.

The doctor smiles at me and makes a juggling gesture. Then he laughs again, slaps me on the shoulder, and marches back into the office.

That evening I let my son sleep in my bed. After he's down, I call D. It's late in Ireland.

"Where are you? You're not on the plane?" Her voice is rising in panic.

I explain what the doctor said, leaving out the part that my son may not be allowed to fly at all, for weeks. "We'll be there next Tuesday morning," I say, hoping that my voice carries an assuredness I lack. "That way we'll still be able to get married on Wednesday. It's not a problem, we just won't have our time together in the west beforehand."

D doesn't hear any of this; her sobbing is too loud.

When I climb into bed my son rolls over and slams me in the head with his cast.

"I'm sorry I can't go to Ireland, Dad," he says the next morning.

"I bet we'll be able to go, kiddo, don't worry."

"No, the doctor said I couldn't fly, didn't you hear him?"

"I know, but—"

"I'll die."

Six days before D and I are scheduled to be married, my son and I go back to have the cast changed. I take the doctor aside. "How is it looking?"

"So far, so good. The swelling has gone down a lot. And already there's bone being created. If you or I had that break there'd be a dozen metal pins in our arms. It's great to be young."

"So do you think we'll be . . . ?"

"Maybe."

"Would you mind going in and telling my son that if you let him fly he's not going to die?"

"Yup, everything looked good, don't worry," I tell D when we connect on Skype. She's in Killarney with her bridesmaid Louise. I can't remember the last time I've seen her face. Over the computer screen I can see the crease between D's eyebrows is deep; she looks strained. She knows I'm not telling her the whole truth.

The longer I see her, the more beautiful she becomes, and then her computer runs out of juice and she's gone.

By the time I get to Ireland, if I get to Ireland, the day before the wedding, D and I will not have seen each other in nearly five weeks, the longest stretch since we met.

Later that evening I make my son take a bath for the first time since he broke his arm. I sit beside the tub and chat with him.

"I'm sorry this happened, Dad," my son says at one point.

"Don't you worry about it, we're going to be fine."

"I hope so."

"Trust me, we will." We chat some more about video games he wants that I won't let him have, and then I get up to make a cup of tea. "Keep your cast out of the water," I say as I leave the room.

"Don't worry, Dad. I know," he says. Within seconds I hear him holler, "Oh, no!"

"What happened?" I rush back into the bathroom.

"I forgot. I started to lie down and I forgot."

"Are you kidding me? I told you five seconds ago!"

"I know, I'm sorry! I forgot!"

"Get out." The cast is dripping.

I call D.

"Where's the hair dryer?"

"Hello, my luv. What? Why do you want the hair dryer?"

"Don't ask. Do you know where it is?"

"Oh, no," she gasps, comprehending instantly. "Bottom of the closet, right-hand corner."

I pat down the cast and wave the blow-dryer over it. "Is it wet inside?"

"No, not really." Neither of us wants the cast to be wet, but we both know that it is. Despite my son's still occasional misgivings about the impending marriage, he is looking forward to going to Ireland. I flip off the dryer. The corners of his mouth begin to turn up and we both burst out laughing.

"Shit."

"Dad, you said the S-word."

Once my son is asleep beside me—before this week he hadn't slept in bed with me for several years—I try to take stock of the situation. I consider the various permutations and possibilities for the next week and what they might mean, both for the immediate future and down the line. After an hour of this my nerves are so on edge I get out of bed and take my first bath in memory.

In the morning, I call the doctor's office, but he's taking Fridays off during the summer.

"Well, maybe it's not that wet," I say to the receptionist. "We can wait till Monday."

"Hold on," the receptionist says, and then a minute later she comes back on the line. "No. If he got it wet, then it has to be changed. The nurse is here, she'll change it, then the doctor can look at it again on Monday."

We go down and Judy, the same attractive blond nurse, slices open the cast; the interior gauze is matted and soaked through.

"You had to get this changed, no question." Judy turns to me, her green eyes glowing. "See how the skin is already beginning to be affected?" She shakes her head. "This is not good." She gets to work on the arm. Her long, loose blond hair falls over my son's shoulder as she manipulates his arm; her thin and well-manicured fingers squeeze just below his wrist. And then my son's arm gets another X-ray.

When Judy compares the X-ray from a few days ago to the new one, the bone looks more off kilter than before. Even my son notices.

"The new X-ray looked worse," he says in the cab on our way back home. "Didn't it, Dad?"

"No." I lie to us both. "They looked exactly the same. We'll be fine."

On Saturday, four days before D and I are supposed to be married, my apostilled birth certificate arrives in the mail. What would we have done for paperwork if my son hadn't broken his arm and needed to stay in New York?

I call D to let her know.

"Has mine come?" D's birth certificate is more complicated. Since she was born in Vienna, it is in German and needs to be translated, reissued, and then apostilled, which adds another step to the already convoluted process.

"We don't have that yet?"

"I told you about it. Did you call that guy?"

"What guy?"

"I have a guy expediting it, it should have been delivered by messenger."

"Oh."

D gives me a name and number and I call.

"Who?" the heavily accented voice on the phone shouts.

I spell the name.

"Oh, yeah. That should be back in a week to ten days," he says.

"No, no, no. We fly in two days, I need it now," I explain.

"Oh, no one told me it was urgent, let me make a call. They're closed today, but I'll call on Monday."

"I really need it, we fly Monday night," I insist.

"I'll do my best," he tells me.

On Sunday, three days before we are scheduled to get married, and a week before the wedding party, D tells me, "My parents want to have the *ceili* at their house."

"I thought it was going to be at the hotel. It was all set."

"Well, they've ordered a second Dumpster, to throw out stuff. They have the room now," she explains.

"It's still on Sunday, after the ceremony, right?"

"Well, we're meeting to discuss that, at my parents' house tonight. There's some thinking that it might be nice to have it after my parents' dinner, keep it all in one setting, at one time."

"Oh."

"You just get on the plane."

On Monday morning, two days before D and I are scheduled to get married in Dublin, my son and I head back to the doctor in midtown Manhattan. Yet another X-ray is taken. The doctor slaps it up into the light board. He silently squints at the giant negative. He compares it to the original film, taking one down and replacing it with the other, then again, and again, back and forth, then he sits down beside my son.

"Lie down," he orders.

My son lies back on the doctor's table.

The doctor wraps his large hands around my son's small arm. He closes his eyes and tilts his head forward, his ear very close to the arm, as if he's listening. He begins to squeeze. My son giggles until he yelps, "Oww!"

"Don't move," the doctor barks. He manipulates the arm some more; my son shoots me a look. When the doctor releases the arm, he sits back and looks up at me. "Let's put a new cast on this arm and get you two on a plane."

"Where is it?" I shout into the phone.

"Someone tried to deliver it at one thirty, there was no one home," the man with the heavily accented voice says.

"We were here at one thirty."

My son grabs my arm. "Dad, the buzzer doesn't work, remember?"

"Oh, shit," I say.

"Dad, you said the S-wo—"

"Please," I hiss at him.

"Would you like me to try and redeliver it?" the man on the phone asks.

"Yes, now. I have to leave for the airport in half an hour, I need that birth certificate."

"I'll call them and see."

"No! Not call them and see. Tell them to get here now! I'm late. Please!" I'm aware that I'm screeching.

In two minutes the phone rings. "I have the messenger on the other line, he's waiting to hear—"

"Why is he waiting, get him here now! Now!"

"He can get there by three, not two forty-five."

"Just get him here now!"

My son and I go downstairs and pile up our bags on the sidewalk. The car service arrives.

"I have to wait a few minutes, something is being delivered," I tell the driver.

"I'm not waiting. Pickup is two forty-five. I have other jobs," the driver replies. He starts the car. I hand him a ten-dollar bill through the window. "It'll just be a few minutes."

"I'll wait ten minutes," he says.

"You should have gotten the good car service, Dad," my son complains. "This one always smells funny."

At 2:59, from around the corner, a short, daydreamy guy in a white messenger T-shirt is strolling slow and easy up the street with a rolling gait. I rush at him. "Are you here for McCarthy?"

"Huh?"

"Are you here for McCarthy?"

He looks down at the envelope. I look and see that my future wife's name is on it. "Nope." He shakes his head.

"That's me," I grab the envelope out of his hand, dive into the car, and we're gone.

At the airport ticket counter I tell my son to pull his sleeve down over his cast and wait by the wall, away from me, because I've forgotten both the letter from the doctor saying that the cast has been bivalved and poses no medical threat to the patient and that he is approved to fly, and also the letter from my son's mother allowing him to be taken out of the country by only one of his parents. Both these letters are still sitting beside the phone where I was screaming to the man with the heavy accent trying to get the translated and apostilled birth certificate. Luckily, no one at the airport seems to care about such formalities, and after I watch my son play a few of the normally forbidden video games, we're in the air for an overnight flight.

My relationship with Ireland has been long and complex. I first arrived in Dublin, with Seve, in the mid-eighties. We were young and free. Ireland was on its knees, in the throes of a deep and protracted recession. We came over from London for a weekend and stayed three weeks. We rented a car and drove, without a plan, moving from one village to the next, meeting welcoming people, playing terrible golf on beautiful courses, drinking too much in the local pubs (enough to occasionally get up and sing), and eventually ending up on the western coast, just outside the village of Doolin, at a small, family-run hotel. It became our spot.

The O'Callaghans welcomed us back like family every year. Seve's and my annual pilgrimage was a stabilizing and rejuvenating ritual. And then one year we were too busy to go, and then another year passed, and then it had been a decade since I'd been back.

Then came the trip when D and I first met. In my absence, the Celtic Tiger had made Ireland rich. I had become a husband and then a father. I was more wary, and weary, than I had been the last time I visited.

Now, because of D, I was traveling to Dublin several times a year. I took her out to the O'Callaghans' in Doolin, but mostly we stayed in Dublin, close to her family and friends. I got to know the city by simply going places as part of daily life. Then we bought a home, a few blocks from D's parents. My relationship with Ireland became more complex, including familial relationships, obligations, and bills.

At times I've resented the incessant pull Dublin has exerted over us, and D's determination to keep Ireland an active part of her life—and consequently our life—has been a source of tension.

"We can't live in two places," I eventually said to her.

"Well, I can," was her response.

The children, like D, have no complex feelings about Ireland. They love being spoiled by Granny and Granddad and relish the feeling of freedom and independence they have here.

My son also loves talking to Irish taxi drivers. And on this morning, after neither of us slept on the flight over, he is chattering away to the driver about all the different places he lives, and why it's still so dark out, and does the driver know that they sell Pringles on the plane and that he had three full tins on the flight over?

We pull up to an ivy-covered wall down a small lane and knock on a heavy wooden door. It's a small hotel not far from where the wedding will take place. That we're not staying in our house is yet another result of our loose planning.

As with most second homes, the purchase was an emotional decision, not a practical one. We stay at our small cottage—originally used to house the workers on the Rathmines tramway line—just a few times a year, though D sneaks home more regularly. But often, when the house sits empty, we rent it out.

When we set our wedding date for August 28, we assumed that we would do the legal ceremony on the Friday the twenty-sixth. When we finally checked, we discovered that the registrar was booked. The closest day we could get married on was Wednesday the twenty-fourth. By then we had rented out the house to a Canadian couple until the twenty-fifth. So we will all be piled into one hotel room on the morning D and I will finally be legally married.

As my son and I enter room six, the heavy curtains are drawn against the dim light of a slate-gray Irish dawn. The unfamiliar room is in complete darkness and my son bumps hard against something.

"Ow!"

"Shh," I whisper.

My eyes adjust to the darkness. D and our daughter are asleep in the large bed that my son has just slammed against. The rollaway cot by the bathroom is empty, the blankets turned down, waiting. Quickly, I get my exhausted son undressed and into the cot. Within minutes he's asleep and I crawl into the large bed beside D. She rolls over and her eyes, puffy with sleep, open. She smiles and moves closer to me, her body luscious with the heat of sleep. She always looks so young when I first see her, and glimpsing her face now, in this shadowy light of dawn, is no exception. Then our daughter's head pops over her shoulder.

"Daddy!"

Six hours later, D wakes me with a shake. The curtains are open and the hotel room is flooded with light.

"Come on, luv. We need to get going. We have a meeting with Patricia in an hour."

We hurry over to Joyce House, to the Civil Registration Office of Births, Marriages, and Deaths, on Lombard Street East. It's a part of town I don't know; the buildings are low and brick, and with the dirty gray sky, it feels like it could be 1930, the way certain streets of Dublin still feel. Past a battered security desk, through a lobby that smells of stale smoke, up a flight of stairs, in the corner of a dingy beige room with worn blue carpet, behind a metal desk by a dirty window overlooking the local authority housing project across the street, Patricia Traynor, a small, middle-aged woman with a charming face, sensibly cut blond hair, and blue eyes behind thick glasses, rises from a metal chair and strides across the room to greet us like we're old friends.

"After all our e-mails, I feel like I know you," she says in a Cavan accent softened by twenty years in the big city. We shake hands and settle into the two plastic chairs across the desk from her.

For all the apparent disregard for detail and organization that D displays, I have never known her to be late for an event, miss a deadline, or forget an appointment. I once asked her why she didn't write things down. "Maybe make a list," I suggested.

"Then I'd have to remember to look at it," she said, "just one more thing I'd have to keep in my head."

Out of a file she slips from her handbag, D produces all of our necessary paperwork. "Sign here," she tells me, pointing to a form I've never seen. "And here." I have no idea what I just signed. D hands the file over to Patricia.

Patricia looks through all our paperwork. "Perfect," she says. "Now I just need to ask you a few questions, and you need to look over the list of possible impediments to marriage."

She hands us a two-sided sheet of paper. There is the predictable warning against marrying if one of the parties is already married or if there is a mental impairment. And then there is a long list of connections between the two parties that cannot exist in order for the wedding to take place. A man may not marry his grandmother, his wife's grandmother, his mother's sister, or his mother's brother's sister or daughter, brother's son's wife, wife's brother's daughter, daughter's son's wife, wife's son's daughter, wife's father's sister, and so on.

The list of impediments to who a woman can marry is similarly restricted.

"I'm not sure, but I think we're clear," I say.

"Now, Andrew"—Patricia looks at me over her glasses—"I need for you to be absolutely sure."

D jumps in. "He's just jet-lagged," she says, patting my knee a little harder than necessary.

"I'm joking, we're safe," I say. I decide not to mention that D's mother's maiden name is also McCarthy and that our ancestors are from the same region of Cork.

We chat a bit more, then Patricia says, "This isn't a highly exhaustive interview, but you seem at first glance to be of sound mind"—she gives me a look—"if a bit sleepy. I prescribe a good night's rest before the ceremony tomorrow."

I feel like I'm in grade school and have just handed in a sloppy book report.

Patricia tells us that she'll be the one conducting the civil ceremony in the morning. Both D and I are pleased by this news. I had neglected to consider who might be marrying us in this legal portion of our two-part, multiday nuptials, worrying only about D's friend Shelly, who will be conducting the service on Sunday.

"And unless you have music, or someone is reading poetry or something, it should last about ten minutes."

"That's all?" I ask.

"That's it," Patricia answers. "Oh, do you have rings?"

"Maybe," D says. "No," I say, overlapping.

"Well." Patricia looks back and forth between the two of us—her face reveals nothing. "You can decide and let me know before the ceremony."

Out on the street, the Dublin August feels like a New York autumn. The wind is blowing, the sky is low, and there's a chill in the air.

"Rings?" I ask.

"Do you not want to wear rings?"

"No, I'm good to wear a ring," I say. "It's just that you said you didn't want a ring, remember? That we didn't need them. We did talk about this."

"Well, I remembered a jeweler I know, she could make us nice ones."

"By tomorrow?"

D calls her friend the jeweler, who tells D that some of her work is on display over at the Kilkenny shop on Nassau Street. We head over. This part of town is always humming. Trinity College, with the Book of Kells, is across the street. A few blocks away, the Grafton Street pedestrian mall buzzes at all hours with shoppers, street performers, flower salesmen, people watchers. The twenty-two-acre St. Stephen's Green, the soul of south Dublin, is a few blocks away.

D quickly finds a ring she likes, but it is slightly large on her.

"We could have that fitted for you," the salesgirl behind the counter says. "When's the wedding?"

"Tomorrow morning," D says, as her phone rings.

"Tomorrow morning?" The young salesgirl is horrified.

But D isn't paying attention; she's on the phone, ordering our wedding cake for the Sunday ceremony. "I'm kind of busy tomorrow morning—" I hear her say.

"Kind of busy?" I interrupt.

D waves me off. "—but maybe I could swing by and take a look at them late in the day, or is there a photo of the cakes on your website?"

The salesgirl watches this exchange, turns her back, and simply walks away from us. I lead D out the door and back onto the street. The idea of rings is discarded without further discussion.

We go around the corner to the Shelbourne Hotel on St. Stephen's Green and head to the bar. There's an elegant, happy chaos to the room. While D sips a glass of wine and I chug a club soda, she says, "Maybe we should switch back the Friday night 'welcome cocktails' to here, instead of the Merrion. There's more atmosphere here. It'll be more fun for the Americans."

"Isn't it all set? Booked and everything?"

But D is already leaning over the bar, asking to speak with the manager.

The girls are sound asleep. My son and I are sitting in the hallway, outside our hotel room, reading *Charlie and the Chocolate Factory,* under a dim lamp. It's one thirty in the morning. We're reading about Augustus Gloop, who falls into the chocolate river and is sucked down a drain. We're both exhausted, but neither of us can sleep. Jet lag has us in its grip. Eventually we go to bed and pass out.

But by eight A.M. we are all up and moving—there is a lot to do, like get married. I rummage through my bag and can't find my razor blades. I have a clear recollection of packing them in New York, but they are nowhere in my suitcase, which is crammed up under the window, on top of my son's and daughter's bags, the contents of which have exploded all over the room.

"I'll be right back," I say, and head to the door. D is calling after me as I go, but I keep going. I need some air—and razor blades.

Outside, it is a bright, cool morning. I feel a thin breeze blowing from the east, while above, rolling white clouds race across the sky from the west. I walk over Leeson Street Bridge and see two swans down beside the canal. The canal used to be the far reaches of town a few centuries ago and it's more residential here than in the center. D used to live around the corner—going for a late-night quart of milk or an early morning, jet-lag-induced walk, these are the first streets of

Dublin I got to know intimately. As I walk, aware of my personal history here, I realize how much I have invested in this relationship. I'm conscious of the rhythm of my steps, the swing of my arms, the fall of my feet. I'm grateful for the few minutes alone. Suddenly I'm singing a Bruce Springsteen song: *May your strength give us strength / May your faith give us faith . . .*

My prayer for the day.

When I return with the plastic razors, D and my daughter are gone. My son is in the breakfast room. In an unspoken agreement that I not see D before the wedding, a series of accidentally well-choreographed things are happening. The girls have gone off to get their hair done. While they are gone, my son and I will dress; my best man, Seve—who arrived yesterday—will pick us up; and we will walk over to the Civil Registration Office. After we leave, D will return and get dressed, her father will collect her, and we will all rendezvous at 10:25, in time to get married.

While I'm shaving I have a clear memory of doing this same thing on the morning of my first wedding. I picture the light coming in from my left and the old bathroom mirror, its chipped corner. I distinctly remember the care and ease with which I shaved and the closeness I achieved. While I'm reliving this, I cut myself badly by my right ear. Blood flows and it is difficult to stop.

"Well at least I'm not repeating the past," I say aloud, trying not to see any kind of metaphorical meaning in this insistent bloodletting.

"What did you say, Dad?" my son shouts from outside the bathroom.

Seve arrives and hustles us out the door. We walk along the Grand Canal, past a half dozen mallard ducks. My son is prancing, skipping, running, up and back along the path. Seve strides beside me; his is a walk I've known so well for so long. There are no two people I would rather be with on my way to get married today. I ask Seve to take a photo of my son and me as we walk. My son isn't interested, and Seve isn't fast enough. My feelings are suddenly hurt. I keep it to myself—I am not nearly as relaxed as I thought I was.

We leave the serenity of the canal and turn onto Fitzwilliam Place. Buses and motorcycles roar past, racing into the heart of Dublin. In the sudden cacophony I feel as if a layer of my skin has been removed; the chaos and noise grate on my now-jangling nerves, my shoulders hunch against the onslaught. Then we can't find the registrar's office.

"Wasn't this your job, Seve?"

We go into a Spar market to ask for help. "Can I get a Coke and some potato chips, Dad?" my son asks.

"It's ten in the morning," I say.

"So?"

"Fine."

"Yes!" He pumps his fist. "Seve, I haven't gotten to have a Coke in months!"

The building we're looking for is just across the street. We're the first to arrive. Suddenly I wonder if anyone will show up.

I know my father won't be here; I never heard from him again—but I didn't expect that I would. My mother and eldest brother, Stephen, won't get in until Friday. Neither of my other two brothers could make it. Peter, a college professor, began his semester this week and couldn't get away, and Justin is absorbed in work of his own. I wish they were here. But the casually affectionate distance that has come to define our relationships prevented me from letting them know just how much their presence would have meant to me.

The glass entry of the Civil Registration Office is at the end of an elegant internal courtyard. There is a small lobby area, and beyond, a blue-carpeted room with six rows of ten chairs each, fixed into the ground, inclining toward the front of the room, where there is a half-moon-shaped desk, with one chair behind it and four chairs around the semicircle. Improbably, the room has an air of hopefulness about it, yet I'm disappointed that the ceremony will apparently take place sitting down. The back wall is covered in wood paneling.

I turn back and look up through the glass doors and see D's three brothers arrive; they're laughing. Then her parents are there, our daughter in her granddad's arms, and three of D's friends—her witness, Jackie, and two bridesmaids, Louise and Karen, D's oldest friends. And then I see D. She is in an elegant silver-blue, form-hugging dress.

I wait where I am, down by the desk. The others come in and there are hugs and nervous laughter. I kiss D on the cheek.

"You look very beautiful," I tell her.

She smiles broadly; she is excited, nervous, self-possessed, and appears to me both very strong and very vulnerable. My son has been jumping around the room, but when the others arrive he becomes quiet and goes to sit in the last row, in the farthest seat on the end. D's parents try to hug him and he resists them. His sister goes to him, but he waves her away. I ask him to come down front, with the others. He refuses.

Much of my son's anxiety about being left out of the family has been addressed again and again over the past months, and he's been in bright spirits since we arrived in Dublin—until this moment. Suddenly, his fears seem to have returned, as I worried they might.

I go to him and whisper, with urgency, "I need you to come down front, now."

"No," he says. His eyes are burning.

I am very close to letting my nerves fuel a lash of anger.

"Please," I hiss. I turn and ask one of D's brothers, Colm Jr., whom my son is very fond of, to sit with him down front.

"Come on," Colm Jr. shouts, waving to my son.

By an act of grace my son rises, shuffles down to the front row, and plops himself beside D's brother.

Patricia appears from behind the wood-paneled wall. She asks us to all take a seat. Seve flanks me on my right, D is on my left, and Jackie is beside her. Patricia sits behind the desk, and without a formal beginning, the ceremony begins.

Patricia goes through some of the legal protocol. I feel a sense of calm about the proceedings that proves to be false when Patricia asks us to sign the binding document, and I begin to sign the wrong line. Seve stops me and points out the correct spot.

Then Patricia asks us all to stand. D and I turn toward each other and hold hands. Suddenly the room is filled with an intensity and gravity that until then hadn't been much more than a vaguely implied possibility but now galvanizes and gathers around us with force. My body begins to heat up. No false calm now; I'm here, and there's a lot going on. D's gaze is filled with purpose; she anchors the room. I look back at Patricia when she addresses me and begins to recite the vows.

I, Andrew McCarthy, do solemnly and sincerely declare . . .

I look back at D and begin to smile in embarrassment, but the gravity in D's face settles me. I begin to repeat after Patricia.

"I, Andrew McCarthy, do solemnly and sincerely declare . . ." I'm somehow surprised that this is what I am actually saying. I don't know what I expected to say, since the specifics of traditional vows were never mentioned in our meeting yesterday, but in speaking these words, without anticipating their pronouncement, I hear them and contemplate their meaning in a way I might not have otherwise. As I echo Patricia, our voices take on a rhythm and I gather confidence.

. . . love her, and comfort her . . .

". . . love her, and comfort her . . ."

. . . in sickness and in health . . .

". . . in sickness and in health . . ."

. . . for so long as we both shall live . . .

". . . for so long as we both shall live . . ."

When I've completed my vows Patricia turns to D, whose gaze on me never wavers. I can't help but grin at her when she begins to recite her vows. The corners of her lips turn up and then she gathers herself again.

When D has finished her vows, we share a look that seems to say, "Yes, we just said all that to each other." It feels as if we are huge and growing—like that night when I was a child, in the snow under the stars in my front yard, and then again in Spain, by the side of the barn while walking the *camino*. I can sense the others around us. Without looking, I know where each one is standing. The room seems to be pulsing. The look in D's eyes lets me know that she feels it too. She exhales deeply, calling on more of the swelling energy, riding the wave. And then she has the largest smile on her face, and then we're kissing.

When we emerge from our embrace, D shrugs, and everyone laughs. Perspective returns to normal and the hugging begins. The laughter is more relaxed now.

Our daughter jumps up into both our arms, D's brothers slap my back, her parents kiss and hug me. Seve shakes my hand with sincerity.

"Congratulations, my friend. Nice work."

My son has moved and sits up against a wall, behind a partition, partially hidden from view. As the others begin to organize toward the door, I go to him, and there are tears in his eyes. I hug him.

"That was a lot, huh?"

"I guess."

"I love you so much," I say.

"Don't say that, Dad, you don't." And the tears roll down his cheeks.

"More than you can ever understand." We sit in silence for a minute, with only the sound of his sniffling. "Come on," I say after a while, "let's go." Seve comes to join us and my son wipes his eyes and we're on the street.

The girls take a cab to the Merrion Hotel, where we have reserved a room in Patrick Guilbaud's restaurant. The boys decide to walk in the blustery midday through Merrion Square. The park is in full bloom. We pass the playful statue of Oscar Wilde reclining on a large stone.

We spend a long and lazy afternoon eating rich food around a large, elegant table, then return to our hotel and all fall into bed. The next morning we maneuver a dozen bags into a taxi and head home.

Everyone silently goes off to engage in their own form of nesting. My daughter is on her bed, changing the dresses on her dolls. My son is up in his loft space, playing with his knights and trolls. D is taking a long bath and I lie on the bed, watching the breeze blow through the tall cypress tree outside the window. It's my favorite view and the first image that comes to mind when I think of our home in Dublin. For the first time this view reminds me of the cypress trees down in Patagonia, the ones at Estancia Cristina, the trees that had been planted to break the incessant winds. It seems a long time ago, my standing by the Catherine River, watching a salmon struggle upstream.

Then, apparently, I laugh out loud.

"What's so funny?" D asks as she comes into the room, wrapped in a towel.

"I was just thinking of Patagonia," I say.

"Wishing you were there?"

"Just the opposite." I reach out for my wife and kiss her properly for the first time since we married. "Feel married?" I ask.

"Half. You?"

"Completely," I say. "I'm done."

"Oh, no you're not, mister."

"Didn't you see him scratching his head all week?"

"I . . . I . . . ," is my only response.

"Call Karen, tell her to stop by the drugstore on her way over," D orders. "We need to be at Dartmouth Square in an hour. The guys are meeting us to go through everything for tomorrow." D shakes her head. "I mean really, luv."

My son was recently away, staying on a farm, and apparently brought home a head full of lice. Maybe in the stress of the week dealing with his arm I didn't notice his incessant scratching, or maybe it's just now that they are suddenly in full bloom.

Karen arrives with something called Clearlice, Pantene conditioner, baking soda, and a fine-toothed comb. I watch D's gentle and affectionate patience with my son as she drops everything and spends an hour tending to him. They laugh when she shows him the comb covered with the bugs that were in his hair.

"Aw, cool," my son exclaims.

"Eew, gross," my daughter squeals.

We're half an hour late when we arrive at Dartmouth Square, where the second ceremony will take place. The square is a hedge-bound, tree-lined green with an open field bisected by a trestle-covered path with an ivy-laced gazebo in the center. It's a simple and elegant neighborhood square encircled by redbrick, Georgian row houses. It could only be in Dublin. We gather under the gazebo. Shelly is there. She is a complex lady, small, redheaded, sarcastic, vulnerable, by turns defensive and loving. She was one of the first of D's friends whom I connected with years ago. I like her a lot. When D suggested that Shelly preside over the ceremony, the idea was greeted with both confusion and a rolling of eyes by nearly everyone. "She'll be perfect," D has maintained from the start. Shelly holds no license to perform weddings, but since the legalities were taken care of with Patricia at the Civil Registration Office, her job is to "bring the spirit into the marriage."

Ronan, a sandy-haired, always fashionably dressed old friend of D's who will "stage-manage" the event, and Peter, a rake-thin redhead and former boyfriend of D's who is handling anything that has to do with our physical presence in the park, are also here, along with D's bridesmaids, Louise and Karen, and the kids, and Seve. Jackie stops by too—she'll sing a song to open the ceremony. Everything that will happen at the ceremony tomorrow will be decided now.

"Okay," D announces, "Andrew, why don't you take over, show everyone what we were thinking."

"Oh," I say. "Okay." We have not discussed this in any way. I look around the obvious staging area. "Well, I think it might be good if Shelly were positioned here." I point to a center area under the gazebo. "The musicians could be over here"—I indicate to the left—"and that way—"

"No. Why don't we put the musicians over here." D points to where I had just placed Shelly.

"Okay," I say, "but if you're going to come in from there . . ." I point off toward the gated entrance to the park.

"No, that's not good, because then people would block her entrance," Karen chimes in.

"Why don't we go back to what we had decided?" Louise suggests.

I look over at Seve, but he won't meet my eye. My son and daughter are chasing a pair of magpies around the grass. One for sorrow, two for joy.

The girls are discussing the binding of the hands and the twelve ribbons that will be used, each one a different color, each representing a different vow.

"Luv, do we want Shelly to explain what each ribbon means?"

"Well," I say, "I think a little education might be a good idea, since not too many people know about the whole tying-the-knot ritual."

D considers this. "Um, no," she says. "It'll take too long. We don't need it. Should we have the big cushions for the kids to sit on in the front?"

"I think kids in front is a bad idea," I say, "they'll get bored and start—"

"Yeah, the cushions will have to go in front," D says; the girls agree and the discussion turns to flowers.

I walk over to Seve. "You're doing great," he says to me.

By six o'clock that evening, we are all bathed and dressed and gathering at D's parents' home for their intimate dinner for forty. Margot and Colm are in their element—entertaining, serving, and laughing, racing back and forth to the kitchen to get drinks. There are flowers everywhere.

"The house looks beautiful," I tell Margot as she zooms past.

"All smoke and mirrors, Andrew, my love," she sings out. "Smoke and mirrors." And she's gone.

D's aunts and uncles are here, her bridesmaids come in and create a fuss, a few of our friends from New York sip drinks and lean against walls. My eldest brother and my mother are here. They arrived yesterday, in time for the welcome drink.

People are milling about, beginning to enjoy themselves, drinking, and then like clockwork, everyone is sitting down, somehow, around the tables that have been set up in the living room. D's brothers are serving as waiters. The starters come out and are cleared and then the main course is presented and I watch everything swirl in front of me.

During dessert, my friend Lawrence, who came over from London, raps on his glass with his knife, silencing the gathering.

"Speech, Andrew, speech!" he calls out. It's just like my old friend to embarrass me.

I rise. "Thank you, Lawrence," I say, my voice filled with sarcasm that some in the room snicker at. Briefly, I thank my mother and brother for making the long trip, and D's family for the evening they've given us, then I sit back down. It's not much of a speech. Luckily, none of D's family are even in the room to hear it.

A little while later, D rises and makes an emotional toast, thanking her parents and brothers and family, and welcoming all the Americans who made the arduous journey. The love she feels for everyone present on this occasion is evident. Around the room, eyes begin to well up, and when she finishes, the room bursts into warm and loving applause, grateful for the release.

D will sleep with our daughter at the hotel next door to her parents' house tonight. I take my son the few blocks home.

We settle at the kitchen table and share a late-night slice of toast.

"Can you cut the crust off, Dad?" my son asks beside me at the table.

"You ate two servings of pâté tonight, for God's sake. I think you're old enough to realize that the crust is the best part."

He takes a bite. "It's actually pretty good."

I tousle his hair and we sit in silence. There is a pure, still place in me that remains mine alone. It is that place I first encountered as a child in my front yard, under the stars, it is the place from which I move out into the world, the place from which so much that is good in my life has sprung. Over the years my willful isolation and separation, my urge to flee, my feelings of being misunderstood and ultimately alone in the world, all grew from a desire to shield that solitary place. But what I've come to see in the past months of travel is that these battlements I've erected ultimately ensure the creation of all they are trying to safeguard against. The revelation of my journeying is that so many of my defenses, so many of the protective choices I have lived by, behavior that has dictated so many of my actions and created much of my persona in the world, are both unnecessary and counterproductive. The realization is at once liberating and already deeply familiar.

The softness of love I have experienced with D has made unnecessary that hard shell of my defensive reaction to the world, and it feels at this moment as if that love has been waiting for me this entire time, just under a silk cloth that took only a gentle breeze to uncover.

I let my son climb into bed with me and we read the final chapter of *Charlie and the Chocolate Factory*. The last of the spoiled children are disposed of, and Charlie, his grandpa Joe, and Willy Wonka step into the Great Glass Elevator and rocket up, breaking through the roof of the factory into the light of day to collect the rest of Charlie's family.

The early morning of our (second) wedding day begins bright and clear. But by the time Seve arrives, white clouds have begun to bunch up and push quickly across the sky. Seve doesn't have much to say this morning, and as I'm putting on my tie, Conor, Louise's partner, arrives in his old beat-up green Mercedes.

"Come on, kiddo, Conor's here," I call to my son, who is up in his loft, playing with his trolls. "We've got to get going."

"To where?"

Seve and I look to each other and laugh. "To get married."

"Again?"

On the ride over, I sit in the back, beside my son. He carries on a running conversation with Conor concerning which *Star Wars* characters are the best lightsaber fighters. We pass Palmerston Park, a lush green with a small playground. I have often played there with the kids but also remember walking there alone, during less happy times, wondering how D and I would ever get through them and what it would mean for us all if we couldn't. I concocted elaborate scenarios of transatlantic visitations and hotel stays—these plans would leave me exhausted and despairing and always I decided to walk back in and try again.

Then we pass D's cousin's house, where we all stayed one happy Christmas. When we drive through Ranelagh, a village D and I used to visit often when we first got together, suddenly, and without knowing why, I am choking back tears, on the verge of completely losing it. I look out the window at the Spar market with the stacks of peat bricks piled high out front. We pass the shuttered pizza shop where we used to eat; when did that close? Then we're under the LUAS tracks that take the commuters into the city center, and when we make a right and a quick left, Dartmouth Square appears in front of us.

The gazebo has scores of roses woven into the ivy, and two large candles in glass cases flank the place where Shelly will stand. Three huge pillows are laid out for the children to sit on. The musicians, a cello and two violins, are getting themselves organized. A large table is set with food, olives and cheeses and vegetables and sliced meats, and wine is on ice. A truck that will serve hot finger food and dripping chocolate to the children is in position. Half a dozen tables with sun umbrellas and chairs have been scattered around the lawn. The most elegant portable toilets I have ever seen are parked just outside the square. All of D's twice-changed—fifty-times-changed—plans are falling perfectly into place.

My son is racing across the open lawn, the way he always does here. I don't know where Seve has gone. The wind is blowing softly and there's really nothing for me to do but stand around and wait.

Then I look up and see a family enter the gate on the east side of the park. They're all dressed up, and then I realize they are here for the ceremony. I turn around and from another entrance, two more couples, dressed sharply, drift into the park. Then suddenly, from all sides, people begin to appear, as if summoned, and within minutes well over a hundred wedding guests have gathered. My mother and brother arrive. D's brothers are here. I see some of D's cousins and uncles and aunts, and other people I don't recognize, and then our celebrant, Shelly, walks up, looking very self-possessed in a deep blue dress. She greets me with a typically self-aware, "Hello, Andrew."

We're ready to begin but the bride's mother has not arrived. Since D's father will walk her over from Shelly's house beside the park, he has been here for some time. I thought D's brother Tom was supposed to pick up Margot, but I see him and his children across the park.

"George." I walk up to D's younger brother. "Any idea where your mother is?"

His eyes grow as big as saucers. Quickly, he pulls out his phone.

I see D's other brother. "Hey, Colm, any idea who was bringing your mother?"

His face goes white. "Oh, Jay-sus, was I supposed to pick her up?"

D's brother Tom comes over. "Where's Mum?"

"There's no answer at the house," George says.

"She probably can't find the phone," Colm says. "Look, I'll go and get her, I'll be back in ten minutes. Just sit tight." And he races off toward his jeep.

A call comes down from Ronan, who is with D. "What are we waiting for? We're getting a little anxious up here. Let's go."

"Just tell them we're getting the musicians set. Don't mention anything about her mother," I say.

People are starting to look at their watches.

And then, marching regally through the gate to the park comes Margot, in a long and flowing black and cream kimono, with dashes of silver and red. The kimono, a gift from D, got stuck in the door as she was leaving home. She didn't have a key with her, a giggling fit ensued, and she spent twenty minutes slowly inching the dress out the door so as not to rip it.

"But we're all set now, Andrew, my love." She grins and strides to her seat.

The musicians begin to play, then a procession is coming up the street and turning in to the park, led by our daughter, in a delicate silk chiffon sheath blowing in the breeze. She is shivering but beaming and walking proud, carrying a small bouquet of lavender, eucalyptus, and sweet pea, leading her mother to be married. Following her are D's bridesmaids, tossing rose petals as they come, and then D, in an elegant full-length, cream-colored silk low-cut dress, also carrying a bouquet of lavender and eucalyptus, enters on her father's arm. She meets me in front of Shelly.

The guests are in a circle around us, some seated on the benches, most standing. My daughter hops up on Margot's lap and settles in; my son is still racing around the park. At several key intervals during the ceremony—twice when his name is invoked, and another time when the ribbons are laid across our hands and the vows spoken—he appears, standing just behind Shelly, and each time when I catch his eye, he grins, spins, and races off, his energy too much to contain.

The sun dapples down on D through the vines from above. In the first ceremony her attention was tightly focused on us, while today she is somehow both intimate with me and accessible to the entire gathering. One of the stones on her simple necklace is twisted and I reach out and set it right. The first ceremony was surprising for the unexpected emotional power it evoked; this time I find myself comfortable in the public nature of the proceedings. I can feel some of D's more religious relatives' silent judgment of our unconventional ceremony, as well as some of D's friends' surprise at Shelly's graceful and eloquent performance. All the varied responses to the love that surrounds us are palpable—and all of them welcome. None of this makes me want to run.

The afternoon is long and loose and exactly what D had said she hoped it would be. All the food is devoured. The wine is drunk. Kids and parents play soccer. A kite is flown. The face painter has created a giant blue butterfly on my daughter's cheek. My son, who loves doing long strings of cartwheels, has learned to do them one handed, his heavy cast on the other arm. Music that comes out over speakers I hadn't noticed has D and her bridesmaids dancing on the lawn. In the course of the afternoon, a few brief and light rain showers roll through. Each time, the Americans rush under the gazebo.

"Oh, what a shame," some say.

The Irish remain out in the rain, which always passes quickly, and proclaim it a "glorious afternoon—gives the grass a little glisten."

When things eventually wind down, we head home for an hour before moving over to the family-run twelve-room hotel beside D's parents' home for the *ceili*.

For months now, D has been telling me I am going to dance, and for months I've been equivocating—"We'll see how my knee is doing," I'd say, or would simply ignore the topic when she brought it up. But there is no avoiding it any longer.

Jerry, who will shout out instructions as we dance, is a small, frail-looking man with wispy gray hair shooting off in all directions. He stands beside four musicians—there's a fiddle, a bodhran drum, a concertina accordion, and a flute. The musicians are seated in front of the fireplace in the restaurant that's been cleared of tables. Chairs line the walls. Windows of stained, leaded glass look out onto the parking lot. The ceiling is low.

Irish *ceili* dancing is not dissimilar to American square dancing, except with better music and an urgency backing it, often fueled by large quantities of alcohol. Jerry lines us up in rows of four and begins to explain the moves and how each line will shift and stomp and twirl and spin and shuffle and move on, swapping partners all the while. His lengthy and complex directions are impossible to follow. Everyone looks at each other and shrugs and shakes their heads. I begin to feel embarrassed. This is a terrible idea. It will be a disaster.

"This one is called 'The Siege of Ennis,'" Jerry calls out. And then the music starts. The bodhran rat-a-tats out an incessant beat we can never compete with, the fiddle rips into a searing pace, the accordion swells below it, while the flute dances above.

Jerry shouts out, "One-two-three-four," and suddenly we are shifting and stomping and twirling and spinning and shuffling and moving on, switching partners, and repeating the process, shifting and stomping and twirling and spinning and shuffling and moving on. Now Margot is in my arms, and then someone I don't know at all, and then Colm steps on my toe, or did I crash into him? Then D is back in my arms and then Seve goes roaring past. Everyone is both focused and laughing. The music is ripping and we're swirling and switching partners again and the music is building and we're spinning and swapping again and again and again and then, impossibly, the music gets even faster and then it comes to a climax and it all stops and everyone is left gasping for air and laughing, hanging all over each other.

"Let's do it again!" I hear myself shout.

Breathing hard, D turns to me with a look of thrilled surprise. She grabs my face in her hands and kisses me hard on the mouth. In this instant, I am all of myself—that shy kid playing in the woods near my home, the guy who snuck into college, and then made those movies, and then found his way around the world. I'm a father and a son. And a husband. In this instant, I am all of it, and I'm happier, and freer, than I ever recall being.

"Now you're Irish," she shouts to me over the laughter.

"This one is called 'Shoe the Donkey,'" Jerry sings out, and begins another set of elaborately impossible directions. Jackets are peeled and ties ripped off. My daughter appears and jumps up into my arms and the band kicks into a jig. I'm holding her and we're swinging and twirling and stomping. Her thin arms are wrapped around my neck and we're laughing. My arm feels as if it will break under her weight as we swing and twirl and stomp, but I won't put her down and I hope she'll remember this for her entire life, because I will.

After "The Walls of Limerick" and "The Easy Brush Dance" and a few more, the band takes a break.

Up at the bar, I try to get the bashful Americans to come dancing. D's friend Bibb and her husband, Sean, are reluctant.

"Come on, you'll love it," I shout, inches from their faces.

I'm either spitting all over them or my sweat is flying onto their faces—either way, they take a step back. When D walks by, Bibb grabs on to her.

"Your husband has turned into Mr. Riverdance," she says.

When I go back downstairs, the band has started again. And there is my son, on the dance floor. He is holding D's father's hand. My son's old friend and new cousin Tristan is holding Colm's other hand. The three are high-stepping and laughing so hard I'm certain they will all tumble to the ground. Eventually Colm has to stop and my son goes off on his own. He is deep in the mix on the dance floor, twirling, kicking, stomping, and jumping, the only child in the sea of pulsing adults. He is without a care.

Much, much later, I try to get him to sleep in one of the small rooms of the hotel. I lie down next to him on the single bed. The music can still be heard through the closed door. He seems so grown-up and still so young. He has never been up this late.

"What time is it, Dad?"

"Almost two," I say.

"Wow."

We lie still in the dark; we're both breathing fast, just from excitement.

"How am I ever going to get to sleep with that music playing?"

"I don't know," I tell him, "but you have to." We're quiet a little while longer.

"I love you so much, Dad."

"I love you so much, kiddo."

"Dad?"

"Yes?"

"I'm glad you got married."

"You are?" I can feel tears burning behind my closed eyelids. "That means so much to me."

"Yeah," my son says, "I got to drink six Cokes tonight."

Shortly before three I find D huddled in a corner with several of her girlfriends. "I don't want to interrupt this coven, but I'm going to bed," I say.

D rises and kisses me. "You all right, luv?"

"I'm good, I just have a little headache. And it's three in the morning."

"I'll be in soon."

I join my daughter, who is in the bedroom next to my son's room. She's asleep in a large bed and I slip in beside her and wrap her up in my arms until she squirms away in her sleep. Soon the door is opened and light floods across the white covers as D enters with a large pint glass filled with ice and water. She shimmies out of her dress and gets into bed on the other side of our daughter. We sigh and reach across our sleeping child and hold hands for an instant in the night.

"I brought you some water for your headache."

She lifts the glass off the side table. I reach over to receive it. Our hands collide in the dark and the full glass falls and spills all over the bed. Quickly I slide our daughter to one side.

"Towels, luv," D says.

I rush to the bathroom and take the two towels and lay them across the bed, trying to soak up as much water as possible, but the bed is sopping. There's nothing we can do. We laugh quietly in the dark.

We climb back into bed. I'm hanging off the edge, rolled onto my side, the wet towel beneath me. D is wedged over on the far side of the bed; our daughter is lying across her chest so as not to get wet. It's three thirty in the morning. We need to get up at eight to catch a plane to Africa.

"Everything you ever dreamed of for your wedding night?" I ask in the dark.

"Perfect, luv," D says.

EPILOGUE

The following morning, D and I left for Mozambique. We regretted having to leave so soon. "We'll miss the postmortem," D lamented. We wouldn't be around her family table when the highlights and lowlights were relived and retold, but as was the case with most of our plans, they were made on the fly and were affected by countless other changes that led to a domino effect, resulting in an early departure we couldn't change.

We flew first to London; then overnight to Johannesburg, South Africa; then on to Vilanculos in southern Mozambique. We spent a day recovering and then we went into the bush. The wildlife in Gorongosa National Park had been all but obliterated by the sixteen-year civil war that ravaged most of the country. Over the past few years, large efforts had been made to revitalize the park and reintroduce game, but things had a long way to go. Still the place was raw and wild and remote. What Gorongosa lacked in overdevelopment it also lacked in effective service, which is how we ended up with a flat tire and no spare by the side of a dirt road at dawn with jungle drums pounding in our ears.

Eventually another van arrived and took us the rest of the way to the airport in Beira, which, like nearly all African airports, was hopelessly outdated and inspired little confidence. Our flight had left long ago, and there wouldn't be another until the following day. I consulted my guidebook and discovered that Beira was "the easiest and best place to catch malaria in all of Mozambique, perhaps the best place in all of Africa." I didn't share this news with D.

Beira had been a stronghold of the resistance during the civil war and it had yet to show any real signs of recovery; it remained a war-torn hive of African chaos. The next morning we returned to the airport.

It took sixteen hours, three flights, and two more bone-jangling rides to travel four hundred miles and reach the small island off the northern coast in the Quirimbas archipelago in the Indian Ocean. The sun had set long before we arrived.

The next morning revealed a tropical paradise—blinding-white, buttery-soft sand; turquoise water rippling up to the shore; a huge blue sky; and palms gently blowing in a soft breeze that took the heat out of the air. For breakfast we had thin crepes and fresh mango. We watched yellow dhows sail across the horizon. We swam in the Indian Ocean. The next day we did it again. We made love in the afternoons and took long naps. We showered outdoors under the purple sky of fading sunsets and had dinner by candlelight on the beach. Stars shot across the sky. We went to bed early and rose late.

We considered staying a few extra days, to make up for the ones we had missed, but then D turned to me. "I miss the kids."

"Me too."

🚶🚶

A few weeks after we returned home, D shook me awake in the middle of the night.

"Andrew, I think I've got malaria."

"Huh?"

"I think I've got malaria," she repeated. "I have a shooting pain in my side, which is very typical of malaria, and the gestation period is exactly right."

"It's probably the Chinese food you had for dinner."

"And I'm clammy."

I felt her forehead. It was fine. "If you're still alive in the morning, we'll call the doctor."

She groaned and rolled away from me.

A few minutes later I heard the patter of our daughter's feet. She climbed up into bed and snuggled down between us. Then my son appeared. "Move over, Dad."

Soon I could hear everyone breathing evenly as I lay awake in the dark, with everything I wanted beside me in bed. I rolled over, and a mosquito buzzed in my ear.

NOTE

When I left the Amazon, I went to Lima, where I met up with Francesco and his wife, Birgit, for dinner. In the course of our conversation, I told him of the young girl. I also told him that several of the passengers on board had expressed interest in helping her, if someone could handle the logistics. Francesco oversaw all arrangements, transferring the girl—who was six at the time, and whose name is Doris—down the Amazon to Iquitos, and then to Lima, along with her father. After numerous medical consultations, the operation on her tongue was performed. Francesco footed the entire bill. Doris has made a full recovery and is back with her family in Hatum Posa.

ACKNOWLEDGMENTS

David Kuhn knew what I meant before I could articulate it, and helped me bring the idea for this book forth. Alessandra Bastagli was the first believer in the book and has been a champion and a dogged advocate throughout. Martha K. Levin and Dominick Anfuso have been unflagging in their support. Aja Pollock was meticulous. Daniella Wexler has been patient and painstaking. I would not be writing anything at all if it hadn't been for Keith Bellows, who was the first to take a chance when an actor asked for an opportunity to write. There are others: Susan Dalsimer, Dani Shapiro, Michael Maren, Nancy Novogrod, Luke Barr, Jayne Wise, Candace Bushnell, Jacqueline Carleton, Lisa Jane Persky, Stephen O'Connell, Lois Wecker, all offered insight along the way. And my gratitude goes to my family, all of them—none asked to be in a book; I hope they will accept, forgive, and understand. Finally, there would be no book without Dolores—for obvious reasons, and for some less obvious ones. I am made grateful, awed, blessed, and humbled by her in equal measure.

ABOUT THE AUTHOR

Andrew McCarthy is a writer, actor and director. He is an editor-at-large with *National Geographic Traveler*. Among other publications, he has written for *The New York Times*, *The Atlantic*, and *The Wall Street Journal*. The Society of American Travel Writers named him the Travel Journalist of the Year in 2010 and presented him their Grand Award in 2011. Andrew made his acting debut at nineteen and has appeared in dozens of films, including *Pretty in Pink, St. Elmo's Fire,* and *The Joy Luck Club*. He lives in New York.